European Distance and E-Learning Network Annual Conference (EDEN 2016)

Re-Imagining Learning Environments

Budapest, Hungary
14 – 17 June 2016

Editors:

Antonio Moreira Teixeira
Andras Szucs
Ildiko Mazar

ISBN: 978-1-5108-5022-4

Printed from e-media with permission by:

Curran Associates, Inc.
57 Morehouse Lane
Red Hook, NY 12571

Printed by Curran Associates, Inc. (2018)

For permission requests, please contact European Distance and E-Learning Network (EDEN) at the address below.

European Distance and E-Learning Network (EDEN)
Budapest University of Technology & Economics
H-1111 Budapest, Egry J. u.1.
Hungary

Phone: +36 1 463 1628
Fax: +36 1 463 1858

secretariat@eden-online.org

Additional copies of this publication are available from:

Curran Associates, Inc.
57 Morehouse Lane
Red Hook, NY 12571 USA
Phone: 845-758-0400
Fax: 845-758-2633
Email: curran@proceedings.com
Web: www.proceedings.com

EDEN 2016 ANNUAL Conference

Re-Imagining Learning Environments

EDEN 2016 Annual Conference

Budapest, Hungary

14-17 June 2016

BOOK OF ABSTRACTS

Including the Collection of "Synergy" Synopses

Edited by

António Moreira Teixeira, András Szűcs and Ildikó Mázár
on behalf of the European Distance and E-Learning Network

European Distance and E-Learning Network, 2016

EDEN 2016 Annual Conference
Budapest, Hungary

Published by the European Distance and E-Learning Network

Editors:

António Moreira Teixeira
András Szűcs
Ildikó Mázár

Editorial co-ordination:

Anna Wagner

EDEN Secretariat, c/o Budapest University of Technology and Economics
H-1111 Budapest, Egry J. u. 1, Hungary
Tel: (36) 1 463 1628, 463 2537
E-mail: secretariat@eden-online.org
http://www.eden-online.org

Supported by the Erasmus+ Programme of the European Union

Introduction

Our current times have been framed by the concept of the *information age*, sometimes also known as the *computer age*. In a networked society as ours, digital technology has touched and changed many aspects of day-to-day life. Several long-standing societal, business and institutional systems have either lost their relevance or have transformed beyond recognition, the music, banking and travel industries being excellent examples.

Education does not stand untouched and we observe emerging and declining paradigms, changing expectations from society, our students now framed as consumers, with new and emerging types of informal learning experiences (take MOOCs for example) and all too frequently operating in unstable economic and policy environments.

The powerful combination of the *information age* and the consequent disruption caused by these unstable environments provides the impetus to look afresh and identify new models and approaches for education (e.g. OERs, MOOCs, PLEs, Learning Analytics etc.). For learners this has taken a fantastic leap into aggregating, curating and co-curating and co-producing outside the boundaries of formal learning environments – the networked learner is sharing voluntarily and for free, spontaneously with billions of people.

How do we as a community of educators respond to these directions? What could it mean for learning and the changing socio-economic demands of society?

We are set a challenge to really understand our learning environments. To create and invent responses that are possibly not even thought of yet. Perhaps there are new business models, new policies, different ways to understand technological influences, new ways to interpret the collaborative and social-networked society that we live in: the learning environment, in its widest sense.

Following up on the results of the EDEN Research Workshop (RW8) in Oxford in 2014 and the Barcelona 2015 Annual Conference, a clear focus has been awarded to the expansion of emerging learning scenarios, identifying an ongoing shift towards greater attention to the importance of context in the learning process. The EDENRW8 report from Tony Bates highlighted that openness needs to go beyond the content-centered focus. What is driving the need for new approaches is the massification of higher education and the need to find new ways to create openness, which requires a greater focus on the contexts of learning. This implies an integrated approach to online education and the various ways of openness in education which are now developing.

More present core questions include the tension between human and machine approaches to learning – raising the important question of what in education is best done by humans and what by machines? New knowledge is also needed regarding how to combine scalability with personalisation, as well as about learning context and contextualisation.

The social and socio-economic context is more important than ever. Society itself can be understood as a learning environment, with questions of learners' connection with the community and the empowerment of the practitioners.

In the new learning environments, the core players and stakeholders – learners, educators, government bodies, educational and learning institutions – increasingly acknowledge the chance for constructive and positive changes.

How do we as a community of educators respond to these directions? What could it mean for learning and the changing socio-economic demands of society? What can we, the community of experienced educators, say about this?

The EDEN 25th Anniversary Conference in 2016 in Budapest aims to evaluate and invent better responses regarding these changing socio-economic demands, the functioning of institutions, the new tools and their usability, the collaborative learning cultures, digital pedagogy – in other words the learning environment in its widest sense.

András Szűcs
Secretary General, EDEN

António Moreira Teixeira
EDEN President

Acknowledgement and thanks are given to the Programme and Evaluation Committee

António Moreira Teixeira, EDEN President, Open University, Lisbon, Portugal
Andras Benedek, Budapest University of Technology and Economics, Hungary
Alan Tait, Chair of the 25th Anniversary Celebrations Committee, The Open University, United Kingdom

Diana Andone, Politehnica University of Timisoara, Romania

Deborah Arnold, University of Burgundy, France

Paul Bacsich, Sero Consulting Ltd., United Kingdom

Ulrich Bernath, Ulrich Bernath Foundation for Research in ODL, Germany

Lisa Marie Blaschke, Carl von Ossietzky University of Oldenburg, Germany

Mark Brown, National Institute for Digital Learning, Dublin City University, Ireland

Alan Bruce, Universal Learning Systems Ltd., Ireland

Helga Dorner, Central European University, Hungary

Maxim Jean-Louis, Contact North, Canada

Andrea Karpati, Eotvos Lorand University – ELTE, Hungary

Elsebeth Korsgaard Sorensen, Aalborg University, Denmark

Sandra Kucina Softic, University of Zagreb, Croatia

Gila Kurtz, The Center for Academic Studies Or Yehuda, Israel

Ildiko Mazar, EDEN, United Kingdom

Gyorgy Molnar, Budapest University of Technology and Economics, Hungary

Fabio Nascimbeni, Universidad Internacional de la Rioja, Spain

Don Olcott Jr., Carl von Ossietzky University of Oldenburg, Germany

Ebba Ossiannilsson, Swedish Association of Distance Education, Sweden

Antonella Poce, University Roma III, Italy

Marci Powell, Past President, USDLA, Marci Powell and Associates, United States of America

Christian-Andreas Schumann, University of Applied Sciences Zwickau, Germany

Sofoklis Sotiriou, Ellinogermaniki Agogi, Greece

Andras Szucs, Secretary General, EDEN, United Kingdom

Ildiko Takacs, Budapest University of Technology and Economics, Hungary

Costas Tsolakidis, University of the Aegean, Greece

Belinda Tynan, The Open University, United Kingdom

Wim Van Petegem, Katholieke Universiteit Leuven, Belgium

Airina Volungeviciene, Vytautas Magnus University, Lithuania

Steve Wheeler, Chair of EDEN NAP Steering Committee, University of Plymouth, United Kingdom

Stavros Panagiotis Xanthopoylos, Brazilian Association for Distance Education – ABED, Fundação Getulio Vargas (FGV-EAESP), Brazil

Denes Zarka, Budapest University of Technology and Economics, Hungary

Olaf Zawacki-Richter, Carl von Ossietzky University of Oldenburg, Germany

TABLE OF CONTENTS

MOOCS ISSUES – EXPERIENCE, UNDERSTANDING, ATTITUDES, HOPES

WORK BASED LEARNING AND TRAINING SUPPORTED BY TECHNOLOGY

SOCIO-ECONOMIC AND CULTURAL ASPECTS IN E-LEARNING

LEARNER NEEDS, CHARACTERISTICS AND THE E-LEARNING SOLUTIONS

ONLINE LEARNING NATIONAL CASE STUDIES

INSTITUTIONAL INNOVATION AND DEVELOPMENT WITH ICTS

POSTERS

WORKSHOPS

DEMONSTRATIONS

BOOK OF PROJECTS – COLLECTION OF "SYNERGY" SYNOPSES

AN INVITATION TO LOOK AT ENHANCEMENT IN TECHNOLOGY-ENHANCED LEARNING

Stéphanie Gauttier, Inmaculada Arnedillo-Sanchez, Trinity College Dublin, Ireland

Introduction

The Internet, e-learning and now mobile learning are seen as opportunities for individuals to access information and engage in learning anytime, anywhere. However, digital devices and technologies are also perceived as detrimental for learning, memory and attention. The role that they play in learning needs questioning. Technology-enhanced learning (TEL) is the use of technologies to support teaching and learning. The term appears almost systematically in research concerned with e-learning without being discussed in itself. To this end, there is a call for drawing more attention to the concept of enhancement, which is at the core of TEL. This paper proposes a discussion of the notion of Technology-Enhanced learning. Firstly, it examines the definition of enhancement and highlights how learners could be cognitively enhanced. Secondly, it discusses the role of technology in learning as seen in the literature, and illustrates how it mainly performs an *enabling* function, rather than an *enhancing* one. The paper argues that technology appears to have a real *enhancing* role when the cognitive abilities of the learner are taken into account, and outlines future research directions for TEL.

Technology can improve learners' cognitive abilities

The transhumanist movement defines enhancement as a way to extend intellectual, physical and psychological abilities of individuals, so that they can go beyond their naturally limited capacities to become transhumans. It has a transformative impact on the individual and aims to increase the capacities, the efficiency of individuals. One way to enhance the individual is to enhance cognition. Cognitive enhancement is "the amplification or extension of core capacities of the mind through improvement or augmentation of internal or external information processing systems" (Bostrom & Sandberg, 2009). Enhancing cognition refers to "the processes an organism uses to organize information. This includes acquiring information (perception), selecting (attention), representing (understanding) and retaining (memory) information, and using it to guide behaviour (reasoning and coordination of motor outputs)", (ibid.). To enhance cognition, one can (a) Select one element of the process, (b) Focus on the process overall; (c) Transform the hierarchy of processes to make it more efficient through the use of technology. It should result in improved learning.

But it is mainly used to provide access to learning, not improve it

Two different roles for technology in learning can be identified in the literature: (a) Technology as an *enabler* of learning whereby learners are afforded access to learning material; (b) Technology as an *enhancer* of learning whereby learners' capacities and performance are improved.

Enhancement has to be considered at design and evaluation stage

Enhancement has to be considered at a technology-design design stage for TEL to be effective, instead of becoming a posteriori concern. Evaluation approaches ought to focus on the intended enhancement, look at the persistency of learning outcome over time. They should also consider the risks associated with intervening on cognitive processes. Indeed, an important downside of enhancement is the impact that enhancing one skill has on parallel or depending cognitive skills which development could impaired, and the enhancement of the learner overall through time. Transdisciplinary research bridging such disciplines as learning, cognitive sciences and neurology is needed to illuminate the impact of enhancement technologies on the brain and learning overall. Studies that consider enhancement in a longitudinal perspective are required to guide educational practices and leverage the power of technology at the most.

Acknowledgements

Financial support of the Eduworks Marie Curie Initial Training Network Project (PITN-GA-2013-608311) of the European Commission's 7th Framework Programme is gratefully acknowledged.

NEW METHODS IN THE DIGITAL LEARNING ENVIRONMENT: MICRO CONTENTS AND VISUAL CASE STUDIES

András Benedek, János Horváth Cz., Budapest University of Technology and Economics, Hungary

Introduction

Our research has been based on the new approaches that have emerged over the latest decade to tackle the issues of using ICT applications in education to activate students. Between 2012 and 2015, we implemented several educational projects related to the development of digital learning environments where students of engineering and economics specialized in teaching were surveyed in order to collect information on the special features of the use of digital curricula and in order to increase student activity in the development project. Based on this research, our presentation focuses on an innovation in the field of didactics, tackling issues related to the learning environment (RE-imaging learning environments). This innovation is expected to play an increasing role in the modernization of secondary and tertiary education. The didactic processes related to the terms *Micro-contents* and *Visual Case Studies* may result in obvious advantages in network learning implemented in a digital environment. They may boost the motivation of students, intensify communication between participants and encourage students to participate in the development of educational contents. The application of micro-contents may be increased both in time and space by ICT support. Applying the relevant text mining methods to a sufficiently high number of texts generated by students provided the necessary empirical base for analysing collections or micro-posts from a theoretical point of view. Diversifying the generation of micro-contents in a new ICT environment (broadband, mobile, increasingly memory-independent cloud services) positions educational contents in a new media. Generating interactive image outputs for micro-contents also has potential for a new didactic innovation. This didactic innovation, currently at the experimental stage, may facilitate the recording and evaluation of computer managed texts in a new system (MEdit). This system is able to display micro-collection contents both as conventional documents and in the form of power point-like slides, at the same time.

Visual Case Studies

Our efforts to include more visual elements in the content of training indicated that creative tasks and the possibility of the complex use of visual elements match the ideas of students about e-learning content. This new curriculum, where verbal and visual elements are presented in a one-to-one ratio, and where knowledge elements are organized into a network, would be scale-independent and structured as a graph. It would also be supported by a mathematical representation to enhance both its theoretical and practical aspects, and users would be allowed to extend it by means of case studies and practical examples.

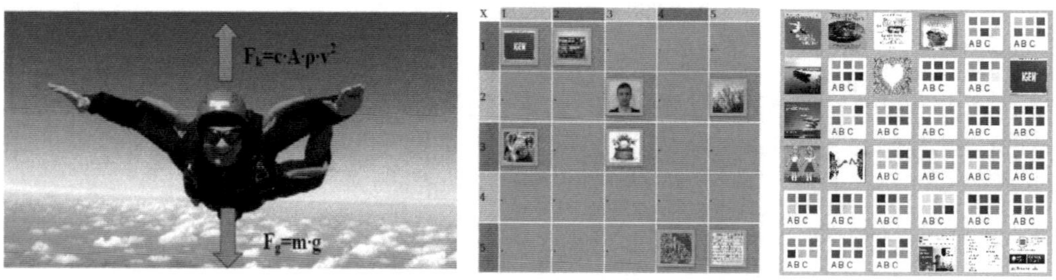

Figure 1. Sample images from a new type of curriculum

ACADEMICS' USE OF ACADEMIC SOCIAL NETWORKING SITES: THE CASE OF RESEARCHGATE AND ACADEMIA.EDU

Efrat Pieterse, Western Galilee College, Hagit Meishar-Tal, Holon Institute of Technology, Israel

Introduction

In the past few years, the Internet has seen the advent of academic social-networking sites (ASNS) such as Academia.edu and ResearchGate. These sites allow users to upload academic articles, abstracts, and links to published articles; track demand for their published articles; and engage in professional interaction, discussions, and exchanges of questions and answers with other users. The sites, used by millions, constitute a major addition to scientific media.

This study investigates the uses and gratifications that academic faculty members derive from two academic social-networking sites, Academia.edu and ResearchGate. It invoked the uses and gratifications theory as a point of departure and adjusted this generic theory, developed in the context of mass-media consumption, to the specific context of academic networks and their singularities.

Research Methods

The study was conducted among 81 faculty members from three different academic institutions on the basis of a voluntary response to an online questionnaire that was constructed for the purposes of the study. It found a difference among these institutions in the extent of use of the various networks and faculty members' perception of the gratifications that the networks give them.

Findings

The findings indicate that researchers use ASNS mainly for consumption of information, slightly less for sharing of information, and very scantily for interaction with others. This finding itself indicates that academic networks do not function as other social networks do. In social networks such as Facebook, interaction with others is the main use; academic networks in contrast, are used chiefly for information consumption and are perceived more as a database of sorts than as a place to establish social or professional relations and interact with others.

As for the gratifications that motivate users to visit ASNS, four main ones were found: self-promotion and ego-bolstering, acquisition of professional knowledge, belonging to a peer community, and interaction with peers. Escapism, a factor that typifies the gratifications that social networks deliver, proved to be weak if not irrelevant in regard to academic networks. The centrality of the self-promotion and ego-bolstering motive stresses the utilitarianism that drives the use of social networks generally and academic networks specifically. The creation of social capital and personal advancement by means of activity on social networks is well known in research on such networks

Conclusions

The behaviour of academics in ASNS shows that they recognize the network as a mechanism for the creation of social capital and for an attempt to transform it into professional capital. In a world where academic faculty members are judged by the number of works that they publish and the number of citations that the works receive an instrument that allows them to influence the extent of their exposure and increase the likelihood of citation delivers much power and utility.

The high score of the *consumption of professional academic information* gratification stresses the importance that academics see in having direct and open access to academic information. The separation between the two social gratifications *The sense of belonging* and *Interaction with professional peers*, and the fact that the sense of *belonging to a community of practice* was ranked higher strengthens the point of need for a sense of belonging than to the need for interaction. The fact that interaction in this environment and academics' motivation to engage in it are significantly weaker than the other uses and gratifications could be explained on the ground that the social potential of ASNS has not yet been fully realized by the academics because they are so new.

ADAPTED LEARNING ENVIRONMENT IN FUTURE EDUCATION

Shimon Amar, Ohalo College of Education, Israel, Frederic Roblin, Steelcase Education, France

Introduction

Into the 21st century, most schools are still using traditional and outdated teaching methods where the teacher is the main source of knowledge and learning is based on memorization of facts. Most learning environments remind old factories or classrooms taken from Charles Dickens stories.

On the other hand, modern working places are equipped with the latest technology. The work is based on cooperation, collaboration and teamwork. The highly competitive working environments create high level of uncertainty and demand adaptive thinking skills and creativity. This reality creates a wide gap between the level of educational system graduates and the level of employees that are demanded in today's economy.

The 21st century provides information that is available and can be found and learned anytime and anywhere, while skills and abilities cannot be learned only in a classroom. Therefore the role and purpose of schools, learning spaces and teachers has to be changed.

These and other insights led the college think tank to suggest a multi-step model named P2PBE (Problem to Project Based Education). This eight-step model combines well-known and familiar learning and working processes. The model includes movement on two main axes: the horizontal axis where the student moves from self-work to teamwork and the vertical axis where the student is requested to move within the framework of his learning from individual outcomes to shared outcomes. This model re-defines the role of the teacher and adapts it to the reality of the 21st century.

The implementation of the described dynamic learning model requires a redesign of the learning spaces, which were planned and processed together with Steelcase Education (Grand-Rapids, Michigan, USA). The new spaces provide our teachers the tools to motivate their students through dynamic and engaging learning experience.

Summary of Findings

Over eighty percent of students and lecturers reported more than a moderate increase in creativity, motivation, ability to get higher grades, and engagement in class while studying in the new learning environment. Students gave statistically significant higher evaluations for practices and solutions in the new classrooms than in traditional classrooms. Significant findings were found in the way students perceived working adequately, or better than adequately, on many of the 21st century skills in the new environment as opposed to the old one.

Conclusion

The 21st century necessitates the design of a special learning environment that facilitates the acquisition of the skills that the education system would like to develop among its learners as part of their preparation for "real life" in a dynamic, rapidly changing environment full of uncertainty. Throughout the world, educators, educational scholars, philosophers, opinion-makers and laymen have tried to come up with suitable pedagogic solutions for the modern era. Questions such as: how to increase motivation and encourage commitment to learning have occupied the best of minds. We believe the present research to illuminate potential solutions that are supported by empirical research relating to a large proportion of the core issues of innovative education, and that indicate possible directions for the future. Moreover, the significant processes highlighted here are extremely important for the training of future teachers in a changing world. The present research sheds light on the role of learning environments in the preparing and training of future teachers in a changing world. It suggests that student teachers can be better prepared for their future educational tasks when their learning environment fits more to the characteristics of the technologically changing world.

TOP-DOWN OR BOTTOM UP: A COMPARATIVE STUDY ON ASSESSMENT STRATEGIES IN THE STUDIO ADAPTIVE LEARNING ENVIRONMENT

Christian Weber, Corvinno Technology Transfer Center, Réka Vas, Corvinus University of Budapest, Hungary

Throughout all situations of life education stays as a stable companion. This seems to stay true with new and changing requirements coming with the new technology enhanced society. But as the learning environments are changing, so are the requirements for education. Technology enhanced learning promises a personalised learning experience and support, and translates the real world's instruction into a computerised learning environment. But by doing so it has to answer the same common questions for instructional design: Should education be provided top-down, starting from the general or bottom-up, visiting the specifics first. And additionally – how should this be reflected in supporting technologies of education?

In class room situations, when applying a top-down approach, a teacher will try to give a general overview first, introducing the big picture paired with an overall motivation concerning both content and outcome, showing the correlation between the different aspects of the particular field. In contrast, a bottom-up way of teaching will tackle the details of a specific area first to develop the topic step by step towards the understanding of the whole area. The approaches of top-down and bottom-up education can be translated into trade-off considerations between behaviourism- and constructivism-based learning. But how can these approaches be built into technology enhanced and technology enabled learning environments? How can testing – which has to be part of a technology enhanced process of learning – reflect these methods? Bransford, Franks, Vye and Sherwood (1989) summarise in a short manner "wisdom can't be told", so no test can define what exactly the candidate knows. But the question is not if wisdom can be or can't be told – as experience can be transferred by communication – but if a learner can make use of it.

Technology enhanced learning needs a connection between what has to be learned, what is tested and what is still to be learned based on the results of testing. STUDIO, an integrated technology-enhanced e-learning solution, offers here the right link between testing and learning. It focuses on providing a continuous feedback loop of learning and testing. Within the system a domain-ontology is used for representing the knowledge to learn. Using the domain structure of STUDIO this paper will first introduce two alternative algorithms for technology enhanced assessment – implementing both a top-down and a bottom-up approach for testing. Using the results of a real world online test in the domain of business informatics, new light on the differences of top-down and bottom-up comprehension of learners will be provided. This paper will detail the main findings of this analysis. The survey is conducted in an environment of blended learning, where students learn through different channels.

The authors acknowledge the financial support of the Eduworks Marie Curie Initial Training Network Project (PITN-GA-2013-608311) of the European Commission's 7th Framework Program.

GAMIFICATION FOR ONLINE COURSES TO IMPROVE INQUIRY METHODOLOGY

Paula Carolei, Universidade Federal de Sao Paulo (UNIFESP),
Eliane Schlemmer, Universidade do Vale do Rio dos Sinos (UNISINOS), Brazil

This article describes the challenges of investigative learning in online courses and discusses how the gamification approach can help to develop the inquiry attitude.

The biggest issues in courses and learning materials are that they are usually too inductive, too explicative and entirely too transmissive and the investigative learning demands several competences essential if we are to overcome this reductive and reactive attitudes and create more critical and engaged citizens.

There are different types of investigative learning, depending on how problems are presented or elaborated. In a problem-based learning approach, there are situations in which problems are proposed by the teacher and the learning process traces a limited movement of investigating and solving problems, which can be more or less open according to the teacher's proposal. There are also approaches that are actually investigative, in which problems arise from students' observation of their contexts and/or social questions considered relevant; in such cases, the teacher may provoke the emergence of the problems, but the entire group will share impressions and create shared and collective questions to engage with.

The inquiry process is aligning the innovation outcomes and it must be based on the societal needs, expectations and ethical values and it should be inclusive, interactive, anticipatory and transparent. Inquiry is based on authorship and the gamification can develop a constructivist approach.

This work analyzes how the essential elements of gamification, agency, immersion and fun can be designed for educational purposes and how it can be of interest to design agency and gameability keeping in mind the competences you want the student/player to develop.

And conclude how the investigation competences as observation, questioning, exploring, explain and evaluate can be developed characters, exploratory actions, including of physical environments using augmented reality, media locative or many sorts of log that can help the online student be more observant of his/her own territory, question and problematize his/her own actions and experiences deductive action and must be proposed with clues, questioning, course log and pattern-seeking, access to information as "mysteries" or simply the attitude of exploring spaces and sharing records and patterns.

More than models and templates, the gamification as exploratory approach can help think another way of design online courses that promote inquiry and deductive attitudes.

DEVELOPMENT OF A NEW ACTIVITY-BASED INSTRUCTIONAL DESIGN MODEL

János Ollé, László Hülber, Eszterházy Károly University of Applied Sciences,
Henrik Sablik, Ágnes Kocsis, Nexius Learning – ELMS Zrt., Hungary

With the widespread adoption of e-learning, the necessity for more research into its effectiveness and quality, and into the operation of an efficient market, has arisen. In order to improve quality and assess impact, it is paramount that methodological approaches are revised and to utilise the findings of previous research on theories of education, instructional design and the psychology of education. Central to instructional design models is the belief that the educational environment and the development of the learning process should be built on describing and analysing student needs and on taking students' particularities into account. Not only do these models determine the students' activities within the curriculum, but they also define the whole process and development of the educational environment and also indirectly influence the learning process. In short, then, the application of modern instructional design models is necessary for relevant, up-to-date and effective e-learning solutions.

Goals and Methods

With the development of our own instructional design models, we have several aims unachievable with previous models. By developing the Nexius model our goal was to create a modern instructional design model, which can also operate in the market and not just in the world of non-profit state schools. The main principles of our instructional design model are the following: individual learning, developing an optimal educational environment for the individual, adjusting e-learning curriculum development to individual requirements and to expected student activities. The development of an e-learning curriculum in an online educational environment is ideal only if the advantages of cognitive theory, educational psychology and project-based development can prevail in developing educational content and in planning education generally. It implements curriculum development via the project-approach taken from the world of business, thus merging the features of project management and instructional design. Not only does it provide theoretical solutions, but it also supports curriculum developers and practical implementation with concrete tools and advice during the course of application. The necessity to develop the Nexius model was driven by practical needs under market circumstances. Although the developers considered each developmental project unique, in order to ensure quality and cost-efficiency it was thought practical to introduce steps which could be standardized. For the development of the model, the developmental experience provided by more than a thousand pages of curricula was processed by those working on Nexius. The projects were analysed qualitatively: small-group and in-depth interviews were undertaken and the work processes of different projects were examined and compared with content-analysis. We mapped the tasks and roles of certain individuals in the process of development. The tasks were grouped, unified and put in logical order. The results were analysed and specified in cooperation with a didactics specialist and we established the modern education-methodological background and its base.

The Nexius Model

The models principle is to represent an activity-based pedagogy based on motivating the students; it attempts to build a bridge with student's existing knowledge while trying to open paths to digital-based motivational opportunities. Compared with previous methods, the Nexius-model approaches instructional design differently. It combines education-methodological support and organizational process focus. The model consists of 6 steps. Each step is completed with the establishment of a well-defined sub-product. These milestones are the exit documents in their establishing phase, and on which the next phase of the process is built, thus they are its access documents. In the model, the sub-steps within the main steps are clarified in full: why they are necessary, how they are prepared, their make up and what requirements they have to meet to be acceptable. The model also delineates the activities of the participants. It separates the different functions, while stressing that a person can have more than one function. The exact number of people participating in the development can vary, although each function has to be present in each case. The methodological, instructional design background of the model is anchored in the curriculum-scheme system, which adjusts the methodological framework and concrete guides – which will be used in practice – to the particular conditions by taking different parameters into account regarding implementation. The curriculum-scheme framework allows for different methodological approaches by taking the educational goals, the particularities of the students and other features into account. Based on the above parameters, we define which 4-4 curriculum scheme out of the three main scheme groups (regulated-, adaptive-, discovery learning) will be applied in the course of development. The practical application of the model has already commenced. Our present aim is to justify the model with research and, depending on the findings, to adapt it. In order to examine the curriculum scheme's system, research is planned which will compare the performance of a single curriculum framed within different schemes, thus providing an opportunity to justify the existence of certain categories.

E-LEARNING DECISION MAKING: METHODS AND METHODOLOGIES

Nikola Kadoić, Nina Begičević Ređep, Blaženka Divjak,
University of Zagreb, Faculty of Organization and Informatics, Croatia

Strategic decision making implementation is still an important problem in higher education (HE). The shift in research moved from goals and activities towards recognizing decision making methods used for decision making (DM) and evaluation of the strategy implementation. The purpose of this paper is to investigate which decision making methods and methodologies are used in the decision making processes in higher education, especially strategic decision making problems connected to the implementation of e-learning. In order to achieve this goal we reviewed 40 research papers. Results show diversity of methods, methodologies and approaches used in the strategic decision making in HE which proves complexity of the topic. We summarize them in four phases according to the cycle of strategic decision making and also recommend methods that can be successfully applied in HE setting based on the literature review presented in this paper and authors' practical experiences. Those four phases are: (a) Identification and research of the problem, (b) Development of the methodology of strategic DM, (c) Implementation and monitoring of strategic decision and (d) Evaluation of the effects of strategic decision. A summary of DM approaches, methods and methodologies as well as specifics of DM in HE and e-learning is given in next table.

Table1: Summary of decision making methods in HE focused on e-learning

Phase of the cycle	Approaches	Specifics of HE and e-learning	Methods and methodologies
Identification and research of the problem	Needs and situation analysis Readiness assessment Diffusion of innovation	Stakeholders' involvement E-readiness Consciousness raising	*Situation analysis (Document analysis)* Case study research Different types of qualitative analysis Structural Equation Modelling (SEM) Social Network Analysis (SNA) Grounded theory Game theory *Educational Data Mining and Learning Analytics (LA)* Methodology for e-readiness assessment *Problem tree with Decision tree* Statistical methods
Development of methodology for DM and decision making	Analysis of potential solutions MCDM Cost-benefit and risk analysis	Benchmarking of HEIs Modelling dependencies and group DM (AHP & ANP with BOCR)	*BOCR AHP and ANP*, PROMETHEE, ELECTRE, TOPSIS Ideal point-based MCDM Multi-criteria variant of cost-benefit analysis Hybrid methodology of risk management – Monte Carlo simulation and Sensitivity analysis Different types of qualitative analysis Factor analysis, Clustering Game theory Goal programming, Knapsack method TRIZ (Theory of solving inventive problems) Decision Tree
Implementation and strategic decision monitoring	BSC, KPI, BPM CMMI PPM	Interpretations of econometrics and use of KPIs and PPM	*BSC Balanced Scorecard* Enterprise Architecture for BPM (Business Process Management) CMMI (Capability Maturity Model Integration) Econometric methods (ROI, productivity, efficiency, profitability) DEA (Data Envelopment Analysis) Total Quality Management
Evaluation of effects of the strategic decisions	Qualitative, quantitative and mixed methods Structural causal models	Stakeholder perspective analysis In-depth case study to find out causes & effects	Qualitative methods – stakeholder perspective, document analysis, internal consistency of the strategy and external effectiveness, benchmarking, *in-depth* case study, Delphi Quantitative methods – econometric analysis, cost-benefit analysis, *multi-criteria analysis and regression analysis* Causal modelling *Educational Data Mining and Learning Analytics (LA)*

SUSTAINABILITY FOR WHOM? PLANNING FOR STUDENT SUCCESS IN OPEN EDUCATION AND DISTANCE LEARNING

Alan Tait, The Open University, United Kingdom

Sustainability lies at the heart of the new UN Development Goals (the SDG's) for the period 2015-2030, and education has a specific Goal, namely *Ensure inclusive and equitable quality education and promote lifelong learning opportunities for all* (UNESCO, 2015).

The very significant growth in post-secondary education demanded world-wide, from some 260m to 400m learners, will need the development of open education and distance learning systems (OEDL) on a substantial scale. Even in Europe, as a developed region, there will be the need to contribute to this priority not only in overall growth in particular in some countries but also in population segments that remain with higher levels of exclusion, and also more widely from the perspective of quality for OEDL.

This paper, which draws on an ICDE report takes student success as a core element of quality for the sustainability of OEDL, and therefore for post-secondary education to contribute to sustainability for our societies in the future. Student success rates are widely reported to be lower for part-time than full-time students, and lower for OEDL than for part-time students as a whole. There is an imperative to improve student success rates firstly for the sake of students who invest their self-esteem, time and money in OEDL programmes, and also for the reputation of OEDL's contribution to educational systems and of the institutions who teach significantly or entirely using OEDL methods. As major effort goes into fulfilling UN SDG 4, OEDL programmes will need to improve student success rates to make a reality of the UN aspiration for significantly higher numbers of successful post-secondary and lifelong learners.

MOBILISING LEADERSHIP FOR INNOVATIVE OPEN AND DISTANCE EDUCATION IN THE 21ST CENTURY

Don Olcott, Jr., Charles Sturt University, Australia and Carl von Ossietzky University of Oldenburg, Germany,
Lisa Marie Blaschke, Carl von Ossietzky University of Oldenburg, Germany

Leadership within online, open, and distance learning (ODL) is critical for transformational and innovative change to occur, and it requires vision, a commitment to core values, and a strong and steady hand in setting the course of change within the organisation. This session will first discuss a definition of leadership and the crisis of leadership facing ODL enterprises today, and then explore Kotter's (2012) eight-step model for leading change as it relates to the context of 21st century ODL institutions:

1. *Establishing a sense of urgency* by examining the market and competitive realities, identifying and discussing crises, potential crises, or major opportunities, and having a sound understanding of emerging and developing market trends.
2. *Creating a guiding coalition* by bringing key stakeholder representatives on board and empowering them to lead the change and to work together like a team.
3. *Developing a vision and strategy* by creating a vision to help direct the change effort, aligning vision and strategy with organizational culture, developing strategies for achieving that vision, and validating it with stakeholders.
4. *Communicating the change vision* by using every vehicle possible to constantly communicate the new vision and strategies, having the guiding coalition model the behaviour expected of employees, and keeping communication open, continuous, and transparent.
5. *Empowering broad-based action* by cross-checking across operational processes and strategic plans, changing systems or structures that undermine the change vision, and encouraging risk taking and non-traditional ideas, activities, and actions.
6. *Generating short-term wins with the long-term in mind* by planning for visible improvements in performance, or *wins*, creating those wins, and visibly recognizing and rewarding people who made the wins possible.
7. *Consolidating gains and producing more change* by using increased credibility to change all systems, structures, and policies that don't fit together and don't fit the transformation vision, hiring, promoting, and developing people who can implement the change vision, and reinvigorating the process with new projects, themes, and change agents.
8. *Anchoring new approaches in the culture* by creating better performance through customer-and productivity-oriented behaviour, more and better leadership, and more effective management, articulating the connections between new behaviours and organizational success, and developing means to ensure leadership development and succession.

GOVERNMENTAL AND INSTITUTIONAL STRATEGIES TO SUPPORT NEW WAYS OF TEACHING AND LEARNING

George Ubachs, European Association of Distance Teaching Universities (EADTU), The Netherlands

The Changing Pedagogical Landscapes study took place from January 2014-June 2015 and was designed to address the following objective:

> *"... to examine to what extent government strategies and higher education regulatory and accreditation, funding, quality assurance, assessment and certification frameworks support or hinder new modes of learning, and in particular increased use of technology in the teaching and learning process. The research resulted in conclusions and recommendations on how these systems – the framework conditions for higher education – can best be tailored to support new modes of teaching and learning."*

Next to recommendations at governmental level, EADTU has been working on the setup of an EMPOWERing university programme to support institutional strategies on the uptake of new modes of teaching and learning. EMPOWER supports collaboration and sharing of expertise between European universities, and provides specialist advice and guidance for institutional leaders on the latest developments in online, open and flexible education. In this respect EMPOWER offers: free independent advice, experience of about 100 trusted experts, guidance for university leaders, expert panels for targeted reviews, support for strategic whole of institution initiatives, and a think-tank for re-imagining the future of higher education.

OPENING STUDIES THROUGH VIRTUAL EXCHANGE – CASE DESCRIPTION

Airina Volungevičienė, Estela Daukšienė, Margarita Teresevičienė, Vytautas Magnus University, Lithuania

Introduction

Openness brings challenges for universities and is introduced in a variety of forms. Virtual exchange (VE) directly contributes to opening up of universities. The aim of VE is to open universities for international studies, to improve the quality of academic processes, but also to share and mainstream socio-cultural experiences in various forms. Teacher collaboration in joint course designing and/or delivery, recognition of student achievements and teacher VE are the main challenges European universities face in organizing virtual exchange. The aim of this paper is to present the case of opening up of universities through virtual mobility by collaboration of teachers in the development and use of OER, in the collaborative development of study modules for VE including student collaborative activities. The described case has been implemented and funded under Erasmus+ KA2 Strategic partnership project *OUVM – Opening universities for virtual mobility* (project No. 2014-1-LT01-KA203-000550). The project partnership consists of 5 universities: Vytautas Magnus University (VMU), Katholieke Universiteit Leuven (KUL), Universita Degli Studi di Pavia (UNIPV), Universidad de Oviedo (UNIOVI), and Universidade Aberta (UAb).

Virtual exchange case description

The aim of the OUVM project is to open university studies for virtual mobility by training teachers and academic staff on how to design MA program curriculum using OER and applying correct licensing; how to establish collaborative trusted relationships in curriculum designing for multicultural exchange; and how to integrate these open education innovations in every day practices. OUVM project training and VE implementation have directly addressed all 7 areas of university activities (Strategy and management; Infrastructure; Curriculum designing; Teacher and academic staff training; Support system; Quality assurance; and Marketing, business and communication), by revising VE procedures at participating universities, creating platform for virtual mobility courses and their marketing, training teachers and support staff specialists on VE curriculum design process and peculiarities, and implementing peer review of VE courses for quality assurance.

Joint course design and delivery is a possibility for teachers to collaborate, share their common practices, and learn from different colleague background, access to resources, and cultural approach. It sometimes is a challenge for teachers who tend to work alone in their course design and/or delivery, as they do not feel well opening their course for others due to various reasons. Thus this collaboration requires openness, professional confidence, trust and tolerance from engaged teachers.

There are several steps students need to implement before virtual exchange. The openstudies.eu portal presents and guides students within these steps. The openstudies.eu portal also aims at presenting and marketing all the necessary information about VE courses for students before they start the learning process; and provides students with the possibility to fill in learning agreement online and submit all necessary documents for valid virtual mobility with proper recognition.

Conclusions

Opening universities via teacher collaboration and student VE is a challenging process where technologies create possibilities and facilitate administrative processes, however coherent preparation and coordination of activities is needed. Erasmus+ funded projects create possibilities for teachers to collaborate in course design and delivery for VE, for students to study virtually abroad, and for institutions to prepare and validate necessary procedures for virtual mobility implementation and recognition.

VE case implementation revealed the main challenges for teachers, students and universities:

- Students – selection and registration for VE at universities abroad;
- Teachers – collaboration in course designing and different academic schedules;
- Universities – recognition of student and teacher VE and virtual mobility.

ADVANTAGES AND DISADVANTAGES OF SPOCS (SMALL PRIVATE ONLINE COURSES): EXPERIENCES WITH ONLINE LEARNING

Gerard Gielen, UC Leuven Limburg, Belgium

A Small Private Online Course (SPOC) refers to a version of a MOOC (Massive Open Online Course) used locally with on-campus students. SPOCs are online courses that are still free and delivered through the internet, but access is restricted to much smaller numbers. Access is restricted to the student groups you are teaching to.

Some SPOCs are meant to support life teaching courses, others are made to replace the reality courses, e.g. for students who are studying abroad or have to combine work with studies or demands more flexible learning pads. In a SPOC as in a MOOC students typically access interactive content at their own pace. SPOCs are online courses taught and assessed by real people mediated by the computer; not just programmed into the computer.

SPOCs support blended learning and flipped classroom learning, which variously combine online resources and technology with personal engagement between faculty and students. SPOCs can include video lectures (educasts), assessments (with immediate feedback), interactive labs (with immediate feedback) and discussion forums.

I worked out a SPOC for my second year students of bachelor social educator at the UCLL (University College Leuven Limburg) for the course *Management and policy of institutions*. The course *Management and policy of institutions* is organized in two ways. Students, who prefer to come to lessons, can do this once a week on the fixed schedule time. They follow 10 two hour-hearing colleges in large auditorium groups. Other can follow the same courses through an online learning platform in SPOCs. I experienced with my own students advantages and disadvantages in working with SPOCs.

- Advantages: An advantage of e-learning by SPOCs is likely that the curriculum can be offered in a more varied way with video, extra information, examples, links to websites, etc. Learners have 24 hours and seven days a week access to the learning environment. SPOC students can participate individual in feedback dialogues with the lecturer and other students through the discussion board; they can ask questions and get online answers and they can participate in activities that are facilitated by real people. SPOC students can test their knowledge through the online questionnaires. Also the lecturer can follow the progress of the SPOC student, he sees when the students have logged in, how many hours they spent on the course, which level the student reached, etc. The knowledge acquired by the specialized lecturer, is not lost (when he leaves the organization) and can be taken over by colleagues.
- Disadvantages: Personal contact with the students is missing for the lecturer. During real courses students can immediately ask questions and get direct feedback. This is not the case through the online course: it takes some time before the lecturer can answer in the discussion board and it is more difficult to answer with a written text than with life spoken words. The tests are self-correcting. But the items of the tests have no feedback information. Stimulating self-learning as goal is not always reachable and is often only a wish from the lecturer due to motivational problems of students. A student should possess ICT skills. Developing quality online courses is still labour-intensive for the teacher. Learning is a social process. Through online learning students are missing this life social network, personal contacts and the peer pressure to study and work motivated for the courses.

Conclusion

Working with SPOCs is an interesting way to let students learn flexible. For motivated and committed students this is a way of stimulating them to powerful learning. SPOCs have advantages and disadvantages. From my experiences I would never force students to choose one or the other way, but offer both learning systems side by side so that the student can learn in the most appropriate way for himself.

EDUCATIONAL SYSTEM INTEROPERABILITY – CHALLENGES FOR OPEN LEARNING AND TRAINING PROGRAMS

Christian-Andreas Schumann, Eric Forkel, Helge Gerischer, Janek Goetze, Thomas Klein, Claudia Tittmann, West Saxon University of Zwickau, Jana Weber, Technische Universität Berlin, Germany, Feng Xiao, Tongji University, China, Jorge Alejandro Manríquez Frayre, Tec de Monterrey, Mexico

Information, knowledge, and competencies are the key driver for the further development in each area of society. Intellectual and knowledge based capital has important influence of investments, innovation and growth in economies. Especially, the knowledge and intellectual resources are becoming increasingly important regarding the transition to information society focused on the digital transformation because information and knowledge will be made available regardless of time and space. Digital learners and coaches are required for the digital society.

Open education requires the willingness of the owners of information and knowledge to make the resources available for use by demanders. There are different forms of motivations to push open solutions of education and training. The spread ranges from the socially competent individualist via the public organization up to the commercial supplier. The reasons depend on the specific target systems including especially strategy, structure and information technology for the open educational approach. But, if the decision for opening the accesses to the own information and knowledge resources was made, a variety of possible relations for the knowledge transfer will be available as single- or multi-channel support services.

The pure doctrine of the past was to integrate functions, processes or systems for using different applications in one extended functional context based on several subcomponents. The learning platform of the first party provider was combined with the content development system of the second party provider and with the document management system of the third party provider and so on. The subsystems will be connected by defined and fixed interfaces. If the interfaces are standardized, each component will be able to use the same interface. Otherwise, the interfaces are unique for the one or few integrated solutions. The result is that the users buy common solutions ready-made. The only way for including flexibility and application-specifics is the customizing approach taking in account that the systems become larger and more cumbersome.

Now, the key question will be how interoperability can be used directly at the point of contact to the customer for open learning and training programs. The chance will be opened to intensify the cooperation with different educational providers by flexible interconnection of educational components using interoperable facilities. The results are the increase of the reusability, the improvement of the openness of the knowledge, the better independence from single providers, etc.

Interoperable systems are a prerequisite for interoperable applications. There are a lot of skills and experiences coming from the knowledge management or software engineering referring to the use of interoperability and already applied in the context of open and flexible learning. Especially, the increase of methodological knowledge was accelerated by re-design of monolithic contents into multivalent knowledge components which are cross-linked for special target groups of learners on demand. The learning objects are put into relations by semantic networks as a kind of knowledge representation.

Recently, the first wave of applications is advancing including the use of system interoperability as well as semantic technology. The experiences by using autonomous and mobile logistic devices without central control based on interoperability and collective intelligence prove that simple rules for the interaction already lead to a first stage of functioning systems. The same results can be obtained for interoperable open education programs.

The approach can be matched with the principles of the more technology-enhanced learning based on Advanced Distributed Learning Initiative (ADL) including accessibility, adaptability, affordability, durability and interoperability without central control system. The concepts was used for developing several study programs provided by an network of educational organizations in the national context and rolled out in different international programs supported by a global network of universities.

OPEN EDUCATION AS DISRUPTION: LESSONS FOR OPEN AND DISTANCE LEARNING FROM OPEN EDUCATIONAL PRACTICE

Ronald Macintyre, The Open University in Scotland, Scotland

This paper reflects on what Open and Distance Learning providers might learn from the Open Educational Resources/Practices (OER/OEP) and Massive Open Online Courses (MOOCs). It is based on experiences working on OER and OEP first at the OU in Scotland (OUiS) and more recently under the auspices of the Scottish Funding Council (SFC) funded Open Educational Practices Scotland (OEPS) programme hosted by OUiS. The paper by exploring the disruptive potential of MOOCs and OER within Higher Education. It considers how disruption might be occurring and asks what is being disrupted.

While it acknowledges lessons for HE it argues the focus on access and scale has obscured other lessons ODL might learn from opening up educational practices. Much of our work has centred on OEP and partnership with organisations outside the formal education sector. As such it has taken the possibilities offered by openness as an invitation to look at the relationship between the formal and the informal.

The paper traces OEPS journey as it explores less apparent but no less important lessons around designing and creating open content through partnership in a way that is cost effective and context relevant. It has treated the challenges of using openness to disrupt where and how knowledge is created as a design challenge. Starting by establishing the "public value" the partner wants to create for themselves and their learners, then looking at what needs to change and how to change it. This means focussing on the transformation process, from the learner's perspective and from an organisational one.

We suggest rather than looking at MOOCs scale and demand side innovation and disruption, openness in education should consider what blurring the boundaries around the academy and the creation of more porous HE providers might to do disruption supply side and curriculum development.

DEAR EDUCATOR, HOW OPEN ARE YOU?

Fabio Nascimbeni, Universidad Internacional de La Rioja (UNIR), Spain

The paper focuses on the change process that university teachers need to go through in order to become fluent in the use of Open Education approaches, understood as part of a broader teachers' development process connected with the crisis of Higher Education systems and with the pervasive impact of ICT and social media. We present and discuss the definition of Open Educator that we have developed in the frame of the Open Educators Factory project, a research action aimed to explore how to transform university teachers from agents of resistance into agents of change for openness in education. The definition takes into account both the objects – teaching resources – and the practices – learning design, pedagogical and assessment approaches – of teachers' activities, therefore representing an attempt to go beyond the use of OER when defining the work of educators in open settings. Subsequently, we introduce a self-development framework for teachers, which takes into account all the dimensions of openness included in the definition and which provides teachers with capacity building paths along each dimension.

UNDERSTANDING LAUREATE'S EUROPEAN HYBRIDITY INITIATIVE

Michael Vogelsang, Business and Information Technology School, Germany,
Marios Vryonides, European University Cyprus, Cyprus, Pedro Lara Bercial, Universidad Europea Madrid, Spain,
Alain Noghiu, Laureate Network Office, Netherlands

Building the Education of the Future

Laureate is the world's leading for-profit education provider with a network of close to 90 institutions around the globe, representing over 1,000,000 students. In 2015, Laureate embarked on a network wide initiative to achieve 25% hybridity by 2019. This goal entails the delivery of 25% of total contact hours in an online format at each institution. This represents a significant transformative mandate for all Laureate institutions. The goal originates in the broader recognition that education is rapidly changing, driven by new learner requirements and the evolution of learning technologies which are entering the classroom. These trends also imply the need for a significant rethinking of classroom pedagogy. In Europe the majority of Laureate's 15 institutions exemplify a traditional teaching and learning profile, hence the organization's hybridity goal represents a major transformational challenge. From a research perspective, Laureate's hybridity goals represents a unique opportunity to study the methods, impact, challenges and successes of online teaching and learning as these evolve across autonomous institutions, connected by a broader organizational imperative.

Research Setup

In order to achieve the 25% hybridity mandate Laureate has created the Laureate Network Office, tasked with helping its institutions achieve their 25% goal by transferring knowledge, skills, best practices etc. between Laureate and its institutions. Each institution has organized resources internally to help advance their own hybridity goal. Individuals associated with this initiative are collectively responsible to help their organizations transform and perform. This entails launching a transitional period for implementation from 2016 to 2019 during which each institution is expected to:

- Re-assess their pedagogy in light of the demands and rational of online and blended teaching and learning.
- Redesign some courses in their programs to be delivered online or in a blended format.
- Train their faculty to acquire the needed skills for online and blended delivery formats.
- Adopt and train the necessary staff in the use of a common LMS (Blackboard).
- Create and administer online and blended learning quality assessment procedures and metrics.
- Track faculty and student performance and satisfaction with online and blended formats.

The coordinated nature of this endeavour is unique and lends itself to a series of comparative longevity studies.

Research topics and questions identified include:

- A comparative study (qualitative) of how key European Laureate institutions reframed their organizations toward hybridity; a comparative study analysing the process and learnings.
- A comparative study (quantitative) of faculty and / or student perceptions, responses to and satisfaction with hybridity.
- A comparative study (qualitative) of the type of blended learning models to emerge at different institutions and their effectiveness.
- A comparative study of student learning outcomes (quantitative) via hybridity vs. traditional learning modalities.

MOOCS FOR MOTIVATION: PROMOTING STUDENT ENGAGEMENT IN HIGHER EDUCATION STUDIES

Steven Warburton, Maria Fragkaki, Sophia Vahora, University of Surrey, United Kingdom

Student engagement in Higher Education is a challenge for most institutions, not only in the UK but in Europe and internationally. One of the reasons that students perform better and are more engaged is when they feel motivated, confident and challenged by their studies, and are rewarded by success. This could be achieved through the raising of aspirations for core study via the successful completion of a short MOOC from a well-known institution. The positive emotional effect of studying within a diverse global community of learners and the value of the ensuing course completion could potentially boost student success on their core courses.

In this paper we explore the relationship between factors that affect learner motivation to study and the potential value of massive open online courses (MOOCs) to stimulate student engagement with their core higher educational studies. The research has used a mixed methods approach to uncover quantitative and qualitative insights from a group of undergraduate level student ambassadors.

Research Instruments

- For phase 1: An online survey was designed to measure a range of sub-processes across four phases of self-regulated learning in Higher Education and more generally in online education. The survey instrument comprised a structured set of 22 questions, each focused on the phases and sub-processes of self-regulated learning from Zimmerman (2000) and of the beliefs, usage and added value of technology in study.
- For phase 2: A *World Café* workshop was designed as a simple, effective and flexible format for hosting group dialogue.

In the first part, we explore whether using MOOCs as a supplemental study activity could enhance their engagement, motivation and confidence. In the second part we examine the pros and the cons of MOOC-style curricula and which student literacies, digital skills and level of self-regulation required to engage successfully with MOOCs.

The results have provided insight into primary engagement factors that underpin motivation in relation to studying and learning. For example, as we might expect, it is possible to achieve improved levels of extrinsic motivation by providing challenging course materials and engaging tasks that are relevant to the students' learning expectations. The data analysis also indicated that good digital skills are recognised as fundamental for learning. In terms of the online learning environment, the participants proposed several attributes that promote students engagement and motivation. Finally, most of the students responded positively when asked about the potential impact that following a MOOC-style curricula could have on their learning. At this stage, there is some confidence that the level of abilities reported in the three phases of the learning process (*forethought*, *performance* and *self-evaluation*) can be transferred to have a positive impact on successful online study (e.g. via MOOCs), particularly where it may be used as a supplemental study activity.

MOOCS AND CHANGE DYNAMICS IN HIGHER EDUCATION

Cathrine Tømte, Siri Aanstad, Jørgen Sjaastad, Sabine Wollscheid,
The Nordic Institute for Studies in Innovation, Research and Education (NIFU), Norway

In 2015, there were 21 MOOCs registered in the national portal www.mooc.no in Norway, most of them covering various aspects of continuing education. In most cases, teacher staff within HEIs designed and developed these MOOCs. An exception is the MOOC in *Mathematic-didactic*, initiated and funded by the government, and with academic and administrative affiliation within two HEIs and their teacher education departments. This particular MOOC offers continuing education in Mathematics mainly at 5-10th grade to teachers who work at schools around the country. Based on this particular MOOC for math-teachers, the present paper aims to explore if this MOOC may enhance pedagogical innovation in the participating/actual teacher educations; and in which ways it may serve as a driver in order to enhance knowledge development in terms of new teaching models or alternative teaching models within the two participating HEIs.

The paper presents preliminary findings from an ongoing formative evaluation study of this MOOC, running from September 2015-September 2016 commissioned by the Norwegian Centre for ICT in Education. Based on semi-structures interviews with stakeholders and coordinators within the two higher education institutions responsible for the MOOC-like course, along with semi-structured interviews with stakeholders from the government side, we addressed various issues. Some of these were background for participation; internal organization and tasks; financial perspectives, collaboration within the institution and with the partner institution and the government; academic and administrative perspectives on pedagogical solutions within the MOOC; routines for knowledge sharing about the MOOC within the institution.

The various stakeholders involved in the actual MOOC apparently seem to hold different conceptions of it; we observe statements such as *it is a MOOC; or a MOOC-like course*; or *it is an online course* and the like. Following this, the governmental bodies are concerned with exploring the possibilities that comes with MOOCs in terms of innovation and reframing informal/unformal and formal learning as various approaches towards continuing education and lifelong learning. However, this point of departure is contrasting the views of the HEIs. These stakeholders are more likely to struggle with connecting the MOOC to ongoing activities within their institutions. We may interpret these diverse understandings and approaches of MOOCs in terms of different perspectives on quality issues, where different aspects of quality are interpret differently, such as quality of academic content; pedagogy; technology; communication and recruitment of students.

Initially, to enhance collaboration and innovation across institutions, the government required the MOOC to affiliate to at least to HEIs. Two HEIs and their teacher education departments became involved, with shared task related to administration and academic content, and coordinated by an overall governmental body responsible for the overall coordination and technological solutions. This approach, including several HEIs to host and develop one particular MOOC, seems to correspond with what seems to be considered as one of the opportunities within MOOCs as flagged by ODL-stakeholders, since it may enhance knowledge development across institutions. As demonstrated in the research literature, missing strategies on an institutional level to integrate MOOCs and link them to existing and mainstream activities within the institution may hinder their uptake. This might be the case in here, and we will pursue this when continuing our study.

DO OUR MOOC'S WORK?
CREATIVE WAYS TO ASSESS INNOVATIVE E-LEARNING PROGRAMS

Elran Michal, Bar Carmel, Bar-On Naama, Elran Yossi,
Davidson Institute of Science Education, Weizmann Institute of Science, Rehovot, Israel

Assessment of learners is important – both of the individual achievements of the learners and the effectiveness of the learning scenario, be it the teacher, the curriculum, the learning environment, etc. We focus on the latter, in an attempt to assess some aspects of two, highly irregular online learning programs in math and science. Assessment of the learners before and after taking part in these programs can give us valuable information about the programs themselves.

The programs, *Math By Mail (MBM) Online* and *Science By Mail (SBM) Online*, are e-learning courses in recreational math and popular science (respectively), for students in grades 3-8, worldwide. The main goals of these programs are to develop high-order learning skills and "out-of-the-box" thinking, and to boost curiosity and affinity to math and science - and it is this that we want to measure. These programs were developed and are managed by the Davidson Institute of Science Education, the educational arm of the Weizmann Institute of Science. Through a unique learning platform within a MOOC-like (Massive Open Online Course) scenario, thousands of young scientists and mathematicians, learn from, and collaborate with leading scientists and mathematicians.

It is extremely important for us to assess the added value of our programs, and learn whether or not they achieve their goals. With regards to MBM and SBM, we want to know what unique knowledge, skills etc. do the students learn. We narrow our focus to specific questions for each course. In order to answer these questions, a new model based on performance assessment tasks was designed and implemented to identify the learning and thinking skills that were acquired during the year within the unique framework of MBM and SBM.

The performance assessment tasks that were developed and delivered online to the participants answered questions that we had about the effectiveness of the programs: Do the students who finish an annual MBM course, grasp the much broader concept of math being a vast body of knowledge and skills? (yes). Does SBM enhance the individual student's "meaningful question asking" abilities? (yes).

Rather than focus on the individual results specific to MBM and SBM, we believe that the model suggested here can be adopted for many online scenario. Performance assessment tasks of the type presented in this paper, are helpful to assess the effectively of programs for a large, homogeneous group of learners. They are easy to deploy online, especially for a large body of learners and hence are also useful for evaluating MOOCs. The direction proposed can be generalized and applied to other MOOC's and similar learning environments.

EXEMPLARS OF COLLABORATIVE LEARNING DESIGN IN ONLINE COURSES

Afsaneh Sharif, Manuel Dias, University of British Columbia, Canada

Abstract

Many instructors promote and support collaborative learning processes by integrating technology into their curricula and establishing interactive environments. There is also a growing trend toward student-led collaborative learning where teachers adopt a supportive role and become learning resources (Wheeler, Yeomans, & Wheeler, 2008). Collaborative learning is based on constructivism, which is aimed at getting the students to take full responsibility for working together, constructing knowledge together, evolving together, and of course, improving together (Dooly, 2008). It also can be based on connectivism, which recognizes the impact of technology on society and ways of knowing. As per Siemens (2005) connectivism is "the integration of principles explored by chaos, network, and complexity and self-organization theories" in which learning in not entirely under the control of the individual; rather, it can reside outside of ourselves and occurs through interaction with various sources of knowledge and participation in different group activities and social networks. In this paper, we present different design strategies and innovative pedagogical approaches that foster collaborative learning through usage of a variety of technologies in Master of Education Technology (MET) program at the University of British Columbia (UBC). MET is a fully online graduate-level program offered by UBC that has attracted students from over 35 countries. The program is designed for educators from different levels and diverse contexts such as K–12 teachers, college and university educators, adult/industry educators, and course/instructional designers. In this paper, we present two MET courses as exemplars of collaborative learning and student engagement in case format. These courses were developed in WordPress, a blogging platform supported by the University, and adopted a similar approach where participants are peers in a professional network and instructors act as fellow peers or facilitators of learning. The content is publicly available with user-restricted access to learning activities. In this paper, we present two courses, ETEC 522 and ETEC 565, in case format that emphasize collaborative learning design online.

Case 1 – ETEC 522: Students as Contributors and Reviewers in a Highly Interactive Course

Ventures in Learning Technology is an online immersion in the global learning technologies marketplace with particular emphasis on emerging markets for learning technologies in public and commercial domains. This course is delivered in a case-study modality from a venture and market analysis perspective, where students examine real-world enterprises and markets while acting as venture creators or analysts. The course culminates with a "venture forum" featuring real or possible venture concepts that learners design and "pitch" to the class. This course is designed to operate as a professional network, a place where social networking techniques are applied to foster individual and collective professional advancement. Students are encouraged to participate in different group discussions and evaluate each other's work.

Case 2 – ETEC 565M: Facilitating Student Collaboration through a Social Medium

Mobile Education is an evolving online course that is examining the impact of mobile technologies on knowledge systems. This course is an experiential immersion in the proven and emerging potentials of mobile technologies and open learning. It is designed to be mobile oriented with the use of a social medium (PulsePress) for short messaging, allowing more efficient communication among learners. Students become proficient with the theory and strategy of mobile education through collective critical analysis of existing technologies, applications, and trends in the global mobile culture specific to knowledge acquisition, generation, and dissemination. Collaborative learning occurs in the forms of collective feedback and curation utilizing different technologies and strategies such as PulsePress and BadgeOS™ plugins.

AN EXPERIMENT OF SOCIAL-GAMIFICATION IN MASSIVE OPEN ONLINE COURSES: THE ECO IMOOC

Eva Garcia-Lopez, Antonio Garcia-Cabot, Luis de-Marcos, University of Alcala, Spain, António Moreira Teixeira, Universidade Aberta & University of Lisbon, Maria do Carmo Teixeira Pinto, Universidade Aberta, Portugal

Introduction

Massive Open Online Courses (MOOCs) represent a disruptive new trend that has brought scalability and openness to non-formal education. In fact, MOOCs have the potential to widen participation in higher education, thus contributing to social inclusion, the dissemination of innovation and the internationalization of higher education institutions.

On the other hand, over time education researchers have conducted many theoretical and empirical studies on the videogames subject. Due to the aforementioned issues, some researchers do not use only videogames to educate; instead they seek to export the positive aspects of videogames to non-gaming educational contexts. This concept is commonly called *gamification*. Some researchers generically defined it as "the use of game design elements and game mechanics in non-game contexts".

This paper presents the results of an experiment using gamification in a real MOOC. This has been developed by an international team composed by researchers from Universidade Aberta (Portugal) and University of Alcala (Spain). The course selected for the experiment is a sMOOC developed by Universidade Aberta (Portugal) in the framework of the ECO project partnership, which draws their pedagogical approach from the iMOOC pedagogical model created by Teixeira and Mota.

Results

The first iteration is considered as *social group* (it includes social network mechanisms but no gamification) and the second iteration is considered as *social-gamified group* (it includes both social network mechanisms and gamification techniques). The results of these iterations, 3.51% of the students completed the course in the first iteration and 5.07% of the students completed the course in the second iteration. Therefore it can be observed that the number of students who passed the course was higher in the *social-gamified group*.

It can be observed that, in all cases, the participation in the platform (blogs, Tweets, messages, etc.) is higher in the social-gamified group than in the social group. In general terms, it is important to highlight that the mean of total interactions in the social group is 117.0281, while in the social-gamified group the mean is 486.82 interactions. This means that the participants interacted more than four times more in the second iteration than in the first iteration.

Conclusions

The results obtained in the second iteration are positive (regarding the percentage of participants who passed the course) with respect to the first iteration but the dropout rates are still low and they considered as "normal". Furthermore, the participation in the platform was higher in the second iteration with respect to the first one. Therefore we can conclude that the use of gamification techniques promote the use and participation of the social platform. It is also important to highlight that there is a need to continue researching in this field including more gamification techniques to reduce the dropout rate.

As future work we are planning to include Open Badges mechanisms, because this kind of reward can be kept after the course finishes, and this could be a good motivation for the participants in the MOOC. The possibility of integrating mobile devices in the courses will also be studied, as done in previous research.

OPENNESS, MULTICULTURALISM, ATTITUDES AND EXPERIENCE IN ONLINE COLLABORATIVE LEARNING

Noga Magen-Nagar, Gordon College of Education, Miri Shonfeld, Kibbutzim College of Education, Technology and Arts Institution and MOFET, Roni Dayan, Ministry of Education, Israel

In the framework of the national ICT program in Israel diverse ICT collaborative programs exist at national and district levels serving the schools, such as Twinning Schools Project, Tec4Schools and Schools Online (Ministry of Education).The current study was aimed to examine the variables that predict integrating Online Collaborative Learning (OCL) in lessons amongst ICT coordinators who participate in such programs compared to ICT coordinators who do not participate. The variables were attitudes towards their students' openness to multiculturalism, attitudes regarding the advantages and the disadvantages of OCL, challenging experiences in OCL and teaching seniority.

The study participants were 315 ICT coordinators. About half of them participated in the OCL programs (44%) and about half did not participate in OCL official programs (56%). The research hypotheses were examined using a self-reporting questionnaire that was developed for this study and was based on validated questionnaires. Path analysis was conducted using the statistical AMOS 22.0 software. Figure 1 presents the research model.

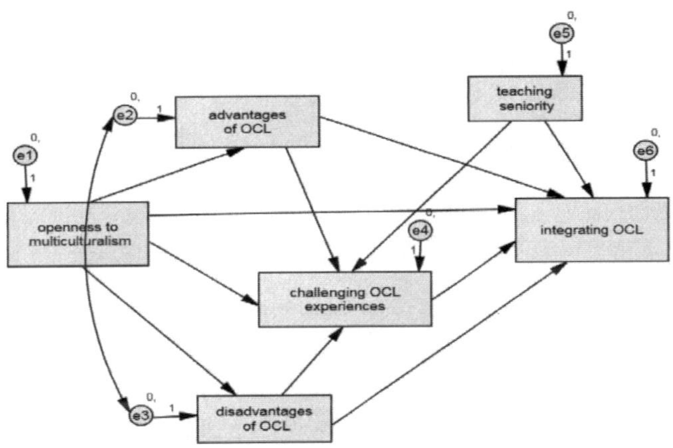

Figure 1. The proposed research model

Amongst ICT coordinators participating in the OCL programs, attitudes regarding their student's openness to multiculturalism have a significant impact on the attitudes towards the advantages and the disadvantages of OCL (β = .54***, β = -.40*** respectively). There is also significant impact on the challenging experience OCL (β = -.21**), but there is no significant influence on the frequency of integrating OCL (β = -.13). Amongst ICT coordinators not participating in the OCL programs, attitudes regarding their student's openness to multiculturalism have a significant impact on the attitudes towards the advantages of OCL (β = .40***). There is also significant impact on the challenging experience, but it is negative (β = -.18**). However, attitudes regarding their student's openness to multiculturalism has no significant impact on the disadvantages (β = -.11) and on the frequency of integrating OCL (β = -.14).

The findings indicate that the attitudes of ICT coordinators regarding their students' openness to multiculturalism is of critical importance to integrating OCL in the lessons, wherein some factors involved attitudes towards understanding the value of such learning and dealing with challenges when experiencing OCL is involved. Amongst ICT coordinators participating in OCL programs, the variables involved indicate a significant process, thus the more positive attitudes they manifest regarding their students' openness to multiculturalism, the lower are the attitudes towards the disadvantages of OCL, the weaker are the challenging experiences of OCL, and the greater is the frequency of its integration in learning. A most important factor found in the research is the attitudes towards the disadvantages of such learning that express a waste of teaching and learning time, creating tension between children and leading to disciplinary problems, difficulties achieving success by the student who is dependent on the group members and active participation. There is no possibility for reasonable evaluation, suitable to all types of students and all subjects. It is possible that by instructing the coordinators and the teachers in general on OCL they may deal with the in-depth application of collaborative learning, so that the disadvantages won't limit teaching and learning.

HOW TO ADOPT THE REMEDIAL CMOOC GUERRILLA LITERACY LEARNERS?

Huion Patricia, Limburg Catholic University College, Belgium

On Why Guerrilla Literacy Learners (GuLL) Need a cMOOC

GuLL aims to expand teachers' repertoires of language teaching. Languages are quite often taught within a linguistic frame where the teacher indicates the mistakes learners have made and where grammar is used to describe these errors. But more and more learners find it difficult to make sense of these rules and create mistakes through unorthodox patterns such as guessing, mathematical calculations, applying correct rules in wrong contexts, applying correct rules too often, implementing rules from one language into another. The teachers do not understand how these mistakes are made and the students do not understand how they can be avoided. They lack a common language.

Gull moves away from language-focused teaching practices and seeks to find out how these unorthodox patterns are created. Through user-centred approaches, narrative coaching, graphic facilitation, art of hosting and digital literacies teachers can create contexts in which students are willing to think aloud and share how they create these unorthodox patterns. We have called these guerrilla patterns similar to guerrilla gardening and guerrilla knitting. Both teachers and learners gain insight into how guerrilla patterns are created and can name them in lay terms such as mathematician, cultural mixer, do-gooder. These lay terms not only serve as a memory bridge to the pattern and make it easier to correct but also become a common language between teacher and student.

But teachers are not trained in these learner-driven, mistake-based approaches. Secondly, we have not discovered all guerrilla patterns yet. That is why we opted for a cMOOC starting from traditional language teaching approaches to Guerrilla approaches, each time asking teachers to reflect on how mistakes are dealt with. In the GuLL MOOC we explain the guerrilla approach through knowledge clips, further reading and watching but more importantly we initiate the conversation about it through the assignments. As such we create a community of practice discussing and discovering more guerrilla patterns. In doing so the GuLL MOOC not only informs about a new didactical approach but more importantly it creates engagement through a strong learner-learner interaction.

On How the Development of the GuLL MOOC Improves the GuLL Adoption

We chose as a whole case the scenario where a teacher, Susan, takes a whole class to London, hops on the tube and sees some of her students are still standing on the platform. As a consequence the GuLL MOOC takes you on a journey where teacher Susan tries to retrieve her students. We wanted teachers to identify with teacher Susan so we chose for animated knowledge clips. We also wanted the learner's perspective to be very clear so we asked a student to do the voice-over.

Finally thinking about our target audiences and making sure teachers would be willing to make this journey to a learner-driven and fail-based approach we added a chapter on existing teaching methods from structuralism/behaviourism, rationalism and cognitive psychology, to social constructivism and alternative approaches such as Freinet, Roger, Montessori and Parkhurst. Thus the MOOC created coherence as the whole case served as a metaphor for the whole learning trajectory and made us connect to the outside world, the teacher's perspective and the student's voice.

THE EVOLUTION OF MOOCS AND A CLARIFICATION OF TERMINOLOGY THROUGH LITERATURE REVIEW

Hakan Altinpulluk, Mehmet Kesim, Anadolu University, Turkey

Massive Open Online Courses (MOOCs), which are based in approach that offers online courses to great masses in an open and free manner, are a recent trend in distance education and are still under debate. MOOCs developed as an extension of the OER movement, changing and transforming in recent years despite retaining certain aspects. This research follows MOOCs, the buzzword of 2012, in an attempt to study the reasoning behind the recent questioning of their effectiveness. Additionally, the evolution of MOOCs is traced, and new MOOCs with new acronyms are portrayed.

HOW A MOOC-LIKE COURSE IS FACILITATING TEACHERS' CONTINUING EDUCATION AND TEACHERS' PROFESSIONAL LEARNING COMMUNITY?

Sabine Wollscheid, Cathrine Tømte, Jørgen Sjaastad, Siri Aanstad, The Nordic Institute for Studies in Innovation, Research and Education (NIFU), Norway

Background and study aim

Within higher education, the supply of Massive Open Online Courses (MOOCs) has rapidly increased, both in numbers and in variation of different types. While the literature on different kinds of MOOCs is growing in general, manifested by a couple of systematic reviews, research on the impact of MOOCs for teachers' continuing education is scarce. Teachers' continuing education is high on the policy agenda in many countries, among them Norway. The government strategy emphasizes school-based programs enabling teachers from the same school to cooperate while taking courses and thus, make advantage of *learning communities* and *collaborative lear*ning. To address the need for teachers' continuing education and to provide a flexible course supply for teachers, national education authorities launched a MOOC-like course in 2015, a course limited to two semesters and addressing math teachers in primary school (grade 5-7). Drawing on preliminary findings from this evaluation, the aim of this paper is to present findings with particular focus on teachers' perspective as users and learners. Drawing on the assumption that teachers are part of online and offline learning communities, we will describe different types of interactions and learning communities, either directly or indirectly related to MOOC-participation. We distinguish between two types of professional learning communities, (a) a type of teacher professional community, which stresses learning together with and from colleagues at the same school, and (b) a type of teacher professional community across different school sites, the MOOC study group. Thus, our specific aim is to describe and explore group interactions between teachers from the same school (analogue), teachers from the same teacher network but different schools, and interactions between teachers in a MOOC-like study group, and how these interactions affect their perception of that particular continuous education program, and further, knowledge transfer at school organizational level.

The study: Method and data collection

The original study is an ongoing formative evaluation study of a MOOC-like course addressing 5th to 6th grade-mathematics teachers in Norway (September 2015-2016) commissioned by the Norwegian Centre for ICT in Education in cooperation with two higher education institutions. To investigate a broad range of topics on two levels, user and governance level, we triangulate both quantitative and qualitative methods and data. Data include semi-structured interviews with teachers, school leaders, pupils and higher education institutions providing MOOC-like courses, observational data of participating teachers in online study groups, document analyses (strategic documents) and a teacher survey. Focusing on teachers and teachers' professional learning communities, this paper draws on interview data of a subsample of teachers, principals and pupils at two primary schools located in a typical middle class area in Eastern Norway.

Preliminary findings

Drawing on interview-data from two case schools, our findings reveal that MOOC-like groups (digital) to a little degree facilitate interactions and strengthen school-based and across-school professional teacher communities, if all participants come from different schools. On the other hand, if teachers from the same school or/and the same existing professional network, participate in the course, this MOOC-like course appear to facilitate school-based professional communities and knowledge transfer. Further data analyses will triangulate interview data with survey data of a larger sample of teachers with the aim to describe different types of group interactions (online, offline) between teachers across and within the same school.

BUILDING TOGETHER EFFICIENT, TARGETED AND LONG-LASTING E-TRAINING: EXPERIENCE FEEDBACK FROM THE UTOP PROJECT

Vincent Beillevaire, UNIT Foundation, Anne Boyer, Lorraine University, France

The uTOP initiative

UNIT (Université Numérique en Ingénièrie et Technologie – http://www.unit.eu) is one of the 8 French Thematic Digital Universities (TDUs) supported by the French Ministry of Education, Higher Education and Research. The TDUs are networks of universities and engineering schools working collaboratively to create a national high-quality educational resource bank for the whole university community (academics and students). TDUs are organised by disciplinary fields and UNIT is the TDU dedicated to Engineering and Technology. UNIT is a Foundation open to all public and private actors of HE in Sciences and Technologies who agree that it is more efficient and rational to mutualise and to share knowledge and projects, and look together for co-financing system in the field of the digital for education.

The *IDEFI uTOP project* is a *multi-partners* project which federates around UNIT its 60 members. This network is composed of actors in digital education such as CNAM (National Conservatory of Arts And Crafts), on-line IUT (University Institute of Technology), Universities and Engineering schools (Telecom Institute, Telecom Lille, Écoles des Mines, ENPC (French National School of Civil Engineering), ENSG, Universities of Valenciennes and Lorraine), research actors in Robotics (INRIA, GDR) and companies (Orange, Aldebaran, Géoconcept). uTOP works as a "marketplace". It's a hub, a place of confluence between training demand and supply, organizing *multi-partners* projects. The uTOP project aims at building an offer of long life trainings on a model, adapted to the French context, of open digital university, addressing the national and international market, first and foremost the Francophony. Its purpose is to become a "bridge" between higher education, business and research worlds.

The uTOP implementation

The uTOP project confirms the concept of *multi-partners digital open university* around three sub-projects of experimental distance training associating economic and territorial players and open projects, in response to required specification (digital and innovative co building training, in response to demonstrated and identified needs, economically viable).

Conclusion

The uTOP project has realized its main objectives and can be considered as a real success thanks to:

- 39 courses and over 2,500 hours;
- 26 internal partners for a common goal and mobilization of over 100 external partners in a multi-partnership approach.

The uTOP project is now an actor located bridging the gap between business and higher education institutions, in the field on online education. In a relatively short time, it succeeds in developing a framework for the facilitation of the collaboration, the promotion of online curricula. The uTOP project supports and funds the development of several online training, some are open and free for the learners (such as the MOOCs previously described) and some others not, some are very short (4 weeks) and some much longer (9 months for master degrees).

Above all, uTOP supports his partners in the implementation of long-lasting economic models in distance training. The creation of profitable trainings allows a return on investment towards uTOP and thus to develop new projects, in services of individuals, companies and economic world.

This initiative shouldn't be limited to France. Next step for uTOP is to extend this approach to future partners in Europe and all over the world.

AUGMENTED LEARNING ENVIRONMENT FOR WOUND CARE SIMULATION

Nelson Jorge, Delft University of Technology, The Netherlands, Lina Morgado, Universidade Aberta, Pedro Gaspar, Instituto Politécnico de Leiria, Portugal

Introduction

This paper describes part of a doctoral study where the effect of Augmented Reality (AR) in nursing student's decision making skills was investigated, by comparing the usage of a virtual simulator (e-Fer) in wound care diagnosis and treatment, with and without the support of AR to visualize the wounds. A literature review was conducted to identify the effectiveness of AR in medical education. In general, AR has shown to be an effective tool to develop clinical skills when compared with other methods, with a greater impact on inexperienced learners, and its transfer to real world scenarios.

Materials and Methods

The e-Fer is an online clinical decision-making simulator used in the initial training of nurses, allowing to simulate the diagnosis and treatment of virtual clinical cases of chronic wounds. The main goal is to promote the healing of the patient's wound by selecting the best diagnosis and treatment solution, in this order. The effectiveness of e-Fer was demonstrated by Costa (2010). In this study an AR component was added, with new clinical cases, creating an augmented learning environment where students could observe the 3D wounds in a more realistic and natural way, simulating real practice. The AR component was created using user-friendly technology, both for the production of the 3D objects and its implementation in an AR mobile application. For this study 6 clinical cases were created and added to e-Fer. The objects for these new cases were produced using *Autodesk® 123D® Catch*, a software that generates 3D objects based on several pictures taken from different angles. After producing the objects the files were uploaded to *ViewAR*, a software that uses printed markers to show the 3D objects in AR, when detected by an *iPad* with the application installed.

A quasi experimental study with pre- and post-test was conducted with 54 first year Nursing students without wound care experience. Participants started the activity by solving clinical cases on e-Fer during 2 weeks. After this period they were split into control group ($n = 24$) and experimental group ($n = 30$). The control group kept solving clinical cases as they were used to in the e-Fer online simulator. The experimental group also solved the clinical cases using e-Fer, but observed the wounds with an iPad using AR. After 4 weeks all data was extracted from e-Fer, processed and analysed anonymously. The Mann–Whitney U test and Wilcoxon signed-rank test were used to compare and analyse the differences in performance, between and within groups respectively. A P value < 0.05 was considered statistically significant.

Results and Discussion

The results after statistical treatment of the data extracted from e-Fer are based on the correct number of answers per clinical case given by students. The Mann-Whitney U test was used to compare groups. No statistically significant differences were found between the two groups in the pre-test, which validates the homogeneity of the groups before manipulating the independent variable, when both groups were using the traditional e-Fer without AR. In the second moment, when the experimental group used e-Fer with AR, statistically significant differences where revealed in all parameters, except for one. The means obtained by the experimental group raised significantly, while the control group maintained their performance. In the treatment phase no statistically significant differences where revealed in all parameters. In fact, it is in the diagnosis phase that observing the wound is critical for a correct decision. In the treatment step, observation takes a secondary role, since it depends on the correct diagnosis previously realized. In this way, observing the wound with AR proved to have a positive effect in the overall diagnosis phase on the experimental group, with highly statistically significant differences ($P < 0.001$) when compared to the control group.

Conclusion

The results showed that AR enhanced students' performance in wound diagnostic parameters, with highly statistically significant differences ($P < 0.001$) in the Mann-Whitney U and Wilcoxon tests.

EXTRACURRICULAR VOCATIONAL TRAINING IN HIGHER EDUCATION: RESUME OF EXPERIENCES AFTER TEN YEARS OF PRACTICE

Thomas Richter, Heimo H. Adelsberger, Pouyan Khatami, TELIT @ University of Duisburg Essen, Germany

With the implementation of the Bologna process in Germany, curricula – originally designed for diploma and magister programs – had to be transferred to three-year bachelor programs. The general purpose was to enable university students to enter the world of works with a qualified (academic) degree earlier.

In the context of the German language speaking countries, unique characteristics were required for the new academic bachelor degree in distinction from the regionally traditional (non-academic) bachelor degrees, which were provided by the industry and the chamber of crafts after three years lasting apprenticeships. Different to the modus operandi *learning on the job* as it is the rather common concept outside the German-speaking countries, the education of apprentices in industry and crafting disciplines is not limited to the particular tasks arising from the daily business in an employing enterprise but, within the particular branch, they are expected to being practically prepared for the full range of tasks from any kind of job. For that purpose, the apprentices are demanded to visit a branch-related school for professionals, which ensure that even very specialized enterprises can employ apprentices. In these schools, lectures are provided on general job-related theoretical knowledge and hands-on training to achieve the full range of practical skills. In order to receive the degree, apprentices must prove their abilities in theoretical and practical exams. The difficult competitive situation for the academic bachelor degree holders particularly gets obvious when it comes to apprenticeships with the purpose to educate assistants for academic disciplines, like biological, chemical and architectural assistants, system programmers, and management assistants in the health industry. Another difficulty for the design of the academic bachelor degrees arose from the demand that education in universities generally is expected to be fully sustainable (timeless). Teaching application-related competences in the framework of academic education as demanded by the industry is understood as a contradiction against this very basic principle: Applications, however mainstream they might be used in a specific field, might easily be substituted as soon as new technologies emerge.

During the redesign of the curricula, most of the theoretical contents from the prior diploma and magister programs eventually were adopted for the new bachelor curricula on the cost of practical experiences, which the students earlier achieved in the context of several seminars, field trips, and hands-on trainings. While the understanding of basic principles and methodologies was focused, practical research skills were reduced to a minimum assuming that these were rather irrelevant for the work in the industry but exclusively required for academic working purposes. Consequently, related practical research skills and experiences were related to the consecutively designed master programs. These were meant to establish the beginning of an intended academic career. It is still not fully clear which specific abilities distinguish academic bachelor degree holders from non-academic bachelors in terms of advantages on the job market at entry-level. Sure, academic bachelors have a deep general understanding of the context and above that, also a basic understanding of typical strategies, measures, and theories, which the non-academic bachelors lack to a large extent. Just, at least for the first years of employment, enterprises still perceive a higher return of investment if employing the cheaper non-academic bachelors who far quicker can fully be integrated within current work processes.

The program *erp4students* was 2006 launched with the purpose to solve the found educational dilemma. Since it was designed as an extracurricular offer, the basic principle of sustainable education in universities was not in danger.

In our case-study-driven extracurricular vocational online training program, we experienced that combining relatively small theoretical lectures in printable PDF-documents with hands-on work on extensive case studies led to the achievement of competences in the field. We further found that group work is not the method of choice when it comes to extracurricular training: In order to successfully complete the courses, the learners need to study in their very own pace. Our learners further expressed to highly value our individual round-the-clock tutor-support because it ensures that they still can make the best out of the rare free time available for extracurricular work once they experience seemingly unmanageable problems. Finally, in our study, we found that the learners' perceptions of and attitudes towards learning are quite similar comparing online programs and traditional learning.

BRIDGING THEORY TO PRACTICE THROUGH A FLIPPED CLASSROOM APPROACH IN AN ENTREPRENEURSHIP COURSE

Ingrid le Roux, University of Pretoria, South Africa

At the University of Pretoria, the focus of a third year Entrepreneurship is on starting up businesses, self-employment and creating employment. While the curriculum is set and allows little foray, lecturers strive to improve the quality of teaching and learning, making the best use of the available infrastructure, class-time and technology. There is a lively debate on the merits of teaching traditional lecture-based classes versus using technology for teaching, and how they can be improved, blended, hybridised or flipped. In the developed world with ubiquitous access to technology and internet, flipped classroom teaching has become synonymous with blended learning and very much the norm. While video lectures are not new, the affordances of videos, screencasts, audio lectures and the like can add real value to a flipped classroom. It is in this arena that a third-year course in entrepreneurship was flipped in 2015, and reported in this article. The study investigates both the instruction method as well as the application of theory through tutorials and focuses on how to apply theory to practice in a representative way in an attempt to simulate a real business experience. Therefore, this study explores the use of teacher created videos that students could watch in their own time at home or on campus and the purpose of the study was to investigate student perceptions of the benefits of using videos and tutorials to link theory to practice. Data were sourced from anonymous written feedback provided by students at the end of the semester. In two questionnaires, students had to rate different characteristics of videos and tutorials using a simple 3-point scale. Those responses were numerically weighted, with 0 for *Not Important*, 1 for *To some extent Important*, and 2 for *Very Important*, the weights added and the characteristics sorted accordingly. The questionnaire also contained open-ended questions where students could reflect on how the tutorials or videos helped them. Written feedback was captured electronically and thematically analysed using computer-based qualitative analysis software, ATLAS.ti™. The same code set was used in analysis of both questionnaires so that themes could be compared between the two. These findings would ascertain how the course components in the flipped classroom contributed to integrate theory and practice. To ensure transparency and validity in the process, coding was checked by two seasoned academics, resulting in minor re-naming of categories. The findings report the benefits that students perceived they gained from taking part in a flipped class approach, as captured in their reflections and the research questionnaire. The qualitative findings were interpreted using the guidelines of Sams and Bergmann (2013), Ash (2012) and Tucker (2012) to understand perceived benefits in an entrepreneurship classroom. Rating the characteristics of the videos, showed in decreasing order: Having another resource in addition to the textbook (53); View it again to understand better (51); Use for revision (50); View again for deeper insight (48). It showed that videos were highly rated as an additional resource. Almost equally important was the ability to view them more than once whether to understand better, for revision or gaining deeper insight. Many students reported viewing slides more than once, and opening the slides at the same time as watching the video on that topic, which was confirmed from logs in the CMS. Before a student can bridge from theory to practice, a solid understanding and knowledge of theory is needed. Videos can therefore be regarded as very successful tools to support mastery of theory. Understanding and learning the theory, particularly within students' preferred learning style, all point toward student initiated activity, representing by far the most salient theme in the qualitative analysis. Considering that lecturing is regarded as passive and lecturer-centred, and videos as lectures that have just switched delivery mode, the students in this study reported the value of different independent learning activities taking place in response to watching the videos, suggesting that the videos used in this course were more student-centred than lectures. A seasoned lecturer knows what the difficult concepts are, anticipates the misunderstandings and from experience uses illustrative examples and applications in an organised well-planned, and -executed video. The tutorials were the opportunities where the application of theory in the real world had most value and two-way bridges between theory and practice were built, with understanding improving further. This confirms the superior teaching value of the flipped classroom, particularly when complicated theory has to be understood and applied in practice, which clearly will not happen to any great extent in a classroom lecture. Not only did the flipped classroom provide opportunities to identify knowledge gaps but also allowed for some lecturer-student interaction, peer-interaction and collaborative learning.

The study has implications for both educators and practitioners. Linking case studies to real business benefit students by exposing them to the world of work and practice. It can be applied across disciplines and is therefore ideally suited in many higher education subject areas. It helps students not only to master theory but also to understand and apply what they have learned in a wider context. The study therefore confirms the notion that education is capable of making a significant contribution to the development of well-rounded individuals ready to enter the world of work.

THE CHANGING NATURE OF COURSE DESIGN AND DEVELOPMENT IN ONLINE HIGHER EDUCATION

Keith Hampson, Contact North/Contact Nord, Canada

Despite talk of *disruption* and *transformation*, a core aspect of online higher education has remained virtually unchanged since the late 1990s: the way that traditional colleges and universities go about designing, creating, and financing in-house online course and content development.

Now, as before, individual instructors assume the bulk of the responsibility for course design and development. While support is now often available from an instructional designer and technical staff, the impact of support staff has been limited by deeply entrenched workplace conventions that, for example, encourage faculty to work alone (and staff to let them). Similarly, funds for course development have been constrained, due to the conventional notion/practice that course materials should be built for use only within the institution from which they came.

The impact of these and other conventions on the potential for high quality instructional content cannot be overstated. The development of more sophisticated forms of digital learning such as personalized instruction driven by analytics, immersive gaming, or the use of rich media, to name but a few possibilities, almost always require a team of specialists, longer development schedules, and considerably more funding than is available in the current approach. Placing the burden on lone educators with minuscule (or non-existent) funding and who are not hired for their strengths in instructional media development is neither logical, nor fair. But more to the point, it is a lost opportunity to leverage high-quality course design to drive improvements in learning outcomes.

Drivers of Change to Authoring and Content

A number of factors are now converging that appear set to reconfigure the role and status of high-quality instructional content which will, in turn, reshape how institutions go about creating and acquiring instructional content.

Quality Course Design and Competitive Differentiation: The number of online and blended courses continues produced by North American institutions continues to climb rapidly. Increased choice for online students has led to true competition between institutions. Competition, in turn, is forcing colleges and universities to begin to develop higher quality, differentiated opportunities for students that can serve as a tangible response to the demands of competition.

Beyond Instructionally Agnostic Software: For much of online higher education's short history, educational software has been used primarily as a cost effective means of distributing repurposed classroom materials (video lectures, slides). But in 2016, new, more advanced forms of instructional software and content are emerging which have instructional strategies embedded within them. These applications have the capacity to improve and scale effective instructional practices, helping educators do more with limited resources.

Increased Transparency: The Internet is making it easier for instructional materials – normally kept out of reach behind password-protected sites – to be available to people outside the institution. The most obvious example of this trend is OER (open educational resources) and its offspring, MOOCs. The trend puts a core activity of the institution – its teaching and teachers – on display in unprecedented ways, opening up the institution and its personnel to evaluation and direct comparison with other institutions.

Media Company Investment in Ed-Tech and Ed-Media: There is growing interest in the digital higher education market amongst traditional media companies, including News Corp. (Amplify), The Washington Post, Bertelsmann AG and Condé Nast. These corporations bring deep experience in packaging and delivering high-quality informational media that will further raise the bar of instructional quality.

These factors act to raise the bar for instructional content in online higher education. Colleges and universities are responding, albeit slowly, by relying more heavily on packaged content solutions and directing more resources to in-house content development processes and resources.

CREATING A SOCIALLY SENSITIVE LEARNING ENVIRONMENT FOR SCIENCE EDUCATION: THE SSIBL FRAMEWORK

Andrea Kárpáti, Andrea Király, ELTE University, Faculty of Science, Centre for Science Communication and UNESCO Chair for Multimedia in Education, Hungary

Promoting Attainment of Responsible Research and Innovation in Science Education (acronym: PARRISE, an EU project for 2014-2017, http://www.parrise.eu) has been developing and testing an integrated framework for Socio-Scientific Inquiry-Based Learning (SSIBL) based on the four components: Responsible Research and Innovation (RRI), Socio-scientific Issues (SSI), Citizenship Education (CE) and Inquiry Based Science Education (IBSE), this last being its core element.

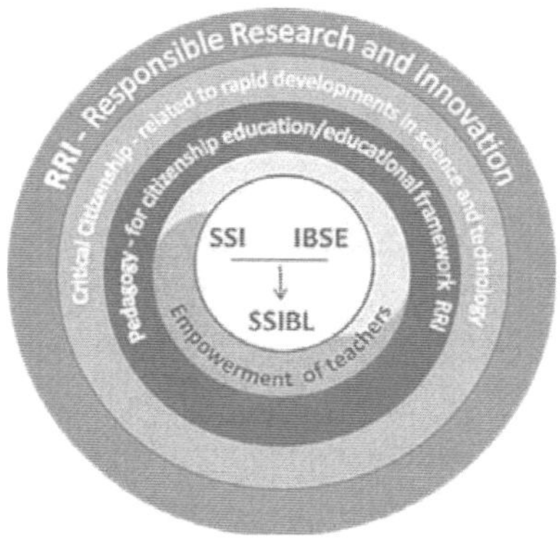

Figure 1. The Socio-Scientific Inquiry-Based Learning (SSIBL)

Adopting this model for science education is important because the relationship of scientific discoveries and innovations and social justice is rarely indicated in Hungarian curricula based on knowledge transmission. In an age of intense citizen involvement in government decisions worldwide about the preservation of natural environment or regulation of energy consumption, communicating socially sensitive issues through science education is increasingly important – and also motivating for students who experience the direct relevance of scientific knowledge for everyday life this way. Our project team works on creating a science education environment that encourages computer-supported, integrative approaches for a multifaceted, interactive and social issue-based approach. Technology is used to increase the collaborative aspects of learning, prepare science teachers to act as responsible citizens of a social-networked society and educate students who are able and also motivated to enter public debates about the way scientific discoveries are used or abused.

This presentation introduces the model and shows its implementation through various educational media during an in-service training program about current results of Physics and shows how they may be integrated in secondary school Physics education. A *formal secondary school learning environment* is proposed that includes real life experiments documented and evaluated through computer assisted devices, and *a variety of informal and non-formal environments* (in science centres, visitor centres of scientific research institutions and technological companies) are integrated to offer hands-on experiences through simulations and mock-ups of research and development tools and supported by an *in-service learning environment* for teachers. The development of educational programs to teach about *New Physics* often involves debates to clarify different citizen, researcher and political standpoints. The case study on the use of nuclear energy presented here will show how these three technology-rich learning environments interact.

Acknowledgement
The project presented in this paper has received funding from the European Union's Seventh Framework Programme for research, technological development and demonstration under grant agreement no 612438.

GLOBAL CITIZENSHIP AND LEADERSHIP IN CHANGED LEARNING ENVIRONMENTS

Alan Bruce, Universal Learning Systems, Ireland

The Impact of globalization on work and learning

One of the key characteristics of the global economy is the increasing fragmentation of production into different activities and tasks along global supply chains. This has profound socio-economic impacts (ILO, 2015). The rise in global supply chains has been facilitated by a significant reduction in trade and transport costs and by advances in information and communication technology (ICT). Together, these forces have transformed the world into an interconnected and multipolar production and trading arena. This makes obsolete traditional national boundaries and limits. The traditional demarcations within jobs and between sectors have blurred significantly. The capacities and skills required have altered. New forms of work and work organization have produced radically new forms of work production, behaviour, methods, and settings. The evidence is that this pattern is accelerating.

This has huge implications for the provision of relevant education and vocational training programs. The impact of ICT supported delivery systems has only made more intense the need to match changing needs to relevant, timely and sustainable educational models that interact positively with this changing world. Upgrading towards technologically and skill-intensive jobs may be the preferred option in the long run to address skills gaps and the impact of vocational change and transformation. But whether or not this is feasible will depend on the productive capacity of an economy. In this respect, policies to enhance technological capabilities, technology transfer and the development of skills, including on-the-job training, are essential (ILO, 2015). This in itself challenges traditional models of learning and educational provision. For learners (and especially those at risk of social marginalization), and those professionals who work with them, there is now an urgent need to re-conceptualize the environments in which individuals work and learn.

Whatever the concerns, it is clear that globalized processes are now a permanent part of the fabric of twenty-first century life. This poses a lot of questions for the principles and practices that underlie the science and practice of learning. The notion of *global citizenship* has recently gained prominence in international development discourse with the recently-adopted United Nations Secretary-General's *Global Education First Initiative* (2012). Among the three priority areas outlined in this global initiative, the third aims to 'foster global citizenship'.

> *Education must fully assume its central role in helping people to forge more just, peaceful, tolerant and inclusive societies. It must give people the understanding, skills and values they need to cooperate in resolving the interconnected challenges of the 21st century.*

If citizenship education remains the preserve of sovereign states, it can be said that many *global trends* present a set of common challenges for all societies and countries around the world. The intensification of globalization is leading to greater collective acknowledgement that individuals and local communities are affected by global processes, and, in turn, that they may also affect them. A global economy would on the surface seem to suggest the need of some kind of global citizenship. The values of public education, critical reflection, access to valued learning outcomes and quality in education all rest upon a direct connection to the policy and principles embedded in the right to learning. The changes produced in both the human and technical aspects of the globalization process shape how global education may now include various learning communities previously excluded by reason of prejudice, discrimination or remoteness. metamorphosis of traditional educational systems to meet unprecedented levels of socio-economic transformation. This also speaks of the critical importance of innovation and vision in addressing the key priorities for developing learning and transnationality to combat socio-economic marginalization. It is of interest that marginalized groups themselves can often be critically important springboards for new innovative learning methodologies. The pervasive globalizing process means no discussion on intercultural learning strategy can be undertaken without parallel international understanding and analysis of how new forms of cultural diversity impact on the learning needs of populations subjected to unprecedented levels of change. Global citizenship as concept and method offers a viable way to liberate education and its associated technologies to serve truly human learning needs in ever more creative and innovative ways.

CORK LEARNING CITY: TOWARD A COMMUNITY WIDE LEARNING ENVIRONMENT

Séamus Ó Tuama, University College Cork, Ireland

Introduction: Cork's Learning Environment both Societal and Educational

Cork has had a wide learning agenda for several decades. As early as 1911 the university was already offering extra mural education. A few years later it was engaging with trade unions offering courses for working men, through the support of the City Corporation (City Council). That tradition took off in earnest in 1947. In Cork throughout the 20th century there were experiments around broadening education and the development of new educational models. From this base the city, through the Cork City Development Board, engaged in a two-year consultation ahead of launching a vision for the city over a ten year horizon called *Cork 2002-2012: Imagine our Future. Imagine our Future* included a *theme* on *Cork as a Learning City*, with an orientation towards an all encompassing flexible learning model: "We see learning as a life-long activity for all our citizens and not as something to be pursued only by young people". This plan established a Cork City Learning Forum representative of a wide range of stakeholders. However its most significant legacy was the establishment of the Cork Lifelong Learning Festival. This festival was launched in 2004 and steadily grew in scale and reach into the community to a point where there are now in the region of 500 discrete activities offered by all types of providers non-formal, informal and formal in an annual week long festival. All activities are free and are open to the public. The participation of ordinary citizens during the festival is impressive. The idea of developing a festival was prompted by key educational influencers. It emerged into a very fertile environment in a city that was already extensively networked and became an instant success. It mobilised and animated a wide range of actors and provided the context through which the subsequent Learning City project blossomed. The idea of a learning city became embedded in public consciousness, there was buy-in for the concept from a wide range of stakeholders and it gathered momentum with the growth of the festival and through international engagement with PASCAL International Exchange (PIE) which also delivered the EcCoWell concept and ultimately opened the doors that led to a 2015 UNESCO Learning City Award. The community wide learning environment is an exciting mix of local innovation and participation and engagement with global networks of cities who are developing their own learning environments under a number of learning cities umbrellas.

RECASTING "WIKINOMICS" IN EDUCATIONAL ENVIRONMENTS – CASE STUDIES IN THE WIKINOMICS PROJECT

Athanasios Priftis, Jean Philippe Trabichet, Haute école de gestion de Genève (HEG-Genève) of the University of Applied Sciences Western Switzerland (HES-SO), Theo Bondolfi, Ynternet.org, Switzerland, Núria Molas-Castells, Universitat de Barcelona, Spain

In the Wikinomics project we revisited the term *wikinomics*, essentially, described a new world of web-based economics where cultural values such as participation, collectivism and creativity are its foundation, in order to tackle one of its main criticisms: wikinomics functioning as an ideology and practice to deliver unpaid surplus value, a subtle form of exploitation of unpaid labour. The Wikinomics project recognizes the contradictions and tensions described above. It acknowledges the field of technical education as the cornerstone and the primary testbed of its efforts. It aims that the trainee reuses its outcomes and has an opportunity to develop expertise in a particular group of techniques, while integrating free culture and wiki-based methodologies to achieve autonomy and collaboration both of the trainer and the trainee.

The Wikinomics project content creation, evaluation and dissemination process embody the existence of a community of practices among VET and other training actors, both at a European and international level. The transfer strategy of the project consisted of three crucial elements, already at the heart of the Wikinomics practices, and transverse all project actions:

- Reuse of good practices in the project that have already been tested at national and international level, both on VET and wider contexts: an example of this is the adoption of the TEDx conferences practice and methods, in order to organise passionate and engaging events that circulate Wikinomics concepts. TEDx organising is not only a dissemination activity but was deployed as a (a) way to connect and spread ideas, (b) space of networking and working cooperatively, (c) learning experience on running inspiring events, d)opportunity for volunteers to participate in wider national and international communities.
- Build generic content, then allow for multiple localised sub-products matching partners needs and languages. In this sense, innovative and open, VET compliant, results were deployed in partners' custom training activities (Wikinomics training module and toolbox, 2015). Inviting partners to reuse generic content and introduce localised sub-products, means that they have a large spectre of open and custom tools and activities to implement, that themselves can reproduce and disseminate openly.
- Introducing collaboration with external communities, scale and team within larger coalitions. This was illustrated, notably by the introduction of the WikiAngels and the TEDx international networks, as well as, the Wikinomics Badges that will be further pursued with more experts and institutions.

Different learning scenarios have been designed and used in our training and implementation activities, in the following structured case studies:

- Switzerland: *The road to Wikinomics;*
- Poland: *Learning how to track changes and limit damage on collaborative websites* and *Tagging and reusing images in a wikinomics way;*
- Portugal: *Creating a Small Business: from business model generation to client development;*
- France and Zaragoza: *Entrepreneurship and companies' innovation.*

The case studies structure included: (a) context: Centre, VET, platform, course topics, (b) Users, (c) Methodological approach, (d) Planning: objectives, competences, schedule, activities, evaluation, (e) Rating: users and teachers and provided results analysis with recommendations. These training activities, as well as, the majority of the project's activities will continue in 2016 providing these case studies with new results. To further advance on collaborative competences in training practices, in the future more details in design and evaluation, as well as, revisited scenarios on collaboration in training activities, would be needed.

HAVE NEW TECHNOLOGIES IMPROVED ACCESS TO QUALITY HIGHER EDUCATION?

Anne Gaskell, St Edmund's College, University of Cambridge, Roger Mills, Centre for Distance Education, International Academy, University of London, United Kingdom

New technologies have transformed educational provision and learning in all sectors. However what has been their impact on issues of scalability, openness and access to education for all? The answer may appear straightforward; information and communication technologies (ICTs) have provided far greater opportunities for all to access a very wide range of educational provision, especially in the higher education sector. However, the issue is not that straightforward; simple provision of opportunities, even when scalable, does not necessarily provide real access and openness for many learners. The emphasis has sometimes been on ensuring the provision of opportunities, rather than considering what the outcomes are for student learning, partly perhaps because the outcomes are more difficult to measure.

The concepts of openness, access and scalability have also changed since the first *Open Universities* were founded, and even more so since the introduction of ICTs. This paper will review how the concepts have changed and the impact this is having. Have all these changes been for the better in terms of student success? The Open University, UK, for example, is closing eight of its 10 English Regional Centres, originally considered essential for student academic advice and support, because it is thought that learners can more effectively be supported from fewer locations and mainly online. While it is too early to assess the impact of this decision (finalised in November 2015), it is worth considering how far all previous changes in concepts and practice have been for the better in terms of student success.

This paper will review some of the key concepts of access, openness and scalability, and their changing nuances and implications. It will also explore tensions arising between delivering open access to online materials, such as Massive Open Online Courses (MOOCs), and the provision of high quality distance learning where internet access is limited.

PERCEPTIONS OF LEARNING ACTIVITIES AND LEARNING OUTCOMES IN A ROSE (RANDOM SHORT-TERM LEARNING ENVIRONMENT)

Keren Levy, Elaine Hoter, David Burg, Ohalo College of Education, Science and Sport, Israel

Frequently situations arise which may cause disruptions of the academic year due to weather conditions, political unrest or military tensions. These shut downs of the educational system may routinely span a week to a few months and may encompass an institution, a region or even be nationwide. There is evidence indicating the importance of the duration of the school year and the adverse effect on student achievements to due to cancellation of school days. This also applies to students in higher education where absence from courses can affect their achievements or lead to a high dropout rate from courses. Day (2015) suggests that the number of cancelled lessons can reflect badly on an institution; while SchWeber (2008) stresses that there are students who would like to continue with their studies even during times of crises. Finally, carrying on with the routine is an important element in coping with emergencies, can help overcome emotional difficulties and trauma, and can contribute to community resilience. On all of these accounts, it is important to avoid depriving students of their right to learn by implementing the variety of (ICT) tools that are widely available to lecturers and students alike. The main challenge is to sustain academic continuity that will lead to satisfactory learning outcomes for the benefit of all students.

A Random Online Short-term Environment (ROSE) is an unplanned online learning environment that continues for a limited period and functions as a seamless continuation of routine face-to-face learning, thus sustaining academic continuity during unexpected shut downs of the educational system. A ROSE is a form of blended-learning (B-learning) that has specific features. Students study in a space which is not always suitable for learning, in which the technological resources could be limited, and the learning process can potentially be disrupted due to the fact that other members of the family share the same space. In addition, there might be occasional external disruptions, as the need to seek temporary shelter, electricity outages etc. Most of the instructors are not versed in transforming learning content to online activities. Planning and actually practicing a ROSE can help to sustain the quality of learning during periods in which it is not possible to conduct courses in their regular venue despite the above challenges.

Our research questions were related to learning activities and learning outcomes:

- What activities were perceived by the students as preferable? How do they compare with the activities that lecturers actually gave during the online week?
- What were student perceptions regarding learning outcomes?

The research indicates the preference of students to activities that involve media (particularly videos) and those that are aimed at rehearsing material dealt with in face to face meetings. As for attributes of these activities, it is notable that the most important attribute is being meaningful and interesting for the student on a personal level. It seems that many students do not believe that it is possible to learn new material in such an environment. Only in one instance namely, activities aiming to rehearse (go over) material taught in face to face meetings, there was a correlation between student and lecturer responses regarding preferable learning activities.

The study showed that there were also discrepancies between the point of view of students and lecturers regarding learning outcomes: Many students stated that due to the workload, they were more concerned with completion of their assignments as fast as possible, and less with actually learning, in contrast to the lecturers, who felt that most of the students learned the material as required.

The study showed general satisfaction of pre-college students compared to the regular students regarding the event and learning outcomes. We believe that this can be linked to the preparation that the students and lecturers in the pre-college went through ahead of the online week and to the fact that their head of department monitored the activities in order to ensure a variety of activities and a reasonable workload.

This research may provide valuable insights into what is needed to done by higher education institutes that find it important to plan and practice implementation of short time online learning environments, in order to prepare for unplanned disruptions of the academic routine.

SITUATED FORMATIVE FEEDBACK – HOW A MOODLE CAN ENHANCE STUDENT LEARNING THROUGH ONLINE FEEDBACK

Niels Bech Lukassen, University College of Northern Denmark and Aarhus University, Christian Wahl, University College of Northern Denmark, Elsebeth Korsgaard Sorensen, Aalborg University, Denmark

This study addresses the conceptual challenge of providing students with good quality feedback to enhance student learning in an online community of practice (COP). The aim of the study is to identify feedback mechanisms in a virtual learning environment (VLE) and to create a full formative feedback episode (FFE) through an online dialogue. The paper argues that dialogue is crucial for student learning and that feedback is not only something the teacher gives to the student. Viewing good quality feedback as social, situated, formative, emphasis is put on the establishment of dialogue. We refer to this type of feedback as, Situated Formative Feedback (SFF). As a basis for exploring, identifying and discussing relevant aspects of SFF the paper analyses qualitative data from a Moodle dialogue. Data are embedded in the qualitative analytic program Nvivo and are analysed with a system theoretical textual analysis method Asynchronous written dialogue from an online master's course at Aalborg University forms the empirical basis of the study. The findings suggests in general that students play an essential role in SFF and that students and educators are equal in the COP, but holds different roles. The students need to take ownership over the learning goals and create a shared understanding of the learning objectives.

EXAMINATION OF THE EFFECTIVENESS OF ELECTRONIC LEARNING ENVIRONMENTS

Erika Jókai, Budapest University of Technology and Economics, Hungary

Importance of impact assessment report on e-learning/e-teaching

This research explores learning management methods in online learning environments that are most frequently used in the national higher education and analyses the students' different learning specialties, customs and efficiency. Analysing the differences of the environments and the students based on these characteristics I make an attempt to create a model determining the efficiency of e-learning environments.

Concept of the research

The basic idea of the research is given by the *added pedagogical value model* expressing the efficiency of traditional school environments. I assumed that after a proper adaptation the model can also be used to evaluate e-learning environments. Therefore I developed a new model based on Kálmán's (2009) model which I expanded with the characteristics of e-learning environments and with the students' characteristics related to online learning. The analysis of the relationships between elements of the model is competent to determine which students' and learning characteristics or which learning environment characteristics influence the result of learning. Former research results suggested that the learning characteristics used in traditional learning environments need to be completed with elements of online learning attitude in electronic environments to define the online learning pattern.

Main questions and hypotheses of the research

I assumed that in courses based on different learning management principles, different levels of performance could be measured; in courses with higher activities and with guided learning process the students' performances are higher. I also assumed that from the learning characteristics the student's ICT experience and his attitude related to online learning primarily affect the student's efficiency in an e-learning environment; i.e. those students who have more ICT-experience and positive ICT-attitude or their efficiency is not affected by the design of the learning environment are more efficient. And finally, I wanted to create a model which could predict students' expected learning performance based on their online learning characteristics.

Conclusions

The analysed sample (826 students of 23 courses from 5 Hungarian educational institutions) has not proved that the highly required activity and the strongly guided learning process could lead to high performance. On the analysed sample the students' highest performances were measured in the partially guided and moderately active courses (requiring not regular but more than one online activity) and I experienced the students' lowest performances in the guided courses requiring a regular online activity. I could not measure significant difference between the performances of the groups based on the students' online learning attitudes. Unfortunately I could not prove that my model was suitable to predict the students' expected performance. But I would like to present my experiences, partial results of my research and I expect further proposals to continue this work.

THE INTEGRATION OF INFORMATION LITERACY SKILLS INTO THE CURRICULUM

Luis Guadarrama, Marc Cels, Corinne Bossé, Elaine Fabro, Mary Pringle, Cindy Ives,
Athabasca University, Canada

This paper discusses the conclusions of the evaluation for the Information Literacy Skills Modules that were integrated into the curriculum of five online Early-European History undergraduate courses offered at Athabasca University (AU). These History courses are offered online and at distance for individualized self-paced studies, where students have up to six months to complete them. AU is an open university where students with very diverse – and sometimes limited – university and professional background, and different ages, enrol in AU courses on monthly bases. At the undergraduate level, there are no cohort groups and no face-to face experience.

The Skills Modules were integrated into the curriculum of the History courses to address serious academic integrity issues students have been struggling with such as plagiarism, lack of experience on writing academic Chicago style papers, documenting sources of information, identifying scholarly articles, quoting sources of information properly, and so on. The skills modules were designed to assist students in producing their research assignments satisfactorily, improving their performance, and avoiding academic misconduct and plagiarism.

Keeping in mind past unsuccessful practices, a multidisciplinary group (a librarian, an editor, a learning designer) got together with the course coordinator to assess the context, discuss previous experiences, and identify a better and more effective solution. Instruction was designed; the skills modules were documented; and learning materials were developed. The skills modules instruction was designed based on the Information Literacy Competency Standards for Higher Education framework (http://www.acrl.org/ala/mgrps/divs/acrl/standards/standards.pdf).

The skills modules were integrated into History courses, along the study guide, and strategically connected to the work students have to produce; the criteria they have to meet; and the expectations they have to satisfy to complete sequenced assignments throughout the course, which reflect the research process. The skills modules were linked to credit assignments to ensure that students could not ignore them. Automated quizzes were designed to reward students' knowledge acquired in the skills modules without creating extra work for tutors. Instructions, rubrics, and evaluation criteria for assignments and examinations reflect the Skills Modules.

Through this exploratory survey we learned that students, who bring to the course very limited experience on documenting sources using Chicago style, strongly agree that the modules helped them to enhance their information literacy skills. Students strongly agree that the modules improved their understanding of relevant academic integrity aspects such as acknowledging the work of others, understanding intellectual property, citing resources, paraphrasing, formatting footnotes, formatting the bibliography of sources, and integrating quotations. Students also agree that the modules improved their understanding about the identification, selection, assessment, and analysis of scholarly articles. In particular, there is a strong agreement that the modules helped them to distinguish between primary and secondary sources of information. Moreover, students agree that the modules assisted them effectively on relevant aspects related to writing their Chicago style papers such as documenting their sources; presenting facts accurately; developing arguments supported by evidence; and drawing conclusions based on the information gathered. Overall, students strongly agree that the Skills Modules helped them to complete their assignments successfully and improve their performance in the course. After analysing the students' grades achieved before and after the integration of the Modules, it seems that the group of most disadvantaged students, who traditionally achieve the lower marks, where the ones who most benefited from the Modules. The data also suggest that despite the Modules were highly beneficial for students, there are still some areas where they could be improved to assist students in developing their academic writing skills.

RE-IMAGINING COURSEWORK MASTERS FOR ONLINE LEARNING BASED ON RESEARCH AND DESIGN PRINCIPLES

Lynette Nagel, University of Pretoria, South Africa

Background

Since the South African government lifted the embargo on delivery of distance education, traditional contact institutions are allowed to present courses or programmes in fully online mode. In order to reach more students from more places, the University of Pretoria with about 50,000 contact students is starting with redesigning suitable existing course-work Masters programmes (CWM) for eventual electronic distance delivery. The identified hybrid programmes are presently being presented with block periods of on-campus activities, supplemented by online activities and materials in the Blackboard course management system (CMS). The ideal is to replace more contact time with electronic activities.

Methodology

Following the ADDIE process of instructional design, the Analysis phase for each prospective programme consisted of interviews with the lecturers to clarify expectations, goals and objectives, and questionnaires. An ICT use and preference instrument to analyse the readiness of students and staff for different types of technology, was rolled out electronically. The results were analysed in order to inform bespoke course design and supportive training resources. Courses are being designed for online delivery with the Community of Inquiry (CoI) framework as guide, in order to address all aspects of teaching, social and cognitive presence. For Evaluation, the CoI questionnaire was used in order to provide a baseline for interpretation of Analysis findings and triangulation. The results of the ICT questionnaires from 2 CWM and a research Masters in three faculties were thus interpreted through the lens of the CoI, in order to pinpoint the areas where the most radical changes in the present delivery modes and improvements to current practices were needed.

Findings and recommendations

In contrast to undergraduate students, the CWM students were all working full-time and can be labelled non-traditional students. It was found that computer literacy and technology access was no barrier to online studies, partially due to the high use of mobile devices (smartphones). Students in different professions used different devices, times and places for attending to online studies, which should inform scheduling of interactions and deadlines for tasks. All CWM students were used to browsing the internet and will be able to access electronic content. While they were not very active on interactive applications, more than 70% used Facebook. With training they should master online interactive programmes.

Use of tools that support Teaching presence (of which the design and organisation aspects were mostly well developed) varied between programmes. On the other side, no facilitated online discussions took place in the courses and limited feedback was restricted to large assignments. While assessment consisted mainly of assignments and written exam papers, there is great scope for introducing online reflective, summative and individual formative assessment, like using Turnitin's available audio feedback and other CMS tools. Group activities mostly lacked.

The amount of contact time can be reduced drastically and the quality of learning enhanced if block week lectures were replaced with recorded lectures using the available ICT tools like Collaborate, or videos in a flipped classroom approach. Premium contact time could be used for interactive higher order learning activities. The use of ICT to support social and cognitive presence will require the most severe changes before contact time can be reduced, as very little such activities were evident. While social presence is the basis for collaborative online activities; sustained communication is needed for students to construct meaning, solve problems and devise new applications. The development of learning communities with high cognitive presence was previously restricted to the contact environment, and will require design of high quality group work and formative feedback processes.

Students should be supported by voluntary pre-course orientation and self-help materials that should address the gaps in use of ICT, the CMS, social media and reflective tools, while alternative assessment practices like journals, e-portfolios and peer review would also need trial runs. In conclusion: the ICT infrastructure and most of the technical expertise needed for online distance learning are already in place. Designing the courses on sound pedagogical and ICT-use principles should ensure a smooth transition to excellent hybrid and online courses.

SELF-KNOWLEDGE AND NETWORKING IN A TRAINING COURSE AND HOW TO MAKE IT IN THE VIRTUAL SPACE

Beatrix Séllei, Budapest University of Technology and Economic, Hungary

Introduction

What do we know about ourselves? How can we develop ourselves or enhance the level of self-knowledge? The main focus of the workshop is building new connections between each other via tests which enhance self-knowledge. As an example we shall use the tools of the positive psychology to pursue happiness and develop positive attitude. In this workshop the participants search the answers for themselves: why it is important to be able to be happy. With my active support and presence the participants gain information about themselves, *where are they right now* in the way to happiness and flourishing. We together have to find out how to enhance the actual level of our happiness. Through my university life and also on personal level I see high interest to the methods of developing happiness or in general self-knowledge. This course can also help renewing learning tools and self-knowledge through self-context.

Description of the Workshop

Nowadays people can learn from different sources almost about everything. One of the key points of learning and being successful in life is the self-knowledge and self-development – claims the positive psychology. How can people enhance their self-knowledge in new ways? Which experiences do people have to develop themselves? Which devices and sources people have to reach a high level of self-knowledge? In this workshop I show some answers for these questions which comes from my practice and I ask some new questions about the topics.

This workshop shows a new concept of learning and tries to define a new environment of learning about ourselves. I shall give a brief summary about my experiences in Finland where I take part in a one week long international collaboration and the aim was to design the new concept, structure and environment of future learning. I would like to spread this knowledge and how I adopted the outcomes to my practice.

I shall give an experience to the participants in one of the fields of self-knowledge. I have chosen the concept of well-being because this is one of the basics of a fulfilling and worth-living life. Well-being is a very subjective and personal field. There is a demand in the society for scientific but easy applicable methods aiming the state of mental, psychological and social well-being. This method is appropriate to reach this goal. I shall show some possibilities how to apply the methods of self-development through internet for lots of people.

According to the positive psychology, everybody is capable to live a complete and happy life. With the emerging world of apps, tablets, smartphones and other internet devices, it is easier to spread the tools of flourishing. With these new internet tools, it is a perfect time to show even more and more people, how to go deeper to the self-knowledge.

The self-knowledge is valuable on itself and this is the basis of networking and making new contacts as we know till the concept of emotional intelligence emerged from the literature. I shall show some ways to link self-knowledge and social networking in a direct way for the participants of this workshop. There are game examples as illustrations which use self-knowledge and share self-related memories. These games help form a new group and there are games based on self-knowledge which aim is to enhance the coherence of a group. There are some applications for both but there is no application which contains all part of this area. We shall talk about these devices and applications in the closing part of the workshop and the directions of developing apps which can reach this goal.

Summary

As outcomes of the workshop participants get a profile about their actual level of happiness and some related emotional features, and which is more interesting that participants get acquainted with a new learning goal and its background. They get also a new perspective about learning – which fits better to the needs of the informational and knowledge-based society.

PEN OR KEYBOARD – AN EMPIRICAL STUDY ON THE EFFECTS OF TECHNOLOGY ON WRITING SKILLS

Benedetto Vertecchi, Antonella Poce, Francesco Agrusti, Maria Rosaria Re, Università Roma Tre, Italy

State of the Art

As stated in the scope of the conference *The social and socio-economic context is more important than ever. Society itself can be understood as a learning environment, with questions of learners' connection with the community and the empowerment of the practitioners.* This means that certain skills, the so called 21st century skills, must be prompted and developed. Writing skills are of paramount importance in this context and, as educators and researchers, we are primarily engaged in understanding the effect the use of mobile devices has on such abilities. The relation between digital tools and writing skills regards different scientific fields, such as education, neuroscience and sociology. Everyone, teenagers in particular, is used to communicate through smartphones, tablets or PCs, writing short text messages. However, in these cases, writing skills are not developed in an efficient and productive way even if they are practiced every day. International studies and research highlight a drastic reduction of argumentation capabilities in writing for people who make too much use of texting, for instance.

Hypothesis, methodology and results

The present study carried out within the module *Writing Methods and Techniques in Education*, hold out at University Roma TRE – Laboratory of Experimental Pedagogy (LPS), starts from the assumption that students can develop their writing and critical thinking skills thanks to specific writing activities. Such activities regard the elaboration of short essays, both by hand and on computer keyboards, with the aim to highlight the difference in results. The general objective of the module, where the experimentation took place, was to improve students' writing skills in different disciplinary and learning contexts. Meta-objectives have been identified in the opportunity for students to improve also their correct use of the language (grammar, morpho-syntax, lexicon accuracy), argument skills as well as critical thinking and creativity skills. Over the lecturing, students have produced short essays on the topics discussed with the lecturer. Assignments were marked by LPS researchers, using an ad hoc essay assessment grid. Short essays written by students were produced in two different ways: by hand or keyboard. All data have been collected and analyzed to highlight the different results in skills development, according to the writing tool employed. From the analyses carried out and the results collected, some main considerations can be singled out: the project learning path aims at successfully developing both correct use of the language (grammar, morpho-syntax, lexicon accuracy) and writing and argument skills, as well as critical thinking and creativity. Computer use in writing activities apparently reduces performances level in the majority of students taken into consideration.

Authors

Antonella Poce coordinated the research presented in this paper. Research group is composed by the authors of the contribution that was edited in the following order Benedetto Vertecchi (State of the Art), Antonella Poce (Research Design, Methodology and Conclusive remarks), Francesco Agrusti (Assessment tool), Maria Rosaria Re (Analyses and findings).

GUIDING STUDENTS TO BECOME LIFELONG LEARNERS: FLIPPED CLASSROOM AND MEANINGFUL PARTICIPATION IN A BLENDED-LEARNING ENVIRONMENT

Teemu Leinonen, Eva Durall, Aalto University, Finland

In this article we present a good practice of combining several teaching strategies such as blended learning, the flipped classroom and self-directed study activities in a MA level course, *Introduction to Media Art and Culture* (IMAC), with the aim of helping students develop lifelong learning skills.

The flipped classroom is a teaching strategy that inverts traditional way of structuring classroom activity with the aim of supporting higher levels of engagement and deep understanding. From this perspective, students are asked to take responsibility of their own learning, to be active subjects in it. In practice, in a flipped classroom, students are asked to familiarize themselves with the course content in advance the course meetings. Time spent in class is then dedicated to practical applications of the course contents through activities centred on questions, inquiry, problem solving, group discussions and students' presentations.

We report how we adopted the flipped classroom model in several editions of the IMAC course through the organization of fishbowl discussions with the students about the homework assignments they were asked to prepare before the classes. The course final assignments consisted in a video essay that the students had to produce in small groups and present to the class. The video essay required students to do research, define a research question and develop a critical attitude towards the topics explored.

The course design included online learning resources and encouraged students develop their Personal Learning Environments (PLE) since, in order to produce the video essay, they had to search information and deeper explore some of the topics discussed during the face-to-face sessions. The combination of teaching and learning approaches based on the flipped classroom, PLE and self-directed learning responded to a hidden-curriculum focused on helping students to carry more responsibility about their own study work they may develop curiosity and skills needed in a self-directed lifelong learning. This approach is asking new role and new patterns of behaviour from teachers, too. For instance, the main character in *The Ignorant Schoolmaster* (Rancière, 1991), Jacotot puts it in words as follows: "To explain something to someone is first of all to show him he cannot understand it by himself" (p.32).

We gathered feedback from the students during and after the course. We analyzed the feedback as well as the video essays submitted by the students in order to assess if the course provided them a meaningful learning experience and if it helped them become lifelong learners. The analysis of the IMAC course shows that the teaching strategies applied during the course helped to achieve the intended goals: give the students a broad overview of the field and help them build critical and informed positions. We claim that the analysis of the final assignments shows that students have acquired relevant skills for engaging in self-directed learning. In this regard, we consider that the research brings an interesting case based on the use of the flipped classroom model.

We must acknowledge certain limitations in the study as well as the need for further research that analyses to what extent the flipped classroom model effectively supports students in developing a PLE-mindset that will help them become lifelong learners. We consider that including the hidden curriculum (positive and negative) debate among the educational community designing and implementing e-learning and blended-learning course is important, since this will have a strong impact on the role of formal education institutions in the future.

IMMERSIVE LEARNING – LEARNING PATTERNS INSIDE DIGITAL CULTURAL IMMERSIVE EXPERIENCES IN SITU

Patrizia Schettino, Università della Svizzera italiana, Switzerland

The paper presents a categorization of visitors learning patterns inside the immersive environment PLACE-Hampi, designed by Sarah Kenderdine and Jeffrey Shaw.

Sarah Kenderdine (2007, 2011) describes PLACE-Hampi in this way: PLACE-Hampi is "a vibrant theatre for embodied participation in the drama of Hindu mythology focused at the most significant archaeological, historical and sacred locations of the World Heritage site Vijayanagara (Hampi), South India."

The paper is focused on how visitors learnt about a new technology, the immersive platform PLACE. As Oliver Grau (2003) wrote, "the platform (PLACE) is in the tradition of panoramas but innovates the way they can be explored, with a new interaction design paradigm".

The study is based on the qualitative data analysis with the software NVivo of 92 interviews and notes of observation about 500 visitors' behaviours inside PLACE-Hampi, during three different exhibitions in Germany and Australia, at the Martin Gropius Bau (Berlin), ZKM (Karlsruhe) and Immigration Museum (Melbourne).

The methodology used is a combination of four different qualitative methods: grounded theory, digital ethnography, narrative inquiry and case study.

From the data analysis, the following types of learners of technology emerged:

- the self-learner by doing (the visitor learnt by trying and making mistakes);
- the self-learner by imitating (the visitor learnt from another visitor, by observing and repeating);
- the peer helped (the visitor was helped or asked for help from another visitor);
- the customer service guided (the visitor was helped or asked for help from a member of the staff).

This categorization describes how visitors learn about a new technology and a new space. My categorization by learning strategies offers a way of analysing this specific aspect of learning in immersive environments: it can be used to compare the learning process about PLACE-Hampi with the *immersive learning* of other platforms.

AMPLIFYING THE PROCESS OF INCLUSION THROUGH A GENUINE MARRIAGE BETWEEN PEDAGOGY AND TECHNOLOGY

Elsebeth Korsgaard Sorensen, Hanne Voldborg Andersen, Aalborg University, Denmark

This study addresses the challenge of inclusion in mainstream schools of learners with developmental and attention deficits and examines the potential of a digital structuring tool, MobilizeMe, to scaffold this process, including the impact and implications associated with the implementation. The study focuses on the discrepancy arising from, on the one hand, the digital and pedagogical affordances for scaffolding the focus learners, and on the other hand, the lack of utilization of these affordances in the context of study. From a case study approach, the paper touches upon the digital functionality of the tool, the pedagogical practice of the teachers and, finally, the consequences of the implementation. Based on the analysis and its findings the study presents a generic model for understanding the elements of the construction of new technology supported pedagogical practices.

TRANSFORMACHINES: TRANSFORMING CITY DATA TO ARCHITECTURAL DESIGN STRATEGIES

George Parmenidis, Nelly Marda, Olga Ioannou, National Technical University of Athens (NTUA), School of Architecture, Greece

An innovative version of the *New Fields of Design and Construction* (NFDC) design methodology course was set in motion at the Postgraduate Program of the NTUA last spring. The intention was to experiment with the existing design education framework of *learning by doing* in an extended learning environment of multiple mediums organized as a representation of the multiplicity of the design praxis.

The course engages participating students in a series of urban mapping methodologies. The corpus of its content consists of a series of mapping tools that are selected by means of their capacity to represent contemporary urban realities. Students are requested to decipher the data they retrieve, compare multiple readings and make connections between the diverse information in a process that depicts the principles of the connectivist model where learning consists of the ability "to construct and traverse networks of connections" (Downes, 2012). Knowledge thus comes in the form of creating visual and conceptual mechanisms, *transformachines* that can turn random information to logical threads by critically joining elements to form reconstructions of the real.

This system of producing knowledge out of random ways of interpreting the urban environment fits the very objective of this course; understanding and managing the complexity of the city. There is a cyclical act both in learning and reconfiguring the realities of the city as students realize that any result cannot be reduced to a single definitive form; rather, it emerges as a dynamic calibration of the unlimited complexities of the built environment and how these can be met in the urban field.

The course also aimed at extending the educational process beyond the limits of the classroom by creating multiple collaborating learning environments for the exchange of content. Thus, the course layout was conceived as an open system of content exchange in multiple intermingling environments that raised student engagement and made them complicit to the formation of the course content. It was intended that students were included in the process of content formation by offering their insights and sharing their references with the rest of the class. Participants have been repeatedly encouraged to contribute in any way they think is more appropriate according to their understanding of the environment.

This process has led to the systematic transformation of learning into e-learning by creating countable verbal and visual structural units. The original three hour long in class presentations were narrowed down to forty minute online lectures that were further dismantled in maximum seven minute videos. A lexicon was also set up to include the terms used in an open to all Google document with suggestive definitions that everyone could consult or even alter what felt unsuited or irrelevant. The visual language, on the other hand, drew more from schemata of thought enriched by additional sensual or digital spatial data. These representational schemes became the visual structural units of the course, for they were able to capture meaning in purely design expressions.

Students' online presence was closely monitored to register their engagement. The results show consistent attendance rates and continuous interaction between parties. The student learning outcomes were examined upon the course's completion to verify whether and how e-learning practices influenced student development by examining the incorporation of the structural content units in their projects. Despite the divergent mapping methodologies that were applied and the different scales of their suggested interventions, all student projects were represented mostly through diagrams and graphs. The visual expressions of the student projects were immensely influenced by the course content tools' inner sense as well as the software that supports them. In addition, a thorough analysis of the two page essays they were asked to submit along with their design proposals on a specific area of Athens highlighted the frequent use of the course terminology as this was presented in the Lexicon and introduced by the mapping tools throughout the duration of the course.

Just like the course depended on its participants to obtain its final form, the mapping and managing of the urban phenomena depended on the personal hierarchies of the people involved in realizing them. What was eventually created was a direct metaphor, the mirroring of one process onto the other.

USING HYPERVIDEOS IN INITIAL VOCATIONAL EDUCATION: EFFECTIVENESS AND MOTIVATION OF INSTRUCTIONAL SCENARIOS

Alberto Cattaneo, Florinda Sauli, Swiss Federal Institute for Vocational Education and Training, Switzerland

Introduction and methods

In recent years the role video can play in fostering and sustaining learning has considerably increased, and the enormous recent success registered by Massive Open Online Courses (MOOCs), in which short instructional videos support lectures, is just one confirming instance among many. However, quantitative confirmation that video is one of the most-used media in schools cannot be enough, and many contributions pointed out the limitations of using videos in classes. In this debate, hypervideo has been considered a video-based tool able to overcome some traditional video limitations, like for example the difficulty to actively interact with the contents or the limitations for reflection or annotation to be supported. Nevertheless, few study addressed the question of how hypervideo can be integrated in instructional scenarios and on evidence-based guidelines to properly do that. Therefore, this is the leading question of our exploratory study on the effects of three different hypervideo-based instructional strategies on learning, as well as the process the teacher passed through when designing the interventions. Learning is considered both under the indices of knowledge acquisition and knowledge transfer in practice, and of motivation and perceived usefulness.

Sample and procedure: four first-year classes of clothing designer students (N = 38, female = 36; M_{age} = 17.16, SD_{age} = 3.40) from an initial vocational school in the Italian-speaking part of Switzerland (Scuola d'Arti e Mestieri della Sartoria, SAMS) have been involved and randomly assigned to four different conditions: (a) Plenary lesson (n = 6), where the teacher used the hypervideo in front of the class as a support for her teaching; (b) Individual use (n = 11), where students individually used the hypervideo in a computer lab; (c) In-group use (n = 12), where students, in groups of three each, have built the interactivities, adding learning materials to the raw video; (d) Traditional lesson (control group, n = 9), where students attended a traditional lesson, without using the hypervideo. The teacher, the content of the lesson (seam anomalies) and the learning materials have been the same in all the four conditions. The raw video was produced by the teacher, who took care of transforming it into a hypervideo, both including the audio and integrating materials and interactivities. All the four scenarios had the same structure, mainly based on three different parts: (a) an Introduction, where the teacher exposed the topic and the objectives, and activated prior knowledge connected to the new topic (10 minutes), (b) a Central phase (50 min. for plenary, individually and control; 85 min. for in-group); and (c) a Closure phase (30 min.), where the teacher and the students summarized the main contents.

Measures: declarative knowledge acquisition was measured through a pre-/post-/delayed-post- test design. The test contained questions related to anomalies of the sewing machine, most of them conceived as open questions about how to manage practical professional situations. The pre-test was submitted one week before the lessons; the post-test immediately after the lesson; the delayed-post-test 1.5 month after the lesson. Just before filling-in the delayed-post-test, students were asked to perform a practical proof too, in order to have a measure of their skills in managing sewing anomalies. Satisfaction, perceived usefulness, and motivation, were assessed through a questionnaire. All the items were based on a 6-points Likert scale from -3=totally disagree, to +3=totally agree.

Results and conclusion

As a preliminary analysis we checked for the groups to be comparable: an ANOVA was performed and results show that the students in the different conditions did not differ. Declarative knowledge acquisition was measured through a repeated-measure general linear model. Post-hoc comparisons showed significant differences between the individual and both the in-group and the traditional conditions, in favour of the first. A one-way ANOVA on the practical proof score showed a significant difference at the 0.9 significance level ($F(3,26) = 2.43$, $p = .09$): Post-hoc analysis revealed all the three experimental conditions outperformed the control group. Satisfaction and perceived usefulness were generally high in all the three groups (Satisfaction: $M = 2.08$, $SD = .73$; Usefulness: $M = 2.24$, $SD = .78$), with higher scores for satisfaction in the in-groups condition and with higher perceived usefulness in the plenary condition, for which the plenary condition significantly differed ($F(2,26) = 4.13$, $p < .05$).

Although preliminary and limited, this study shows that hypervideo represents an effective way to learn and an incentive for student's motivation, and inform us about the opportunity to integrate – and to further investigate the use of – hypervideo in an instructional scenario, especially in those contexts like vocational education where theory and practice have to be related one to the other.

CURRICULAR DEVELOPMENT AND ICT: FROM TECHNOLOGICAL DEFICIT TO METHODOLOGICAL DEFICIT

Fernando Albuquerque Costa, University of Lisbon, Portugal

The way the main aspects of the information society are dealt with in school and how the young are being prepared to act socially and in such a professionally fluid and constantly changing context are crucial questions that today's teachers and educators cannot ignore.

As several national and international studies seem to indicate, even in wealthier countries with a long history of teacher training, there remains a big deficit in how teachers are prepared to exercise their profession, especially from the methodological point of view. Not only does the use of digital technologies in educational practices continue to be much lower than one would expect, in view of the investments made, but there is also a glaring lack of guidance as regards how they should be taken advantage of, which leads to irregular usage that is not in accordance with the main theoretical principles underlying the constructivist framework of these countries' national curriculums.

Preparing teachers to use the digital technologies in their educational practices is not merely a technical question of how well they master the technologies. Moreover, the way this issue usually ends up being tackled in conventional training gives us strong evidence that the strategies for professional development implemented are ineffective from the methodological point of view. In other words, even after attending the training programmes provided, the teachers and educators continue to have big doubts about what ICT can be used in education, and why and how ICT can improve their pupils' learning. We believe the essential question lies in the way the teacher training has been designed and its obvious ineffectiveness to properly prepare the teachers.

Given the diversity of the curricular areas in which the technologies may be used, the different phases and stages of teachers' careers, and the wide range of perspectives they have about what teaching and learning comprises, and how to incorporate ICT into this process, we always considered it strange that these multiple factors were not specifically incorporated into teacher training.

Based on the fact that these differences are of crucial importance in the teaching practices of teachers and educators, in this text we propose the outline of a framework of thinking that will allow us to identify and characterise the different kinds of pedagogical intervention using ICT that can be useful when it comes to designing the training.

INTEGRATION OF VIRTUAL LEARNING ENVIRONMENT INTO THE EDUCATIONAL PROCESS

Sandra Kučina Softić, Ana Ćorić Samardžija, University of Zagreb University Computing Centre, Croatia

Virtual learning environment can have an important role in the learning and teaching process. But its implementation into the educational process depends on teachers' knowledge about technology and ways how to integrate it into educational process. In this paper the results of higher education teachers' satisfaction with the VLE Merlin and its support are presented. VLE Merlin is set of learning platforms for higher education in Croatia which is maintained by the E-learning Centre at SRCE.

Today, technology is more than a tool; it underlines and influences most of the activities in our lives: the way we learn, work, communicate with others, search for information, spend our free time etc. We are faced with a growing use of ICT in education, especially in higher education; however there are a lot of questions and issues that are still open and essential to dealing with e-learning effectiveness. One of the most important prerequisites is to provide continuing and sustainable support to teachers. Teachers often face obstacles when planning to use ICT and e-learning technologies in their teaching. In order to ensure successful e-learning and e-teaching, institutions should provide solid e-infrastructure and support to teachers and students. Perhaps the most basic e-learning requirement is an adequate technical infrastructure to deliver e-learning courses. The course management systems and virtual learning environments which are easy to use have encouraged the adoption of e-learning. Teachers want technology that is easy to use so that they can focus on their subject matters. And besides that, they want immediate help and answers when they face obstacles.

Integration of virtual learning environment into the traditional environment can strive to minimise boundaries of the educational process, making it more flexible, enabling the acquirement of new skills and competencies, but the process of creating a better educational scenario also requires adjustment, reorganisation and investment. Definition of VLE by JISC (2008) uses the term Learning Management System (LMS) which needs to be designed to act as a focus for students' learning activities and their management and facilitation, along with the provision of content and resources required to help make learning activities successful. In most universities the VLE is a part of the *blended learning* experience where students still have face to face lessons but increasingly which are increasingly augmented with online activities and tasks using a VLE.

One of the first goals of the E-learning Centre at the University Computing Centre University of Zagreb SRCE was to establish and provide the university with an e-learning platform and e-learning technologies. The e-learning platform, today VLE, is continuously maintained, upgraded and built on. Organized and sustainable support to users is very important in use of new technologies and is one of the priorities of the E-learning Centre. User feedback is very important, therefore the E-learning Centre continuously takes steps to collect and reflect on it. In this paper we will reflect on data gained from a recent survey on teachers' satisfaction with the VLE Merlin.

This research confirms that there are factors that influence teachers' attitudes towards ICT and e-learning and their implementation in the educational process. If the teachers are not aware of the technological possibilities and the way how it can be integrated into educational process, the use of technology does not innovate the learning and teaching process. The majority of teachers use e-learning as an extension of their classroom courses, to provide course content online and distribute learning materials, course information and schedule, as well as to communicate with students. They are more likely to adopt new technologies if they see that technology offers them a better way to do their work and achieve goals. When it comes to the production of e-learning materials, teachers generally rely on themselves, their colleagues and friends and sometimes they also use the technical support available at their institution or at the E-learning Centre at SRCE. Available and sustainable support and infrastructure is of great importance to teachers who are using e-learning and can be a motivator for experimenting with e-learning technologies.

HOW SOCIAL NETWORKING EXPERIENCE RELATES TO SOCIAL PRESENCE AND ATTITUDE OF USING SNS IN EDUCATION

Jieun Lim, Jennifer Richardson, Purdue University, United States of America

The purpose of this research is to explore the effects of students' social networking experience on social presence and attitude of using Social networking sites (SNSs) for educational purposes. As online learning has increased a number of researchers have focused on the need to integrate techniques to strengthen students' social presence in online learning. SNSs have been suggested as an effective tool to increase social presence. However, despite the positive expectation that social networking activities and social networking sites can promote social communication and collaboration, little is known about students' prior experience with using SNSs and how their social networking experiences impact (a) their social presence and, (b) their perception of using SNSs for learning. To fill this gap, the following research questions were examined in this research:

1. How are students in online courses using SNSs?
2. Does students' intensity of use of SNSs influence their social presence in online learning?
3. What are students' perceptions about using SNSs for educational purposes?
4. Does the intensity of use of SNSs effect students' perceptions about using SNSs in educational environments?

To investigate the effects of students' social networking experience on social presence and their perceptions of using SNSs for educational purpose, students (n = 82) were surveyed.

In this research, we determined that most students are familiar with SNS environments and view SNSs as an integral part of their daily life. The findings of this research showing that most students are accustomed to SNSs may imply that students can extend their use of SNSs to the educational setting without much difficulty or needing to learn the basics of SNS functionalities. In addition, the students indicated social relationships as their dominant purpose for using SNSs, but this research also demonstrated that students do consider SNSs as a place where they can also gather and share information more generally.

This study also identified positives correlation between the intensity of using SNSs and students' perceptions of using SNSs for educational purposes. This result shows that more experiences and familiarity with using SNSs are likely to be an important factor in students' positive perceptions of using SNSs for educational purposes. When we consider that most current undergraduate students are familiar with SNSs, the findings propose a positive expectation that current and future students may be open and ready to use SNSs for educational purposes on a technical level.

Next, overall, the students revealed a positive attitude toward using SNSs for educational purposes, indicating it could increase motivation for learning, increase learning community intensity, and communication and collaboration with peers. This result coincides with the previous research which indicated that students revealed positive perceptions of using Facebook page as a supportive tool for learning.

Interestingly, no significant relationship was found between the intensity of using SNSs and students' perceived social presence. This contradicts what limited information is available relating SNSs and social presence, including the idea that the use of SNSs may have effects on students' social presence by enhancing the abilities of open communication or experiences of web community. The lack of significance may be attributed to the fact that survey items for social presence have focused only on students' perceptions about their social presence rather than what student actually do.

Together with previous research and our own results, it is safe to say that adopting SNSs for educational purposes is a real possibility as a means to overcome issues such as isolation or lack of community, given continued advances in SNSs capabilities.

USE OF BIG DATA IN EDUCATION EFFICIENCY ANALYSIS

György Molnár, Zoltán Szűts, Dávid Sik, Budapest University of Technology and Economics, Hungary

This paper attempts to address the relevant use of Big Data from the point of view of education. Big Data is a popular term used to describe the growth, availability and analysis of both structured and unstructured information. Everyday a huge amount of data is being collected from web-browsing and searching, social media, and similar activities all in order to be stored and analyzed. Big Data provides both challenges and opportunities among others for governance, scientific and education sector.

This paper starts from painting a global picture about Big Data. It firstly presents the characteristics of this new paradigm, discusses the machine learning and the most common open source software used in Big Data environment, Hadoop. Secondly, it presents a way of determining the efficiency of some special educational applications using Big Data. Thirdly, it examines the usability of Big Data paradigm in everyday life through the example of Waze mobile application. Finally, according to the analysis and conclusions future development plans and guidelines are presented.

Every day 2.5 quintillion bytes of data are created. 90% of the data in the world today have been created in the last 2 years alone. We continuously produce data – Big Data – during our online lives. Data comes from several sources: sensors, smartphones, GPS devices, social media sites – to name few. Data created by users in social media can be used to determine sentiments.

In order to efficiently analyze huge datasets in almost real-time, computers should be used. This is achieved by machine learning systems that automate decision making on data. The general idea is using training information to deal with data, and automatically producing outputs: recommendations or groupings. Big Data also includes image processing, natural language processing, speech recognition, data mining, but the study presented in this paper is based on semantic analysis. Hadoop, an open source software is often used in Big Data environments. It enables distributed processing of large data sets across clusters servers.

In order to give account of application of Big Data in education efficiency analysis, the authors carried out a survey among 110 students of Budapest University of Technology and Economics on the use of social media. The survey was carried out to support our hypothesis that students nowadays argue about educational issues in social media and these opinions can be analyzed.

The Big Data sentiment analysis presented focused on teaching-learning issues discussed (Moodle, Wikipedia) on Twitter. The results of the research may be suitable for building a framework of a micro or mezzo learning environment that lays on connectivism.

Besides this original research, authors introduced another efficient use of Big Data in informal learning, Waze. Waze is a GPS software based on driver's community involvement. It depends on drivers to input their own data (beside the one sent the devices) about road and traffic conditions. The system then in real-time analyzes the data and alerts other users about dangers and offers optimal driving routes to avoid traffic.

REPOSITORY OF INSPIRING SCIENCE EDUCATION PROJECT FOR SPACE AND ASTRONOMY IN SCIENCE EDUCATION

Panagiota Argyri, Model High School Evangelika of Smyrna, Greece

Abstract

Astronomy is one of the most exciting and rapidly evolving branches of science. Astronomy has influenced our history and culture through its practical applications and its philosophical and religious implications. Historically, not only scientists and students, and generally people are huge interested in the achievements and advances of space science. Space Science research seeks to increase our understanding of solar system and universe. In order to support teaching astronomy and space in science education presented a brief description of ways that classroom teachers can use repository of Inspiring Science Education project (ISE) to enhance space education and develop students' scientific inquiry skills in astronomy observations.

Introduction to Inspiring Science Education portal

Inspiring Science Education (ISE) portal (http://www.inspiringscience.eu) provide digital resources and opportunities for teachers to help them make science education more attractive and relevant to students' lives. Through the Inspiring Science Education website and the activities organised by the partners, teachers can help students make their own scientific discoveries, witness and understand natural and scientific phenomena and access the latest, interactive tools and digital resources from within their classrooms.

Key outcomes of the Inspiring Science Education project:

- Access to online, interactive tools and digital resources from all over the world that can be used for science teaching.
- Templates, scenarios and methodologies to support science teachers and teacher trainers in their drive to make their teaching more exciting, fun and relevant for students.
- A platform that can be used by students and teachers alike to take science teaching beyond the classroom and into the realms of extra-curricular learning.
- A variety of eTools and digital resources that provide opportunities for students to collaborate with each other (in or out of the classroom) or with others outside of the class.
- Inspiring Science Education is all about providing the tools to make science education.
- ISE is providing digital tools to space and astronomy in science education.

EXTENDING LEARNING ENVIRONMENTS IN HIGHER EDUCATION: ONLINE PEER-TO-PEER COUNSELLING IN PROFESSIONAL DEGREE PROGRAMS OF SOCIAL WORK

Patricia Arnold, Munich University of Applied Sciences, Germany

There has been a lot of discussion about the role of digital media in higher education. Principal advantages of incorporating educational technologies into higher education teaching are generally conceived to manifest themselves at three different levels: (a) *efficiency* can increase as regards cost-effectivity, time-effectivity, sustainability or scalability, (b) *enhancement* of both the learning and teaching experience can occur by multimedia, more international and authentic learning resources, (c) *transformation* may be achieved with substantial qualitative change in learning and teaching processes or radically new processes.

This paper will deal with a transformative change in learning environments in higher education by digital media: the method and the accompanying platform that will be investigated in the paper do not radically substitute traditional learning environments like for example Massive Open Online Courses do but actually merge different learning environments into one – the classic higher education learning environment and the more professionally oriented learning environment with actual real life professional challenges. Key to such merging learning environments is the method of *online peer-to-peer* counselling and a special web-based platform *kokom.net* (https://www.kokom.net) to support such innovative and collaborative learning experiences.

The method *online peer-to-peer counselling* and the accompanying platform *kokom.net* is used within a Bachelor degree program in Social Work that targets professionals in the social work sector who lack an academic degree and search for an opportunity to study alongside their jobs. The purpose of using the method of online peer-to-peer counselling is twofold: Firstly, in our digitized society online counselling by now constitutes an important field of social work practice and students need an opportunity to experience an online counselling setting themselves to actually grasp the potentials as well as the drawbacks of online counselling. Secondly, and perhaps even more importantly, by practicing online peer-to-peer counselling with the support of the specialized platform kokom.net students acquire a method that is well established in social work practice and they come to know a platform that transgresses the confined space of higher education as it is also a well-established platform used in the social work sector by professionals.

The paper describes and analyses the use of the online peer-to-peer counselling method and platform within the study program as part of a comprehensive case study. The case study aims to unpack the special effects that such an extension of learning environments has in detail. Three different areas will be of particular interest here: (a) the perspective of learners, (b) the perspective of teachers, and (c) the knowledge transfer from university to social work sector. Methodologically, the case study will draw on evaluation data form surveys, document analysis of student generated reflective e-portfolios and notes from teacher discussions by means of participatory observation.

The structure of this paper is as follows: Firstly, the special method of online peer-to-peer counselling in the context of online counselling as an area of growing importance in the field of social work will be outlined. Subsequently, the case itself is presented as to the context and merger of learning environments. Discussion of the case takes place in the next section, with the aim to assess the impact of the method and the platform usage from the perspective of students, teachers and a possible knowledge transfer to the social work sector. Conclusions in the last section will highlight main insights and bring this paper to a close.

HOW DO FACULTY MEMBERS REACT TOWARDS THE USE OF PERSONAL MOBILE DEVICES BY STUDENTS IN THE CLASSROOM?

Hagit Meishar-Tal, Holon Institute of Technology (HIT), Alona Forkosh-Baruch, Levinsky College, Israel

Introduction

Recently many students enter classes with mobile devices and use them as a learning support tools. On one hand, mobile technology can be seen an opportunity and conducive to authentic, meaningful and experiential learning, but on the other hand, it can be seen as a nuisance which interferes with class management, distracts the students' attention and diverts them from learning.

The goal of this study was to examine how faculty members cope with students bringing mobile devices into lessons, in a situation that lacks an overt policy regarding this phenomenon. We were interested in whether faculty members initiate incorporation of mobile devices in their lessons, if they forbid usage of these devices, or if they are indifferent regarding the phenomenon and do not interfere in their students' behaviour regarding the utilization of mobile technologies in their lessons.

Method

The study was conducted using a quantitative method. The research tool included an online questionnaire distributed among faculty members of two teachers' education colleges in Israel. Respondents included 152 teacher educators, 86 from one college and 66 from the other college; of these 121 were female and 31 men.

Findings

The findings show that in spite of the growing scope of mobile devices (mostly smartphones, but also laptops and tablets) the initiated usage by faculty is not as widespread respectively. Most faculty members do not respond to the perceived change in the noticeable change in availability of mobile devices for students. They do not change the course of the lesson and do not adapt it to the new possibilities posed by these new technologies. However, most of them do not prevent the students from using these means in a spontaneous and informal mode.

Discussion

The possible reason for this may faculty's mixed attitudes towards mobile technologies: on one hand, they acknowledge the advantages in using these devices in the lessons, but on the other hand they are also aware of the disadvantages in using it. Another reason that faculty do not respond to the change in their classes lays in the fact that most of them lack the knowledge regarding the utilization of mobile technologies in effectively in class. They report that their knowledge of the different possible uses of mobile devices in class is mediocre at best in most categories.

ONLINE COURSES EVOLVING TEACHER EDUCATION PROGRAMS

Miki Kritz, Miri Shonfeld, Kibbutzim College of Education Technology & Arts, Ilan Nagar, Hemdat Hadarom, Israel

Online Teaching in teacher training colleges has become part of training towards schools of the future. Colleges are opening more and more massive online courses. Skills to integrate technology into learning are becoming increasingly important both for the college students' studies and for their ability to fit into the schools of the future. The Ministry of Education considers the student's ability to fit into schools today, not to mention the schools of the future, as one of its main goals: and that colleges will train graduates who will be able to lead changes and implement technology in schools. These courses receive much investment and financing from the developers. Therefore, it is important to assess the contribution of the online courses for teacher trainee's literacy. Thus it was interesting to compare the different models of courses provided by the college in different populations and in recent years (2013-1016). The research analysed the contribution of the various methods of online courses (Hybrid, Online, MOOC's) for a length span of several years, at a width span of various student populations, undergraduate and graduate students. It examined the attitudes and perceptions of students in various courses in several areas: the teaching process, the contribution of online tools, self-study, satisfaction, contribution to the learning course, implementing different learning tasks, and the use of technology for teaching and learning.

The study was conducted in courses taught for undergraduate and master's degree (nine different courses with 695 students). Examining the perception of the students about the contribution of the course learning, student achievement, and the visible benefits of each model, enabled re-examining the desired models. In addition, change in a specific course over the years and among different populations enabled a thorough examination of these models. The study used questionnaires based on the MOFET research network, students' achievements, courses' outcomes and interviews with students from all courses. Preliminary Results showed that the students appreciated both courses and the scores were high. Analysing the course products and activities showed no differences in activities pattern in individual assignments, while in the collaborative assignments, especially those requiring discussion, there were differences. In class discussion only few students participated but in the online course most of the students participated. In addition, students from the Hybrid course emphasized the ICT tools they learned to use while students from the online course emphasized self-learning, peer teaching and various pedagogical strategies. It seems that students understood the importance of such courses. As one of them wrote "It enabled me to take responsibility on learning, to get involved in learning and to put efforts in learning".

Much has been researched and written about the pros and cons of online teaching. Its wide availability and improvements are rapidly increasing and are confronted by the fear of its disadvantages, such as the loss of the social component and the experience of F2F human encounter, or its lack of suitability for certain learning styles and students. Research of different models of online learning could lead to a better and more balanced approach toward online learning.

OPENING UP HIGHER EDUCATION: QUALITY ASSURANCE FOR INNOVATIVE APPROACHES

Stamenka Uvalić-Trumbić, Senior Advisor to the US Council for Higher Education Accreditation; Former Chief of Higher Education Section, UNESCO

Institutions are being urged to innovate in the provision of higher education, notably through online delivery, while some governments are encouraging the emergence of new providers. Quality assurance systems have been slow to catch up, so this burst of innovation is being restrained by having to satisfy QA criteria designed for an earlier era.

We report on three initiatives that address this challenge. First, the US Council for Higher Education Accreditation, through its International Quality Group (CHEA/CIQG), has designed and pilot tested a *Quality Platform*. This was expressly conceived for innovative higher education provision – variously described as *non-institutional* or *post-traditional*.

Although quality higher education is quality higher education in whatever form it takes, designing a QA system for innovative provision means focussing on the most essential criteria. For the Quality Platform these centre on the articulation and achievement of student learning outcomes. We describe the pilot implementation of the Quality Platform at the DeTao Masters Academy in China, an organisation conducting high-level training outside China's conventional higher education system.

The other two initiatives are guides of more general applicability written in the form of Frequently Asked Questions. One, *A Guide to Quality in Online Learning* (http://teachonline.ca/tips-tools/guide-quality-online-learning), addresses the use of online technology in regular credit programmes. The other, *A Guide to Quality in Post-Traditional Online Higher Education* (http://www.idea-phd.net/images/doc-pdf/Guide_to_online_post_traditional_highered.pdf), addresses the challenge of QA for more informal approaches such as MOOCs and OERs.

QUALITY CULTURE IN BLENDED LEARNING: SELF-ASSESSMENT AS A DRIVER FOR CHANGE

Hilde Van Laer, Koen De Pryck, Chang Zhu, Yves Blieck, Vrije Universiteit Brussel, Belgium

This paper proposes a methodology for self-assessment of online and blended learning programs (OBL) in adult education at the institutional level. It is based on applied research on the quality of OBL in formal adult education and continuing vocational education training, funded by the Flemish government (Belgium): the *Adult Learners Online! Blended and Online Learning in Adult Education and training (ALO!)* (www.iwt-alo.be).

Adult education centers in Flanders offer education for a highly diverse audience. Due to its flexibility of access and learning modes, blended learning is becoming more and more attractive for adult learners, especially for those who have to combine their studies with work, family and social responsibilities.

Not only the learners but also the institutions of adult education are characterized by great diversity. The number of enrolled students can vary substantially, as well as the amount of OBL programs they offer. Some centres have more than 10 years of experience with blended learning programs, while other institutions are in the early stages of adopting OBL in their programs. Given this diversity, a contextualized quality approach is required.

In the first section of this paper, we explore the literature on how a quality culture can be supported and implemented in education and how self-assessment procedures can support this implementation. In a second section, the construction of a contextualized self-assessment methodology for adult education centres is described. In the last part of this paper, we suggest future directions for our research.

IMPLEMENTING A MODEL AND PROCESSES FOR MAPPING DIGITAL LITERACY IN THE CURRICULUM (ONLINE BADGES)

George Evangelinos, Anglia Ruskin University, Debbie Holley, Bournemouth University, Mark Kerrigan, Anglia Ruskin University, United Kingdom

The paper discusses a process for embedding digital literacy in the curriculum by utilisation of a meta-framework defining digital literacies that could be delivered through technology-enhanced learning designs. The work builds on previous research that investigated the EU Digital Literacy DIGCOMP framework for its appropriateness to be used as a framework for the description and measurement of the digital capabilities of students and staff involved in tertiary healthcare education. Digital literacy is delivered as a graduate attribute through the utilisation of technology-enhanced learning activities that deliver aspects of the curriculum in a pedagogically-appropriate, technology-enabled way. An example of how this process had been utilised to map the digital-literacy characteristics of pilot programmes of study is presented. The study highlighted key aspects of the student experience and quality assurance implications when applying this process into practice.

INTERNATIONAL STUDENTS' BEHAVIOUR IN VIRTUAL COLLABORATIVE LEARNING ARRANGEMENTS

Wissam Tawileh, Technische Universität Dresden, Germany

Summary

This paper compares the behaviour of students from two different countries in a common Virtual Collaborative Learning course. Using the open source web analytics engine Piwik, browsing behaviour of students from Germany and Jordan in a closed learning social network was tracked and analysed. The results show differences in students' browsing behaviour and usage preferences. They provide implications for design adjustments of the learning arrangement.

Study Design

The course *Collaboration in the Virtual Classroom* is offered as a Virtual Collaborative Learning arrangement where students from Germany collaborate with students from partner universities abroad. In the summer term 2015 it included eighteen business students from Germany and eight computer science students from Princess Sumaya University for Technology in Jordan. Students' activity on the platform was tracked with their permission during the intensive virtual collaboration phase (20.04.2015-18.05.2015) using the web analytics tool. This could recognise 93.6% of all visits and 98.1% of all actions tracked during the virtual phase to be form Germany and Jordan. The recorded statistics were segmented and compared to explore variation in the browsing behaviour between students from Germany and Jordan.

Results

Students' Engagement

- Online Presence: A comparison between the total visits from Germany and Jordan exposes a common trend between both countries over the course duration. A slight decrease in the number of visits from both countries can be observed as the course proceeds, which can indicate an increasing students' orientation, as they tend to perform directed rather than exploratory visits and accomplish their intention in fewer visits.
- Online Activity: German students conducted more actions during their visits than their Jordanian peers. In more than a half of their visits, Jordanian students' viewed less than six pages, while 47% of the visits from Germany called more than 10 pages per visit. Jordanian students frequently "checked-out" the platform and left after a short navigation, while German students interacted with course content more extensively.

Students' Preferences

- Time Management: The highest average number of actions conducted in one visit was on Saturdays for German students and on Fridays for Jordanians. The distribution of actions' intensity over the weekdays indicates constant effort during the visits. German students preformed 56% of their visits between 8AM-5PM, while 49% of the total visits from Jordan were recorded in this timeframe. Jordanian students visited the platform after midnight till early morning (16% between 12AM-7AM) more than German students (9%).
- Technical Devices: Students from Jordan visited the learning social network from mobile devices much more frequently than their German peers. The number of actions performed from mobile devices was lower than the number of visits in both cases. Jordanian students mainly used mobile devices for frequent short visits.

Conclusion

The results show a variation in students' online behaviour between Germany and Jordan. While Jordanian students recorded more frequent short visits to the learning platform, German students spent more time in the social network during their visits and interacted more with the course content. However, the overall trend shows active participation from all students with daily visits and frequent actions even on weekends. It was demonstrated, how web analytics can help collaborative course designers and instructors to follow groups' activity and consider enhancements in the design of international Virtual Collaborative Learning arrangements.

DIGITAL LEARNING IN HIGHER EDUCATION – "LESSONS FROM AMERICA"

Gerard L. Danford, Haaga-Helia University of Applied Sciences, Finland

This research grew out of a 2014 academic sabbatical held in the U.S. In-depth face-to-face interviews were completed with 85 experts (institutional leaders, faculty, instructional designers-technologists, open educational resource experts, librarians, consultants, analytics experts and learning managers). Institutions represented included; 11 research universities, and 28 universities/community colleges (public, private, not-for-profit, and for-profit). In addition, educational consultancies and MOOC providers (Coursera) were involved. 35 video interviews were produced (plus transcripts) to complement the empirical research. That supplementary material was made freely available online (www.onlineedureport.org).

Digital Enrolments in U.S. Higher Education

Digital higher education enrolments in the U.S. are growing faster than higher education enrolments as a whole. Digital enrolments account for 3/4 of the total growth in higher education, and 13% of all higher education students are exclusively enrolled in digital courses. The overall growth rate for digital enrolments is approaching +4% per annum. By comparison, traditional enrolments are declining, which represents a challenge for the continued sustainability of some institutions.

The author has determined that three dominant drivers are at play (demographic, economic and competitive). Furthermore, each of these primary drivers is exhibiting unfavourable sub-conditions. In fact, there are simultaneously three or more unfavourable sub-conditions occurring within each of the dominant drivers.

Learning Outcomes

Learning outcomes are a highly contentious topic within U.S. higher education. Up to recently, outcomes were primarily driven by a necessity to meet accreditation standards. However, a more substantive application of outcome assessments at the program and course levels is currently on the agenda within many institutions. However, there are numerous learning outcome criteria which can be deployed/measured, and those criteria are often institutional, program, and course-specific. According to experts interviewed in this research, digital learning has received a disproportionate amount of scrutiny with regards to learning outcomes. As a result of this scrutiny, the subject of learning outcomes is currently a top research priority.

Impact on Costs

U.S. higher education costs per student have risen faster than inflation for decades. Average full time tuition was $9,410 in 2015-2016 (+2.9% on previous year before adjusting for inflation). Furthermore, digital learning is regarded as the best hope for cost-savings based on; reductions in labour costs (fulltime and adjunct faculty), scale economies due to larger class sizes, and less face-to-face interactions.

Conclusions

Digital learning not only appears to increase the attainment of credentials, but also increases the efficiency by which students attain those credentials. Therefore, students are attaining credentials earlier and faster if they are engaging with digital learning. However, one major challenge is concerning the availability of adequate data (analytics) to reinforce these findings.

ICT IN THE FINAL YEARS OF SECONDARY SCHOOLING: POLICIES AND ASSESSMENTS IN AUSTRALIA AND VIETNAM

Tran Manh Tang, Dorian Stoilescu, University of Western Sydney, Australia

Introduction

This study aims to contribute in analyzing, comparing and understanding of knowledge and skills of curriculum, policies and assessment in ICT education in both countries, by using comparative education methodologies. First, it analyses the content of the curriculum in both countries and show the difference that these countries have in defining ICT curriculum. Second, it exhibits ways in which the officials in both countries attempt to provide adequate resources and skills in ICT curriculum. Third, it endeavours to determine more precisely the distance between the current ICT requirements for ICT high school teachers and the actual level of performance by teaching staff. As such, it is hoped that this project in comparative education will make definite contributions to the understanding of ICT curriculum in high school teaching and learning.

Findings

The importance of ICT curriculum was heavily emphasized by the Vietnamese government in numerous documents. Nonetheless, these aspects were not critically and practically implemented. By contrast, VMOET (2009) does not articulate specific educational objectives for ICT in education, and does not have a practical procedure in place for evaluating content delivery. The objectives for ICT education in Vietnam may be well-intended, but are lacking clear definition in important ways. In Australia, the Digital Education Revolution (2008) documentation provides evidence that the four dimensions of Kozma's (2011) framework gives us a thorough perspective. The ICT infrastructure access is in place for a wide use of digital teaching and learning resources. As well, it provides an adequate framework of using adequate tools for processing information and a foundation for knowledge, communication and collaboration in all areas of curriculum. In addition, ICT leadership policies ensure a coordinated plan to provide schools with infrastructure, learning resources and teacher capacity to address 21st century educational challenges. ICT professional development ensures teachers have the skills and tools to design and deliver knowledge and skills that meet student needs and mobilize the benefits and resources of the Digital Revolution. Further, learning resources are mandated to stimulate and assist student learning outcomes, including collaborative and interactive activity guides, and instructional and reference materials. The objectives of ICT education in Australian documents are different. They reflect a concern to develop positive attitudes towards ICT as well as the development of knowledge and skills and information technology processes, expressed in terms of three major objectives: to appreciate ICT as an essential and relevant part of life; to develop students' ability to work with ICT; and to advance students' knowledge, skills and understanding. The Australian priority is the process of learning and application, with no evident moral or ideological political objectives. Incidentally, the ICT Stage 6 mention of *developing students* appropriate language for the effective communication of ICT education is not mentioned in the current Vietnamese ICT curriculum.

The Australian curriculum framework embodies assessment as an integral part of the learning process, aimed at optimizing the learning process. For instance, in Stage 6, assessment is described as the process of gathering evidence of and making judgment about students' needs, strengths, abilities and achievement. Information gained through assessment provides feedback to students and teachers, leading to more effective learner-centred programs and ultimately improvement in student learning. The assessment in Stage 6 gathers information on student development and achievement, helps to plan further learning experiences, and gives teachers a starting point to evaluate the teaching program and also target particular learner groups. In Vietnam, curriculum documents base ICT education assessment on teaching objectives and basic syllabus requirements. Student mastery of basic ICT knowledge and ability are assessed; the teacher should also improve assessment methods in order to enhance student learning. The standards see the purpose of assessment being to enhance students' all-round moral, intellectual and physical education development. The syllabus also envisages improved methods of assessment as a means of encouraging students to study harder.

THE ROLE OF THE ASSOCIATION OF ARAB UNIVERSITIES IN PROMOTING ELEARNING IN THE MEMBER UNIVERSITIES

Sultan Abu Orabi, Abdallah Al-Zoubi, Association of Arab Universities, Jordan

Many initiatives and numerous experiences have emerged in recent years in the field of open and distance learning in the Arab world, and several open and online universities have been established, most notably: (a) Al-Quds Open University, Palestine; (b) Saudi Electronic University, Saudi Arabia; (c) Hamdan Bin Mohammed Smart University, UAE; (d) The Open Educational College, Iraq; (e) Open University of Sudan, Sudan; (f) Virtual Syrian University, Syria; (g) Arab Open University, Kuwait; (h) Takwin University of Distance Education, Algeria; (i) E-Learning University, Egypt.

However, open and distance learning carries serious concerns to Arab governments and quality assurance agencies. These include safety of national systems, legitimacy of providers toward protecting users from fake providers, program quality, etc. In addition, numerous challenges and barriers that confront open and distance learning in the Arab world which can categorized by lack of management and policy issues, human resources, financial, technical and delivery systems, pedagogical and student support services. Future trends of open and distance learning in the Arab world include expected growing enrolments in accredited lower cost programs, and increased emphasis on lifelong learning to meet the rapidly changing skills needed.

Major reform is needed to overcome such challenges:

- Integration among Arab open and distance learning universities to benefit from shared experiences.
- Universities should have an awareness policy regarding the culture of the open and distance learning institutions, namely values, morale, interrelationships, commitment, diversity, and a sense of belonging. It is also important to eliminate employers' reluctance to accept online qualifications.
- Partnering with local, regional and international institutions to provide good facilities to deliver the best courses.
- Upgrade infrastructure and resources and coordinating efforts among universities to decrease expenses and spread risks.
- Opening up new paths to allow online graduate students to pursue further education and transfer credits from traditional universities.
- Setting stringent rules and regulations in order to ensure the authenticity and integrity of student work.
- Establishing centres to design, develop and produce e-Learning materials and follow up upon students and staff progress to provide continuous feedback.
- Revising promotion and incentive systems to support the process of change, and ensure high motivation of teaching and supervisory staff.

The Association of Arab Universities has recently been active in resolving some of the challenges that face open and distance learning in Arab universities by opting for cooperating with European universities in one Tempus project entitled *Enhancing Quality of Technology-Enhanced Learning at Jordanian Universities* (*EQTeL*), with a wider objective of promoting reform and modernization of higher education in Jordan through the introduction of a national quality assurance system for technology-enhanced learning. The other project is an Erasmus+ new initiative entitled OpenMed with an overarching goal of raising awareness and facilitating adoption of Open Educational Resources (OER) and Open Educational Practices (OEP) in the Arab Mediterranean region, with a particular focus on Egypt, Jordan, Morocco and Palestine. The aim of the presentation is to present the efforts of AArU to promote and disseminate open and distance education in Arab member universities and to coordinate efforts to find solutions to problems and challenges encountered and to offer opportunities for its members through its international channels and networks.

SCHOOL DISPLACEMENT: LEARNING OUTSIDE BORDERS

Ana Mouta, Ana Paulino, Hélder Quintela, JP-inspiring knowledge, Portugal

This text explores the extent to which classrooms are being transformed as a consequence of learning changing paradigms. Its borders are here considered, in order to open the dialogue on the future of formal education and the scenarios that may (not) be intentionally designed to preserve and revive cultures. Current policies are briefly identified to understand what is still driving the decisions on the Education field. All this context gives support to the presentation of a framework – the ik-Model – that has Pedagogy as its central axis. It is displayed as an approach that enables the iterative reasoning and acting towards wider and deeper learning opportunities, fuelled by an inspiring and contextualized look upon peoples' needs and wills, cultures and roots, globalisation, networks, and displacement. Throughout the presentation, some examples will be shared regarding the potential of the framework to help designing learning scenarios based on mastery, participation and collective signification. A case study from Bolivia is briefly presented to question the learning age grouping and how the challenges of breaking age barriers to learning may be intentionally revised using the ik-Model. From Jordan, we learn how to blend different learning resources and how teachers and students roles are naturally reconceived in a scenario where they have the opportunity to master their actions and profoundly develop their accountability. In this example, present and future perspectives mix, as well as *real* and *virtual* worlds to foster girls and women empowerment. In Portugal we understand the power of role-taking when it comes to integrate *the new* and how contexts of *learning* and *applying* content may not be conceived as static ones. In the conclusion, learning (dis)placement is explored considering the messages from the examples described before, where narratives and learning stories are assumed as the most wanted outcomes from meaning.

DESIGN CHALLENGES FOR AN E-LEARNING ACCREDITATION SYSTEM FOR THE REPUBLIC OF MALTA

Anthony F. Camilleri, Knowledge Innovation Centre, Alex Grech, StrategyWorks, Malta

In the context of the most recent Higher Education Strategy for Malta, the Maltese Government has put emphasis on the goals of promoting the development of e-learning as a means of widening participation, attracting foreign fee paying students to study in Malta, and ensuring quality provision across all institutions and their programmes. As such, the Maltese government is examining the design of a national accreditation system for e-learning in Higher Education, with particular emphasis on non-traditional forms of education such as MOOCs, as a way to achieve these goals.

This paper describes the first two steps of a design thinking approach: considering the challenges and opportunities which are informing the thinking of policy-makers, and examining the scenarios which may arise out of each one, with the aim of providing a basis for future ideation, prototyping and testing of an accreditation system.

The paper proposes the possible objectives of such an accreditation system for e-learning, taking into account the various policy imperatives at national and European levels, as well as the socio-economic environment of the Maltese Islands. It then considers the various challenges which may be faced in designing such an accreditation system, in particular focusing on three sets of issues. Jurisdictional issues consider the issues an accreditation agency has in ensuring it has full authority and ability to accredit programmes which may be unbundled, and offered by various providers across different borders. Quality management issues are involved with the specific differences between e-learning and "traditional" processes, and thus, what kind of providers and/or programmes might fall under an e-learning accreditation regime as compared to the quality assurance regime already in place for institutions and programmes. Data and Trust issues consider how such an accreditation system can fit within existing recognition and quality assurance tools including the European Qualifications Framework, European Credit Transfer Scheme, European Standards and Guidelines for Quality Assurance in Higher Education and the diploma supplement, while at the same time gaining broad recognition from the stakeholders standing behind these same tools.

The paper concludes with a set of recommendations to governments, in particular the Maltese government, listing key success factors for a successful system for accreditation which will allow for stimulation of the growth of e-learning in Malta while at the same time offering adequate protection for all users of the system, and full transparency of its processes.

DIGITAL CREATIVITY FOR NET GENERATION STUDENTS: RETOOLING THE ART AND DESIGN ENVIRONMENT AT SCHOOL

Andrea Kárpáti, ELTE University, Faculty of Science, Centre for Science Communication and UNESCO Chair for Multimedia in Education, Ágnes Gaul-Ács, KAPTÁR Visual Arts Workshop and Archive, Hungary

In arts education, the "iconic turn", the steady increase of images and icons in communication and the appearance of multimedia art works became an agent for paradigm change in the 21st century. Beyond fine arts, contemporary curricula focus on visual communication that includes digital graphics, photography and video. Research has consequently intensified on the skill structure and developmental stages of the "new child art" and the need for a suitable learning environment soon became evident. In Hungary, digital pedagogy has only targeted the visual arts in the last decade when tablets and smartphones began to offer numerous imaging options that invaded social web pages. Digital child and youth art has by now become a curriculum component in many countries and the art studio has integrated e-learning technology and pedagogy. This paper summarises Hungarian experiments in developing a new, creative learning environment for art and design education.

In a longitudinal study to describe the *traditional and digital visual language of children and adolescents of the 21st century*, we have asked some educational institutions where digital technology was regularly used for teaching and learning, to do the drawing tasks using digital tools as well as traditional ones like pen, pencil and paint. In Kindergarten, with children aged 2.5-6, we experienced no problems with digital technology use. Pen and pencil images are richer in detail and manifest better proportions, while digital ones developed on interactive whiteboards and tablets show more signs and symbols, complex composition, and sharp colour contrast. *New arts media motivate for collaboration* with classmates and children far away, and thus model the contemporary workspace.

The *Hungarian Diagnostic Assessment System, eDIA*, developed by B. Csapó and Gy. Molnár at Szeged University, Research Group on the Theory of Education, was used for testing and also for developing visual skills. eDIA provides an internationally unique educational environment for interactive online testing through dynamic, multimedia tasks. Tasks for art and design education were also developed, focusing on colour appreciation, spatial perception and creation, and visual communication using still and moving images, infographics and scientific visualisations. Through this assessment environment, we have been able to reveal skill components of visual competence areas, identify talents and deficits, support teachers in developing individualised educational programs and monitor personal development paths. Spatial relations may best be observed during action in real space – or in dynamic, interactive virtual space. Therefore, we included the *GeoGebra 3D, dynamic geometry software* in our battery of testing tools for spatial abilities to provide dynamic visualisation options. We compared task difficulty in a traditional paper based and in static and dynamic virtual learning and assessment environments. Student results were similar, but the dynamic digital environment was more suitable for demonstration and practice. Especially for girls, showing phases of a spatial manipulation makes it much easier to understand a spatial problem. In the current research phase we experiment with solutions to develop spatial skills through experimentation in digital space.

In interactive digital art education environments, cognitive skills involved in perception, design and creation are targeted simultaneously, just like in real life. Visual skills are in focus, but other competences are also tested, revealing the interdisciplinary significance of art education. For art education, digital imaging offers an excellent opportunity to educate for safe, expressive and aesthetically pleasing self-expression. Creation with traditional tools is important for skills development and the preservation of cultural heritage, but it is the digital media that children and young adults will regularly practice. School art and design studios must therefore be furnished to satisfy the need for digital self-expression in a motivating and technically up-to-date environment.

THE IMPACT OF THE NATIONAL ICT PROGRAM ON THE SCHOOL FROM THE VIEWPOINT OF THE ADMINISTRATION – A CASE STUDY

Wasserman Egoza, Targani Tami, Herzog Academic College, Israel

The National Computerization Program

The Israeli national ICT program (also called *Adapting the Educational System to the 21st Century*) is a program that was formulated in Israel by the Ministry of Education to promote pedagogy and learning in the school using ICT and its implementation in the curriculum. The Science and Technology Department of the Ministry of Education built a long term program which was presented to the Knesset Educational Committee in April 2010. The program is a multi-year plan which was implemented gradually, starting in the peripheral areas of the country. The program is based on a computerized model of innovative pedagogy (Information and Communication Technology – ICT). The goal is to implement the best pedagogy on a systematic level in the school while teaching 21st century skills to the pupils.

The purpose of the study

The purpose of the study is to examine the process of implementing changes in the school as it is reflected in the application of the ICT program. The study examined the all levels in the school: the administrative staff, teachers and students, from the point of view of the administrative staff of the school.

Method

The study was conducted using the qualitative method and the paradigm of constructivist interpretation. Eight staff members from several elementary schools in Israel participated in the study. The research tools were semi-structured in-depth interviews. The interviewees were asked questions relating to the implementation of the computer in education.

Findings

Analysis of the interviews showed that there was a *change in the school following implementation of the program.* This change was felt on several different levels: *Administrative*, *teacher* and *pupil.*

- *The Administrative level* – the research findings indicate that the principal is the significant figure in the implementation process of the program. The importance that the principal places on the aims of the program influences the amount of activity on behalf of the subject and on the extent of change it achieves in the teachers. It also emerged that the principal and the administrative staff have discretion how to activate the program in their school and allows for a certain amount of school autonomy in the implementation process.
- *The teacher level* – The research clearly showed a change in the teaching process that was expressed by the teacher rethinking his teaching methods. The change is dependent upon the teacher, according to his knowledge and motivational level. The need for using discretion was emphasized along with the need for rethinking the old methods of teaching. It was also found that the program resulted in an advancement of team work, sharing learning materials and cooperation between the teachers. A subject that was brought up by the interviewees as a suggestion how to improve the program was to increase pedagogical guidance such as training programs and continued professional development as a tool for improving ICT instruction.
- *The pupil level* – From the findings it can be said that the ICT program in school improves the pupil's learning experience and raises the motivation of the pupil. In addition, the program broadens the pupil's knowledge and allows for adaptive teaching. The ICT program narrows the gap between the media that is familiar to the pupil from home and the media found at school. Implementation of the program carries with it a message to the schools and may contribute to improving the teaching process.

DEVELOPING AN IRISH PROFESSIONAL DEVELOPMENT FRAMEWORK FOR TEACHING AND LEARNING, IN THE CHANGING HIGHER EDUCATION LEARNING ENVIRONMENT

Geraldine O'Neill, Terry Maguire, Elizabeth Noonan,
National Forum for the Enhancement of Teaching and Learning, Ireland

Introduction

The context of higher education is changing. The learning environment in which staff are working is in a state of flux as it responds to new socio-economic and political drivers, including the accelerated development of the digital world. In order to be responsive to this change, staff need to be adaptive and to continuously develop new knowledge, skills and attitudes for their own and their students' learning environment. As a consequence of this, there has been much focus internationally on the development of new flexible frameworks for staff professional development (PD). There have been many international drivers for the development of these frameworks, for example, the European Standard and Guidelines (2015). In Ireland, there have also been many drivers (i.e. Irish Higher Education Authority, 2014) to support the development of a national framework that both prepares staff for their own changing learning context and is inclusive of a wider understanding of professional development. Therefore, in response to this, one of the *National Forum for the Enhancement of Teaching and Learning's* key work plans was to develop a national professional development framework that would recognise, enhance, inform and support staff in a changing learning environment.

Methodology

In 2015, the National Forum carried out an extensive nation-wide consultation process, based on an earlier review of international professional development frameworks and an exploration of Irish accredited and non-accredited activity. 40 written response submissions were received from Irish higher education institutions, organisations (such as student union bodies), networks and individuals. In addition, there were 20 institutional face-to-face consultations with staff and students. For different perspectives, seven interview-style meetings were held with professional bodies to learn from their experiences and approaches to PD. The data from the interview notes, written submissions and group-discussion notes were analysed using a thematic analysis approach.

Findings

The five key themes that emerged can be broadly synthesised into the following findings: (a) The Irish higher education sector was in favour of a more transformative professional development approach, which acknowledged the spectrum of accredited and structured/unstructured/ collaborative non-accredited activity; (b) There was a strong view that professional learning not only happens in structured events, but within the context of professional practice. In addition, the wider institutional and socio-political context strongly influences professional development; (c) There was a need for a values-driven framework. Based on the consultation, the values underpinning the framework were that it should encourage inclusivity, authenticity, scholarship, learner-centeredness and collaboration; (d) The model for the framework should represent the changing pathways of the diverse staff involved in teaching in higher education. Staff should engage in a cycle of reflection, based on evidence-based practice, as they move through the different phases of their professional development; (e) Five key overarching domains were identified for inclusion in the framework: Personal Development: Self; Professional Identity, Values and Development; Professional Communication and Dialogue; Professional Knowledge and Skills; Professional and Personal Digital Capacity.

Conclusions and Next Steps

This paper sets out some of the key themes that emerged from a national consultation on a new professional development approach in Ireland. It emphasises the importance of being responsive to the complexity and changing context of practice. Based on this consultation a PD conceptual model, national guidelines and a resource for individual staff have been developed and have received further feedback. It is planned to pilot this new national professional development approach in September 2016.

CURRENT SITUATION OF E-LEARNING IN HIGHER EDUCATION: A CASE STUDY

Yasemin Gülbahar, Hale Ilgaz, Ankara University, Turkey

Introduction

E-Learning is gaining popularity year by year and almost all big universities providing online programs and courses nowadays. Due to high population in Turkey, there is a huge demand for e-Learning especially from the disadvantaged groups who needs to work while studying, and who are not able to come to school due to several reasons. Hence, universities are providing different programs according to these demands. On the other side, for similar reason, having high numbers of formal students, universities suffer from inefficient number of instructors and classrooms. Thus, in most of the universities the courses which should be delivered to all the enrolled students are turning to be provided online.

Ankara University offers various online programs which are supported by Distance Education Centre. These programs vary between vocational, undergraduate and graduate degrees. Ankara University Distance Education Centre supports this e-Learning process by providing learning management systems, virtual classrooms, interactive content and communication tools.

This research study is conducted to reveal readiness and satisfaction levels of online students and investigate possible differences between grade levels, gender and student status (formal or online).

Research Methodology

This research study was based on a survey methodology in order to reveal different aspects of various programs for all students. Hence, e-Readiness was administered at the beginning of the semester whereas e-Satisfaction was administered at the end of the semester. The population for this study was composed of 10,262 students who were enrolled in various distance education programs or online courses in a state university. Two scales, namely *e-Readiness Scale* and *e-Satisfaction Scale*, which were originally developed by the researcher, were used to collect data for this study. The e-Readiness scale was aimed to reveal the participants' level of readiness for e-learning before course starts. The e-Satisfaction scale was aimed to identify participants' level of satisfaction about the e-learning process and administered at the end of the semester. One way ANOVA, Scheffe, and descriptive statistics conducted on actual data sets. Before starting analysis phase, all improper data has been deleted from all datasets.

Discussion and Conclusion

Findings revealed varied results for different groups. These differences have many reasons like age level, subject field, instructional content provided, ICT competencies, communication and interaction expectancies and assessment preferences. It is difficult for formal learners to keep up with both face to face and online courses at the same time especially when the time for the course offered didn't match with students' expectations. It is also difficult for lifelong learners to handle e-Learning besides work and family responsibilities. Under the light of these facts, these findings are somehow interpretable through known variables and of course besides many obstacles there are many options for future implementations in order to eliminate existing and potential problems. As educators we are trying our best for those who do not have any other chance than e-Learning for being educated. More ubiquitous learners are desiring e-Learning than ever and we know what they expect and how they can be satisfied with their e-Learning experiences. Hence, based on the results, training of instructors, enhancing the quality of content, and enriching existing materials and resources can be set as first steps that we have to take for providing a better e-Learning experience to our students and further strengthen our e-Learning implementation.

THE TU DELFT ONLINE LEARNING EXPERIENCE: FROM THEORY TO PRACTICE

Nelson Jorge, Willem van Valkenburg, Sofia Dopper, Delft University of Technology, The Netherlands

The development of online courses at TU Delft is based on the Online Learning Experience (OLE), a pedagogical model that guides the development of our courses and strives for increasing quality. The creation of the OLE was an important step for TU Delft, contributing to the development of online courses in a more systematic and consistent way, guiding all course teams through the realisation of several shared educational principles.

The main goal of the OLE is to improve the quality of our online education by setting course design guidelines to support course teams, based on 8 principles. At the same time, the OLE can be used as a tool to promote reflection before the course starts to set expectations, and in the end to evaluate and improve the next run.

The OLE radar graph is a tool to promote reflection and critical thinking, offering the opportunity to improve an online course. The exercise should be done by the course team and support staff before the course starts, in order to anticipate opportunities for improvement and at the same time establish expectations, taking into account several aspects (e.g. the number of learners, their needs and the specificities of the course).

In order to generate these course insights to be analysed and discussed during the course development process, the OLE guidelines are used as criteria, rated on a scale from 0 (*not at all/inexistent*) to 5 (*exemplary/excellent*). The results (%) are then plotted on a radar graph to get a visual insight of the course. Feedback from all players involved in the teaching & learning process is collected after the course runs, including student's data (collected from surveys and extracted from the learning management system), to compare and draw reflective conclusions, contributing to an improved version of the next run of the course.

Insights from teachers and support staff developing online courses were gathered during a seminar hold at the TU Delft in October 2015, where the tool was discussed and tested. The input received from the participants allowed us to create visual representations of our types of courses, plotted on a radar graph, as shown in Figure 1.

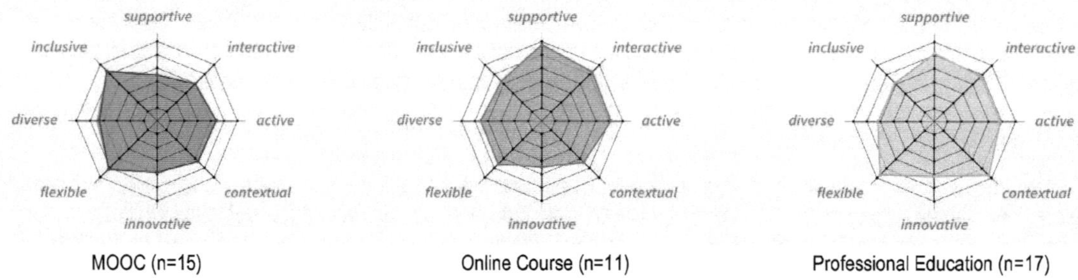

Figure 1. The OLE radar graph for 3 types of courses: MOOC, Online Course & Professional Education

In these examples we see that different types of courses originate different radar graphs. While an online course should be highly supportive with learner-teacher interactions, it's not expected that a MOOC reaches this level considering the massive number of participants. MOOCs can be seen as flexible and inclusive courses open to anyone in the world. In the Professional Education course example we see that contextual is the highest ranked principle, considering that learners expect to work on real world cases and apply what they learn directly into their practice. Flexibility is also an important principle, considering the needs of this specific target group, namely working professionals with a busy life. Although these examples don't apply to real courses, it revealed itself as an interesting exercise to gather perspectives regarding different types of courses.

The OLE guidelines are already an important instrument used by course teams and support staff for the design and development of TU Delft online courses. Many fruitful discussions have risen concerning the OLE, bringing up important concepts to consider and creating awareness regarding online learning practices and education in general. Putting the tool into practice in a reflective and insightful way has shown similar perspectives when thinking about different types of courses. The next step is to implement the OLE in a more systematic way.

FROM SANDBOX TO LEARNING CENTRE: A CASE STUDY IN NEW LEARNING ENVIRONMENTS

Deborah Arnold, William Perez, Université de Bourgogne, France

Introduction

The bac@sable is a new learning space for Continuous Professional Development (CPD) in the field of digital pedagogy, launched at the University of Burgundy in April 2015. The concept lies in the combination of physical and virtual spaces conducive to discussion, exchange of practice, experimentation and discovery. The idea was thus to create a non-classroom: to provide a pleasant, functional, modular space in which to run a wide variety of activities. These range from the more formal training courses and workshops for small groups to barcamps and *digital pedagogy surgeries*, with educational technologists on hand to meet individual or collective needs, with an open door policy twice a week. Coffee and tea are obviously a must! This project is part of the University of Burgundy's overall strategy, at the convergence of two related action plans: the blueprint for real estate (SDIA) and the blueprint for information systems (SDSI), the latter of which includes a dedicated *digital pedagogy* strand. Within this strategy, the bac@sable is the flagship project for supporting innovation in teaching and learning through the use of digital technology.

Why and how we did it

The bac@sable project was thus undertaken to meet the needs of faculty, to provide a space conducive to discussion, exchange of practice, experimentation and discovery. The idea was to create a physical and virtual space for continuous professional development (CPD) going beyond the "traditional" training course. From our experience in training and accompanying staff in digital pedagogy, we know that traditional training courses have only marginal impact for a number of reasons: there is no obligation for French academics to train in (digital) pedagogy, many have time constraints. The solution had to be both structured and flexible, the environment pleasant and stimulating. Desk research, site visits and consultations with faculty and students contributed to the overall design and equipment choices. As in many universities, square metres are hard to come by and in times of budget restrictions, a new purpose-built building was not an option in the immediate future. A number of locations were shortlisted within existing premises, the choice finally resting with a room accessible at ground floor level and close to the cafeteria. A floor plan was drawn up and various furnishing and equipment solutions tested before purchase. The room itself underwent refurbishment and the final touches provided in the form of specially commissioned artwork to support the digital theme, including a QR code as a piece of art! A team of 4 educational technologists was designated to design the CPD programme and run the bac@sable. It is a modest space, but carefully designed in a modular fashion to adapt to different uses. A meeting area with movable tables to seat 4-12 people; a screen to project from up to four laptops or tablets; two "digital sofas" with sockets for recharging mobile devices; "seatables" (chairs which can become tables). The virtual learning space to support the community consists of a dedicated area in the university's LMS and a series of social media channels (Facebook, Twitter, Scoop.it).

At the time of writing, the impact of this initiative can be seen at several levels:

- Among faculty, a growing interest in digital pedagogy and satisfaction with the solutions offered.
- Considerable interest from university management, not only in relation to the CDP support in digital pedagogy, but also the *demonstrator* aspect, to inspire and inform choices for the future learning centre.
- Considerable interest from the wider community thanks to the social media communication campaign.

Next steps

One of the major projects in the University of Burgundy's digital campus strategy for the coming years is the creation of a Learning Centre. This project involves the total rethinking and renovation of one of the existing main libraries, as well as the development of other spaces including faculty libraries and the Language Centre. The bac@sable is to be relocated from its experimental location to one of the faculty libraries, thus increasing its visibility and contributing to the objective of encouraging more staff and students to use the libraries.

THE ASSESSMENT PROCESS AS A CORNERSTONE OF QUALITY ASSURANCE IN HIGHER EDUCATION: THE UOC CASE

Ana-Elena Guerrero-Roldán, M. Elena Rodríguez, Xavier Baró, David Bañeres, Ingrid Noguera,
Universitat Oberta de Catalunya, Spain

Introduction

Internet has long since opened new teaching-learning scenarios that are promoting renewed insights about quality assurance. Universities are analysing the impact of flourishing net-based course formats, such as MOOCs, and are working to ensure the quality and certification of the learning processes involved. According to the Bologna competence-centred model, in traditional and new teaching-learning scenarios, the assessment process will be the challenge with respect to previous stages of the European educational system. The ICT that teachers are employing in their daily tasks are enhancing learning methodologies; nonetheless, new approaches need to be considered from the perspective of e-assessment.

The Assessment Process as a Quality Accreditation

In this paper we analyse the assessment process as a quality accreditation tool based on two main premises: the educational and technological ones. A formative assessment model is the most suitable approach to analyze competences acquired through learning activities or examinations. ICT can make the educational system more reliable and credible as their use can improve the authentication and authorship of learning acquired over the net. This is why we believe that the e-assessment process is a cornerstone of European Higher Education.

The Universitat Oberta de Catalunya (UOC) is a fully online university with learners disseminated across the world. The main goal of our case study is to define and to analyse an e-assessment system, focusing on the process of learner's authentication and activities' authorship in online learning environments. We analysed whether our learners are who they claim to be and if the activities were executed by them. During two academic courses several methods and techniques were applied in two pilot studies involving 200 students in a real environment. These techniques included data capture based on learners' authentication (i.e. learners' identity, personal digital certificates, facial recognition) and learners' authorship identification through activities (textual forensic analysis, plagiarism from the net, keystroke patterns).

Preliminary Results

Students feel more comfortable with a fully online assessment instead of moving physically to the university. They feel comfortable in providing the personal data needed for personal authentication (photograph, voice recording and a keystroke record). The verification techniques included in the pilot reinforce the student's trust in the rigour of the assessment system and, subsequently, in the degree certification.

Teachers realize that learning activities and assignments should be carefully designed for e-assessment processes. They also notice that the possibility to collect evidence and additional information on the academic progression of their learners allow them to better assess students. From the university point of view, adding student authentication tools and authoring analysis to an e-assessment process improves the quality of the assessment and allows the university to truly verify that competences are acquired by the learners being awarded academic credentials through activities. The tested e-assessment system provides increased credibility to the university and greater recognition from both the educational community and society.

UOC wants to share with EDEN audience its study cases and their results, which are the basis to a Horizon 2020 proposal on e-assessment quality lead by the UOC, and jointly presented with 18 partners from European universities, quality agencies, research centers and businesses. The proposal has been selected for funding, thus underscoring the importance that this issues holds in HE. The awarded project is called *Towards an Adaptive Trust-based e-assessment System for Learning* (TeSLA).

TELL ME YOUR STORY: A MOOC MODEL FOR REDUCING BIAS THROUGH PERSONALIZING CULTURAL NARRATIVES IN SMALL, COLLABORATIVE, MULTICULTURAL STUDENT GROUPS

Elaine Hoter, Ohalo College of Science Education and Sport, Nili Alon Amit, Kibbutzim College, Jen Sundick, David Yellin College of Education, Manal Yazbak Abu Ahmad, Sachnin College of Education, Reina Rutlinger-Reiner, Talpiot Academic College, Israel

Introduction

Once literary studies in the western world focused on a dominant literary culture and highlighted the classics. With the breakup of the literary canon, more space has been given to women's literature and literature written by minorities. Nonetheless, with the mass migration to Europe and shift in world cultures, many immigrant and minority students feel alienated from the culture in which they live and very little literature is taught in the schools and colleges that gives prominence to those students' native cultural backgrounds.

The MOOC setting that we have developed exposes students to diverse multicultural literature and leads them to respond to and share ideas regarding the literature and in particular cultural issues. Based on the TEC Model, the MOOC incorporates work in small multicultural groups where students experience collaborative discussions and shared projects on literary and cultural issues.

Course Description

The course *Minority Literature Written in English* is one of the MOOCS offered by the TEC Center. The course consists of 100 student teachers from five teaching colleges throughout Israel, Jewish, Moslem, secular and religious. In the planning stage of the course, the lecturers meet in person for a two day getaway, and work collaboratively in person and online throughout the year. The collaborative aspect extends to the lecturers as well, who model for the students positive multicultural cooperation: the workload, both in terms of preparation and delivery of the online sessions, is divided and the lecturers contribute their own areas of expertise. Each lecturer takes responsibility as faculty facilitator for small groups of six students comprised of participants from all of the teaching colleges in the course, including Arabs, Jews, secular and religious students from different religions and cultures in Israeli society.

The literature studied includes short stories and poems dealing with the topics: *Spiritual Journeys, Home, Family, Love and Marriage, Identity, Intergenerational Relations and Food*. Most of the texts read in the course are written by Arab and Jewish writers and relate to issues that draw on the various geographic, cultural, and religious backgrounds of our students.The assignments encourage students to share their own experiences, knowledge, and anecdotes with other group members, either orally in breakout rooms during the lesson, or in writing as group assignments. This creates an authentic learning experience in English as a foreign language and allows for task-based written and oral exercises to be performed collaboratively by students from different backgrounds and beliefs. The collaborative strategies and understanding and appreciation of the other, which are critical in Israeli society and indeed the world, are invaluable tools that these student teachers can transfer to their own future students in the classroom.

Research

The students were required to keep a reflective journal throughout the course as well as participate in forums and social media discussions carried out in the small multicultural groups. We have examined this material in order to understand the heuristic process the students undergo in this course, their collaboration with students from other cultures, as well as how the course influenced them. The poster will present the model we have developed for reducing bias through personalizing cultural narratives in small collaborative multi-cultural groups together with the analysis of the students' reflective journals and participation in the social media.

TEACHING TO TEACHERS: A MOOC BASED HYBRID APPROACH

Rosanna De Rosa, University of Naples, Alessandro Bogliolo, University of Urbino, Italy

Sakai-Miller (2015) encourages educators to get to the heart of 21st century teaching by asking themselves three questions about the lessons they are preparing: What? So what? Now what? According to Sakai-Miller, in order to empower students, we need to empower teacher first thus realizing a virtuous cycle to disrupt old paradigms and move the education forward. The pivotal key is to shift from the paradigm of acquiring knowledge to actually using it; bringing theoretical ideas into practice. To help teacher to uptake the innovation age challenge, we need to solve the digital isolation of all employers in the education field, thus transforming them into an active community.

Considered as a transversal skill, teaching Coding to teachers has been considered as a relevant way to restore the centrality of the teacher in the Italian school system through a highly scalable process of teaching/learning among the diverse actors involved: coding ambassadors, teachers and digital animators, pupils as final users.

Starting from the perspective described, a special MOOC on Coding has been offered to test and deploy a hybrid approach where the virtual dimension was articulated in synchronous and asynchronous activities throughout the use of hangouts for living the experience in real time. In this context, the MOOC platform (Emma, euroepanmoocs.eu) was used to re-arrange the lesson and its instructional design in a form of a loop.

In the case of MOOC on Coding both the MOOC teacher and participants share a common understanding of their mission in the world, a sole vision of the future education, and a clear objective to be reached all together. The similarity with the Alinsky model of *community organizing* is impressive. Here a self-selected community is able to self-organize using the community at the same time as a medium and a message to enlarge the participation and to scale up the benefits of becoming a whole in a bottom up constructivist and connectivist experience. Common needs, self-recognition, peer-reflection, co-construction and empathy are here the keywords of a successful MOOC. This result seems to be counter-intuitive since the MOOC roots are deeply radicated in the ideas of openness and scaling up at a global level. Which, of course, are both brilliant ideas, that indeed do not exclude the possibility of scaling up education within specific communities.

As a preliminary conclusion, we can say that this hybrid model was able to ensure to over 6,000 participants a high level of engagement, participation and learning.

EMBEDDING MOOCS IN UNIVERSITY COURSES: EXPERIENCES AND LESSONS LEARNED

Sólveig Jakobsdóttir, Grímur Bjarnason, Kristinn H. Gunnarsson, Dóra Dögg Kristófersdóttir,
University of Iceland, Iceland

The focus so far on the discussion of effects of MOOCs on education in Europe, with associated opportunities and threats, has largely been on pedagogy and learning in a more abstract way rather than on more concrete effects, for example the opportunity to use MOOCs as a tool for professional development for teachers. The role of MOOCs can be an important one in this respect, not the least in the area of ICT in education where the need has been great for teachers all over the world. In this poster, we will describe the experiences of embedding MOOCs in a graduate course on distance education at the University of Iceland (UI) School of Education in spring semester 2016. One purpose of this integration was to expose students to the opportunities involved before graduation so they could be more aware of what might be available for them in their future professional development. Also, those experiences provided materials for critical analysis based on theories, research and pedagogical models in distance education as well as ideas for the design and development of online courses.

In the spring semester 2016, there were 23 active students (12 males, 11 females, age range 25 to 63) in the course which is 10 ECTS. Students got an overview of generations of distance educational pedagogies and a list of reports and journal articles on MOOCs in education. The MOOC project was the first assignment (2.5 ECTS, 25% of the final grade). The majority of the participants had never signed up for or completed a MOOC and were not aware that such courses existed. Six teams of students were formed (3 to 5 students in each team). A list of potential MOOC providers and individual MOOCs were provided and teams identified potential MOOCs of interest from each provider. The teams got six weeks to complete the project.

There were 17 MOOCs from 7 different providers selected. In all cases only one student chose each MOOC except for one MOOC on teaching with Moodle from Moodle.org, which was a topic of high practical interest to many of the students, some of whom were aiming to create a Moodle course in another assignment later in the course (Moodle is also the most widely used LMS for schools and universities in Iceland). There were seven different courses (41%) run in the Coursera platform, four (24%) by edX, two by OpenLearning, one by FutureLearn, one by Alison, and one by PR Academy. The content of about 41% of the courses (7) were related to ICT and media in education and/or distance or blended learning. Whereas the other 59% had content in relation to varied themes including language, physics, sustainable development, and personal development.

All six groups did online presentations (via Adobe Connect) in mid-February outlining their experiences and turned in their final report about a week later. In the poster, major themes and conclusions from these reports will be introduced. In addition, three students gathered additional data with phone interviews among the cohorts participating the course in spring 2014 and this spring. Data will then be presented for example on whether and then how the cohort of 2014 applied their experiences of participating in MOOCs. An overview of pros and cons of embedding MOOCs in university courses will be provided.

USING OERS, PERS, BLENDING AND FLIPPING TO DELIVER A COMPUTER SYSTEMS MODULE TO YEAR 1 STUDENTS

Michael O'Rourke, Athlone Institute of Technology (AIT), Ireland

The key aim of this project is to incentivise higher education students to engage with a Year 1 Computer Systems module through a blended and flipped classroom approach. Attendance at the traditional lecture is in decline for a variety of reasons. The concept for this module is to encourage self-directed learning (SDL) through reading Proprietary Educational Resource (PER) material and watching Open Educational Resource (OER) video in advance of class assessments. The actual class time is used for discussion of the content of lessons using PowerPoint summaries, watching related videos, online assessment and laboratory work. The project aims to measure and evaluate the effectiveness of this approach.

ICT CONTESTS AS A ROAD TO COMPUTER LITERACY OF OLDER PEOPLE

Olga Grishina, Elena Sidorova, Plekhanov Russian University of Economics, Russia

Plekhanov Russian University of Economics has always embraced all new tendencies of changing environments. ICT-backed learning has become an inseparable part of educational process for Plekhanov digitally equipped full-time students while the whole principle of distance education at the Faculty of Distance learning is based on technologies. The more recent achievement is the programme aimed at digital education of older people which was introduced several years ago to eliminate digital division between generations and has been successfully functioning up to now. To encourage retired people in their usage of ICT even more, Plekhanov University in collaboration with the Council of the Federation Committee on Social Policy and the Union of Pensioners has launched a series of computer quests and championships for them on its premises.

Currently pensioners make up one third of the population of Russia but only 15% of them possess the skills of working on the computer. The Council of the Federation Committee on Social Policy fully understands that only by enhancing the computer literacy among older people they may improve the quality of their life and better integrate them into the society, in accordance with the principles of *active aging*.

So the Faculty of Distance Learning of Plekhanov with its *Silver generation* project has been involved in the programme for 4 years. The main aim of the programme is to encourage and support older people in their usage of Internet services. In order to make computer training more challenging the pensioners were offered to compete for the title of the champion of Russia on the premises of Plekhanov at the final stage.

Project

Before the organisation of the championship it was necessary to formulate its purposes and identify the age groups. As in Russia the retirement age for women starts at 55 and for men, at 60 the same criterion was agreed for the participation in the championship. The second criterion was that only people whose previous work had not been connected with computers and who had successfully finished the computer-training courses could take part in the championship.

From the organizational point of view the competition consisted of three main stages. The first one was distant – the pensioners had to prepare a presentation *Information technologies in my life* in MS PowerPoint 2007/2010 at home and then sent it to the organizational committee. The best presentations were selected and their authors were invited to the regional centres of the Russian Federation to participate in the second stage. And so only the winners of the second stage could come to Plekhanov Moscow to take part in the finals.

More than 2 thousand people from 59 regions took part in the preliminary stage and 150 pensioners – the winners of the regional stage (2 people from each region) and 6 foreign teams from Belarus, Belgium, Slovakia, Abkhazia, Kazakhstan and Uzbekistan – participated in the finals. On the first day the contestants had to make a presentation in MS Office PowerPoint and format the text with graphs and pictures in MS Office Word in accordance with the template. Then they were supposed to find certain information with the help of the search engine, pay the utility bills and get the appointment to the doctor on *State services.ru* website and to find the information about banking products for pensioners on a bank site. The second day was devoted to the role-play *For all occasions* where teams of pensioners competed with Plekhanov students. With the help of *Consultant-Plus* law reference system the teams had to complete the marriage agreement and to answer the questions on spouses' mutual responsibly. The involvement of students benefited both sides as older people can share their experience and young people help with the computer skills. In general Plekhanov students are active participants of *Silver generation* project helping older people out of classes as volunteers.

Conclusion

The computer contest has demonstrated sincere interest of older people in the programmes like that. Such events may serve as a good incentive for older people to get computer training, which contributes tremendously to the idea of active aging, promoted by the government. Besides, they may encourage the authorities especially in the regions to develop computer courses in order to embrace as many people as possible. The fact that computer literacy may help a retired person live a fulfilling life and be in demand in the community should no more arise any doubts.

KNOWLEDGE IN MOTION BETWEEN FORMAL EDUCATION AND PROFESSIONAL PRACTICE – HOW TO DESIGN FOR LEARNING ACROSS BOUNDARIES

Anne Mette Bjørgen, Line Kristiansen, Lillehammer University College, Norway

Introduction

We examine how adult students perceive their learning between formal educational settings and work. We are especially interested in how learning has potential to be realized between learning contexts by using digital technology. We pursue these issues by exploring the relationship between our didactic approach and how students use and experience the learning resources and methods. We draw on analyses of selected courses at Lillehammer University College in Norway as examples. These courses are aimed at different groups of professional workers in order to develop their professional competences; ambulance workers, employees of municipalities, public health coordinators. Our didactic-pedagogic approach aims at inspiring students to reflect on own practice and to connect learning in formal education with learning at their workplace. We investigate how students experience and perceive their participation in different activities involving a range of learning resources, for instance video lectures followed by dialogical groups (online or offline), and peer-based learning on written work. We also study how they view learning resources as relevant in developing their professional practice and professional competences.

The following questions guide our study:

- How do adult learners experience their participation in continuing education?
- In what ways do they find the course content, methods and learning resources relevant in relation to their professional work and professional competence development?

Based on a socio-cultural perspective on online learning, we discuss and suggest some relevant criteria to promote learning across contexts. We argue that learning criss-cross formal and informal learning contexts, and that it is vital to approach formal educational settings and workplace settings as being connected rather than separate learning contexts.

Methods and data

Our data include surveys and focus group interviews. The surveys contain data from evaluations of about 150 students from two different courses. The surveys also include some qualitative data as we encourage students to tell in their own words how they experience methods and content. We use a thematic analysis approach to analyse the interviews.

Learning across contexts – some vital aspects based on empirical findings

Our ways of facilitating courses are inspired by research highlighting the importance of promoting opportunities for adult learners to link between theory and practice and to reflect on this, to express own ideas and perspectives, and encouragement to improve thoughts, ideas and arguments in assignments. We put particular emphasis on a mixture of obligatory and voluntary elements as a design principle, in order to engage the students to reflect, share and participate. Our surveys as well as the interviews show that a majority of the students experienced that the courses had contributed to change their professional practice.

Based on our results, we suggest a student-centred approach where methods and learning resources engage students to participate in activities that urge them to reflect on own practice. We also suggest a solution that expands learning spaces and merge learning contexts in order to provide students with opportunities to draw on and develop own experiences, knowledge and skills by using a range of contextual resources.

THE SIGNIFICANCE AND POSSIBILITIES OF INTERNATIONAL COOPERATION BETWEEN INSTITUTIONS OF HIGHER EDUCATION

Éva Sándor-Kriszt, Anita Csesznák, Budapest Business School, Hungary

The significance and importance of international relations is increasing for the institutions of higher education of our homeland. It is comprehensible, since, as a natural consequence of globalization, we are experiencing the augmentation of international cooperation in all fields. Hungarian higher education has roots too dating back to centuries. We have many foreign students today. Establishing and maintaining connections abroad has become so easy and usual in our day, no wonder if the role and possibilities of international cooperation have expanded.

We can see a particularly significant increase in the role of international cooperation contemporarily. It is due to many factors, but all are consequences of globalization. Hardly any event in the world lacks international consequences.

It is clear for experts on higher education that universities and colleges have numerous functions supplementing teaching and research. Institutes in higher education are centres for knowledge and skills. Moreover, they have to respond to the ever changing demands of society and provide learned and skilful experts for the job market. Generally speaking, they have to contribute to the social, cultural and economic maintainability of the state. Higher education can fulfil these tasks only by applying a multi-layered system of cooperation and cooperating tightly with other institutions. The professional cooperation built and maintained with foreign institutions can be especially fruitful in this respect.

We can compare many fields in higher education, curricula, course materials, new methods and systems of teaching, and we can count on further exchange of teachers' and of course, students' experiences. Higher education is constantly changing all over the world and hence requires much attention and creates many challenges. Though often inconvenient, we all see its benefits. Exchanging each other's experiences on these topics might also be fruitful.

International cooperation has many forms and levels. Cooperation formed or functioning at the highest levels influences cooperation at lower levels. For example, an institute or just one of her employees may benefit from a ministerial level cooperation agreement. However, we wish to focus on lower, institutional (or even departmental) level activities and relations, since we are active at this level and have great possibilities here too.

Cooperation is really rewarding if it satisfies the following requirements:

- well defined particular activities belong to its scope,
- it is operative, planned and nursed,
- institutes have designated persons responsible for the cooperation.

Opportunities of cooperation

- formal call of leaders and comparing notes,
- exchanging faculty,
- exchanging or adopting course materials,
- exchanging students,
- joint programs.

THE IMPACT OF LEARNING TECHNOLOGY ON STUDENTS' LEARNING

Egoza Wasserman, Miki Kritz, Einat Rozner, Asmaa N. Ganayem, Dorit Barat, Smadar Bar-Tal, Miri Shonfeld, MOFET Institute, Israel

Technologies have the potential to improve learning. However, they might disrupt learning processes if they are used incorrectly. The poster presents research on the impact of online environments on the learning process (e.g. MOOCs, online learning, virtual worlds and mobile apps). The presented intertwined studies are carried out by an academic interest group at MOFET institute, a national inter-collegial centre for the research and development of programs in teacher education and teaching in colleges. These studies include mixed research methods, based mainly on self-report questionnaires and text analysis. The studies focus on the impact of an assortment of technologies and learning environments on the learning process. Learning refers to cognitive processes, as well as to affective aspects, e.g. motivation. The populations include secondary and postsecondary students as well as pre-service teachers.

Online courses have become increasingly popular in the last decade. Distance learning differs from traditional learning in many aspects. Massive (multiplayer) online courses have already taken two main and very different teaching approaches: the passive and the interactive approaches. In the passive approach, students mainly watch videos of class lessons and experience some interaction in discussion groups. Assessments are usually limited to multiple choice tests and sometimes to delivering tasks. In the interactive approach, the aim is to foster active learning and inquiry tasks. Assessment of the many tasks relies mostly on peer assessment from an educational standpoint. Interaction is one of the most significant components in the learning process in general and one of the cornerstones in on-line learning processes in particular. Distance learning is reflected in four types of interaction: student-teacher, students-students, students-teacher, and learner-materials. Virtual worlds provide a place for "real" meeting with the teacher and the students. Research points out that using virtual worlds enhances students' motivation and engagement, facilitates collaboration and provides immersive, experiential learning opportunities unavailable in traditional learning environments. Virtual worlds in any form are widely used knowledge- and social-interaction platforms and will probably be a part of the social-technical system people use for teaching and learning in the foreseeable future. However, there are challenges in using this technology; also, its effectiveness has not yet been found as sufficient. In the poster, we will share our experience in enhancing teacher's presence, interactions and peer assessment in massive online courses and virtual worlds. The study will present how the distance learning influences the student in terms of effective learning, motivation and development of thinking and learning skills using online environments and the various types of behaviour in the online interaction that occurs in the professional teaching community using those environments.

In addition, the poster includes mobile apps usage on learning. Studies present inconclusive results regarding the advantages of implementing mobile apps in the learning process as well as their potential for improving learning, in spite of their popularity. Other studies focus on the challenges and obstacles of apps on the learning purposes. The study proposed herewith examines incidental learning (i.e. unplanned or unintentional learning) among multicultural students sharing an online course. The study will focus on the WhatsApp application impact on learning, adding information on the value and obstacles of using this app in relation to an online course in which all students participate. Studying the use of WhatsApp for learning purposes via the student's viewpoint can contribute to developing new teaching methods, thereby making learning more accessible for more students.

REDEFINING THE STUDENT EXPERIENCE: INFORMATION-SEEKING BEHAVIOUR – THE COMPLETE PICTURE

Sandra Tury, University of London, United Kingdom

There has been an increase in importance and focus on the *student experience* in higher education recently. In the UK it is regularly mentioned in university surveys, league tables, in recruitment and marketing material, and strategic planning documents. According to Morgan (2016), the student experiences "encompasses all aspects of student life (i.e. academic, social, welfare and support) with the academic imperative at the heart of it" (http://www.improvingthestudentexperience.com). However the striking feature of many surveys of student experience, such as the Higher Education Policy Institute (HEPI) and Higher Education Academy (HEA) annual report on student academic experience in the UK, is the focus on the institution's own provision for campus-based students and on learning and teaching or assessment and feedback. There is much less evidence gathered for distance learners and it is unclear whether distance learners are part of surveys, and in fact looking at some of the HEPI/HEA survey questions such as those relating to contact hours, one can assume that they are not.

This gap may have arisen because distance learning has been considered an adjunct to the dominant provision to student communities primarily based on campus. The increase in scale and diversity of the student community, the importance of distance learning for access to education, and the economic importance of distance learning to higher education institutions necessitate the consideration of the student experience of for distance learning students. According to Unwin et al. (1998), over half of conventional universities are currently involved in postgraduate distance learning provision.

This article is based on detailed research from a completed doctoral study which investigated the information seeking behaviour of distance learners registered with the International Programmes of the University of London (formerly the University of London External System) which is the second largest provider of distance education in the UK (has over 50,000 registered students from 180 countries).The research employed a combination of quantitative (questionnaires both online and by post) and qualitative (laboratory-based observational study using think-aloud protocol) methods and one-to-one interviews using open-ended semi-structured questions. The population comprised 1,000 distance learners registered on seven different Social Sciences and Humanities programmes. All participants were registered online library users. A total of 649 out 1,000 (65%) responded to the survey. They resided in 81 different countries. Statistical analysis using a chi-square test for independence was used to measure the significance of the variables.

Of the 33 factors relating to the distance learners' student experience examined by the research, only two are briefly analysed and reported in the paper and include: learners' success at accessing the University of London's Online Library resources, and the reasons for choice of information the frequently used.

It is recommended that in order to enhance the student experience in distance learning, an alternative and more holistic approach which incorporates the learner's information seeking behaviour (ISB) should be adopted.

MONITORING A LEARNING COMMUNITY IN A HYBRID ENVIRONMENT: A SENTIMENT ANALYSIS

Ilaria Merciai, Marco Cerrone, University of Naples Federico II, Italy

As Facebook publishes figures showing that social networks have reduced the degree of separation of people on the planet from 6 to 3.7, it is a platitude to say that they are powerful communication tools. However, the literature on their impact within MOOCs is still emerging, where the learning community already resides within its own space on the MOOC platform and where teaching units are accompanied by a forum for requesting clarification or information.

In a recent MOOC on the EMMA platform (www.europeanmoocs.eu) – *Coding in your classroom, now* – Facebook was used as an additional learning environment, to post and share information on content related to the course, to comment lessons and assignments, or simply to share a common experience and outcomes.

The user-community network that has developed around the course has grown from the 6,000 learners enrolled on the course to reach a population of 100,000.

The community started to exchange information about their area, schools and classes, and to use the learning experience on the MOOC to share and build knowledge and even plan meetups in their local area.

Sentiment analysis, with key word, online expressions, concept, contexts, shows that socials acted as a powerful tool not only for dissemination of the course but also for informing thousands of people about the innovative features the Emma platform was experimenting. Last but most importantly they became a powerful tool for sharing best teaching practice in the field.

This paper presents an exploration of the learning community on this course and evidence for some of the observations we make, trying to understand what impact this hybrid model of MOOC delivery has on the creation of the learning community and student engagement.

TPACK OF EXPERIENCED MATHEMATICS TEACHERS IN LOW SES SECONDARY SCHOOLS

Dorian Stoilescu, University of Western Sydney, Australia

Several studies show the importance of equity in mathematics education, in contrast with what normal educators would perceive mathematics as a neutral area. Educating mathematics teachers in order to help them lay into practice notions of social justice becomes an important objective and technology has its important role. Because of the increasing number of years of schooling, and high school becoming mandatory, mathematics education no longer targets only intellectual elites. Furthermore, computers offer an environment that allows a dynamic context and lets instruction become more engaging and interactive. Becker and Ravitz (2001) surveyed 1,215 schools with 4,100 mathematics teachers of grades 4 to12 to see patterns and frequency of using computers. The results show that, during 30 weeks, only 11 percent of participants reported using computers more than 20 times. Even in these cases, the use of computers was for playing games, typing in word processors, or reading materials from CDs. As well, pedagogy is changed, as computer technology is involved to explaining, testing, and giving feedback to students.

Mathematics teachers often invoke the role of technology in motivating their students in learning mathematics. Therefore, integrating technology in mathematics education becomes essential to motivate multiple categories of students. Thus, through participant narrative, the specific objectives of this study are to: (a) Identify ways of using technology in mathematics education classrooms in a multicultural school with low economics status; (b) Identify whether various identities are included and/or excluded/silenced in the process of integrating technology in secondary school contexts and to what extent; (c) Identify systemic aspects and structures, including policies, pedagogies and practices that reinforce or perpetuate this inclusion/exclusion; (d) Explore teachers' opinions about their views of integrating technology in mathematics education; (e) Use the TPACK framework in order to describe the expert teachers in low SES schools.

This study is a qualitative research. I will select five teachers from two schools. I will combine case study with ground theory. In the first stage, I will study each teacher separate and construct an individual case study. In the second stage, I will do a cross case analysis to see common aspects and differences between the five teachers. In the third, I will try to redesign the TPACK aspects of using the TPACK framework and prescribe ways of efficiently using the framework, by using the grounded theory. A mentioned before, the main criteria for selecting the schools and the teachers is that they represent a community with an ethnic diversity and a low socio economic status. The two secondary schools selected in this study are from the Greater Western Sydney which has a great number of new immigrants, both from working and middle class. I will look for secondary teacher who have at least five years experience of working in secondary education and are regularly using technology in their mathematics classrooms.

Introducing technology in mathematics education has received mixed reviews. On the one hand, researchers saw integrating technology as an opportunity to make mathematics more accessible for various social categories of students. On the other hand, studies have shown that technology as amplifying social pre-existent inequities. For instance, it was noticed that students from poor economic background have during their classrooms only exercises that emphasize low skills and rote memorization. First, researchers mention that often teachers in these schools are not adequately trained or are from the minorities themselves. As well, researchers mentioned that often technology is only introduced only perfunctory, without adequately attempting to redesign or reshape it later based on local feedback.

THE E-CAMPUS-PROJECT – THE TRANSFORMATION OF A STUDENT ADMINISTRATIVE TOOL INTO A PERSONAL LEARNING ENVIRONMENT

Mikael Reberg, Mid Sweden University, University Library and Learning Resource Centre, Sweden

Summary

The web technologies of the present time together with the diverse plethora of digital applications for mobile technologies offer unique opportunities to design mobile and flexible Personal Learning Environments (PLE). Even though the concept of PLE doesn't have a widely established single definition, the common factor seems to be the potential for offering new ways of using digital technology for student-centred learning, and are typically described as a collection of different applications, usually web based and collaborative (*social*), which aims at foster self-regulated and collaborative learning. A PLE should offer the learners possibilities to

- learn with other people;
- control their learning resources;
- manage the activities they participate in;
- integrate their learning.

In 2010, Mid Sweden University decided on an educational strategy for the coming years 2011–2017, in which e-learning was established as one of two main areas for strategic development. E-learning should be a part of the educational activities carried out on campus as well as a part of the courses given on distance. An important part within the framework of the strategy was that Mid Sweden University should have a presence on the Internet that could be understood as a *digital campus* or an *e-campus*.

The *e-campus-project* started in 2013 with the ambition to build an e-campus for students. This digital environment would be organized around the existing student administrative tool *The Student Portal*. Together with a new personalised interface the portal would be developed towards potential integration with other learning resources and learning support services located on the university websites, including the university library services, as well as the learning management system Moodle and GoogleApps licensed to the university. Functions for personalised schedules, possibilities to access transcripts of learning achievements and functions for course registration as well as resources for booking rooms for group work should be easily accessible. Students should have the possibility to easily communicate with each other and with their teachers via group or programme sites and messaging systems.

Also, based on the increasing adoption of smartphones and iPads, the demand for mobile access to this new environment was obvious. The new environment should therefore have a responsive interface.

In conclusion, the possibilities to transform the existing environment into a PLE is present and vital.

The poster presentation aims at further the discussion on the concept of PLEs and the different solutions for digital learning environments among universities by presenting the key elements of the personalised and responsive interface in this still ongoing project. The poster gives an overview of what functionality is present in the digital environment and what possibilities exist in the coming steps of the continued development.

READING AND WRITING IN VARIOUS TECHNOLOGIES FOR LEARNING PURPOSES

Hayley Weigelt-Marom, Alona Forkosh-Baruch, MOFET Institute, Israel

Today's educational settings require students to use a variety of technologies (e.g. devices, software, applications, etc.) for learning purposes. Most of the learning that utilizes these technologies involves reading and writing. Each technology may involve different scopes, forms and genres of reading and writing. For example, searching the web mainly involves writing words or short sentences as opposed to writing a coherent message or moreover a full text using a word processor. Additionally, learning technologies may include (inertly or via add-ons) assistive technology programs (e.g. text to speech, speech to text programs, spell checkers) which can change students' reading and writing performance and preferences.

The preliminary study herewith aims to better understand the influence of various technologies used for educational purposes on students' reading and writing. Results were collected from self-report questionnaires of students and their teachers. These included questions regarding the type of technologies used for learning, frequency of usage, questions concerning the scope and genre used for reading and writing while utilizing different technologies, usage of assistive technology, and questions regarding technological preferences. Results and implications for educational settings will be presented in the poster, verbally and graphically, as well as recommendations for further research.

The study was conducted as part of the work of the *Technology in Education Interest and Research team* at the MOFET institute, a national intercollegial centre for research and development of programs in teacher education and teaching in colleges in Israel.

DEVELOPMENT OF SHARED KNOWLEDGE IN A VIRTUAL REALITY ENVIRONMENT FOR COLLABORATIVE LEARNING

Laura Kiss, Balázs Péter Hámornik, Máté Köles, Budapest University of Technology and Economics, Hungary

Collaborative learning task in virtual reality environment

The virtual training demonstrated in this session is targeting the future founders of startups. In the world of innovative small companies usually the members of a team are representing various professions and working in interdisciplinary teams. Technology is important in a startup and teamwork plays a key role in the long-term success.

The research to be presented was conducted in Virtual Collaboration Arena (VirCA) which is an open and modular virtual reality management software. VirCA is designed to support collaborative work in virtual environments. The paper presents a 2 hours long training task for teams in virtual reality that includes individual and team tasks and measurements of shared team mental models. In the experiment two collaborative settings were used: a virtual and face-to-face. The collaborative learning task consisted of three phases: (a) discussion of team roles (leader, developer, and marketing/communication specialist), (b) cooperative work, and (c) collaborative work. The sample consisted of 18 people in 6 teams (mean age was 25.28 years, standard deviation 3.41 years). A team consisted of 3 participants with the roles described previously. Three of the groups worked in traditional setting and three of them in virtual reality.

Research questions and results

We have investigated the characteristics of the collaboration and measured the development of shared mental model both in traditional and virtual environment. We used test-retest method to evaluate the development of the preliminary mental models to the end of task completion. We calculated the accuracy and similarity of the shared team mental models within the teams and defined the differences of the two conditions. Our hypotheses were the following: (a) the virtual teams' shared mental models do not significantly vary neither their accuracy nor similarity compared to the traditional teams'. The knowledge about the team collaboration is equally similar and accurate in the two different conditions. (b) The collaborative learning task has a significant effect on how the similarity and accuracy of the team mental models develop. We assumed that after the task the team mental models would be more similar and accurate than the initial ones.

To measure the similarity and accuracy of participants' shared mental models we used the method of Banks and Millward (2007). We found that the two similarity values were not significantly different from each other $t(4) = 0.532$, $p = 0.623$. The mean accuracy of the teams also did not show any significant difference ($t(4) = 1.031$, $p = 0.999$). We could confirm our first assumption was proved to be true; the virtual teams' shared team knowledge was as similar and accurate as in the face-to-face condition.

To study how the collaborative learning task influenced similarity and accuracy of the team mental model we have calculated Paired Sample T-Tests and correlated the means' result of the initial and final questionnaire of the team mental model. Our calculations showed that no difference appeared after the collaborative learning task either in similarity ($t(5) = 1.559$, $p = 0.18$) or accuracy ($t(5) = 0.804$, $p = 0.458$) of the shared team mental model. Our second hypothesis was not supported by the data. After the collaborative learning task the team mental model showed no significant change.

Conclusion

We have found evidence that the VirCa could be used as effectively as a face-to-face training setting, which is an important step towards to the application of VR technology. Virtual trainings can be a next step from e-learning materials towards a learning environment that could provide more presence and less constraints with incorporating our knowledge of web based learning settings also.

CHANGING LMS: HOW TO MANAGE CHANGE ABOUT TECHNOLOGICAL INNOVATIONS IN HIGHER EDUCATION

Eva P. Gil-Rodríguez, Ana María Delgado García, Mireia Leg Gil, Universitat Oberta de Catalunya, Spain

Although there is a considerable body of written literature available on how to implement innovation in businesses and organizations, and, at the same time, many technological innovations are being applied within the field of teaching and learning, we do not find many references to innovative experiences implemented on a large scale within a university and generalized to its faculty and students. Normally, technological innovations are intensively used by a small proportion of the faculty and it is very difficult to generalize them to the rest of the teaching staff. As a result, the benefit that would be gained from their implementation for the other students is lost.

Resistance to technological change is a phenomenon that has been extensively documented in all types of organization. However, certain measures have also been documented that may tend to minimize this resistance: mentoring, training, information and assistance actions are required so that the time and the learning curve required are reduced as much as possible, and the technological change is made as smoothly and comfortably as possible both for the faculty and for the students. However, it is also necessary to articulate the interests of the various agents involved in this technological change process, which normally also entails a culture change in the organization.

This communication presents the Universitat Oberta de Catalunya's experience in generalizing an innovative experience, namely, its new virtual classroom environment, in the Faculty of Law and Political Science. In order to achieve this generalized implementation, a series of steps have been followed and a number of specific actions have been designed that have succeeded in progressively integrating the faculty in the new environment, following a user-centred design and continuous improvement cycle that has also enabled the virtual classroom environment to be refined. Thus, the needs and concerns of all the agents involved in the change have been taken into account: from the faculty and the e-learning research centre to the faculty and students support services and, it goes without saying, the University's Information Systems.

Although the lack of success in initial implementation could be attributed to the system's lack of technological robustness – still in a non-stabilized beta version – the classroom stabilization actions only achieved a level of generalization in the University of 44%. Therefore, as a first conclusion, we can say that even though technological change has obvious benefits and no technical drawbacks, it does not take place spontaneously but, on the contrary, requires institutional actions to promote it and ensure effective implementation. Then, we will give an account of the actions undertaken to address the change to the new virtual classroom environment, and we will also explain the results that have been obtained with these actions, increasing the level of implementation from 44% of the classrooms to 91% in one year.

BLENDED LEARNING BEFORE A LEARNING ENVIRONMENT CHANGE: PRE-DEPARTURE TRAINING FOR MEDICAL EXCHANGE STUDENTS

Nynke de Jong, Laury de Jonge, Marijke Kruithof, University of Maastricht, The Netherlands

Introduction

Maastricht University encourages medical students at master level to gain international experience. An Internship in a non-western country poses different problems and challenges for students as compared to the usual internships in the Netherlands and neighbouring countries. Around 150 medical students leave our university to non-western countries each academic year. The aim of the university is to send these students well-prepared to their institutions abroad: the internship on the tropics should be safe for patients, but also for students.

In the past students had to follow an (obligatory) course in tropical medicine. This course focussed on some important tropical infectious diseases and public health aspects, but not so much on personal preparation, for instance safety issues and dealing with cultural differences. Because of a change in the curriculum this module was not obliged anymore. At the same time, the lack of sufficient preparation of medical students for foreign electives was a national topic of discussion. Therefore the urge was felt to develop a new module, which focussed not only on tropical diseases, but could also contribute to personal preparation for foreign electives.

Background information

Master medical students can leave for their internship to various countries in their 1st, 2nd or 3rd year. The pre-departure module should therefore be offered to students at different study levels, but should also be *time-tailored.* Students need to finish the module just before they leave, so they know to which country they go (just-in-time-learning). As a consequence, students can apply knowledge of the module to their country of internship: contextualisation. This contributes to the well-preparedness of students.

Content and structure of the "pre-departure module"

The content of the module is developed by (tropical) doctors. It consists of the following topics: logistics and safety, infectious diseases, mother and child health, and culture. The structure of the pre-departure module is flexible because of the need of a module for different levels in training of the students and the complexity of different times of departure. For this reason an *open* online module, on a secured platform *Blackboard*, was chosen. *Open* means that all students of Maastricht University can enrol themselves in the module at any time. At the introduction page of the module students find basic information about the entire module. The procedure of the module is explained and supported by different files. From the start students follow the (sub)topics of the module one by one. The structure of the modules is fixed. At the end of a topic, students make an assignment or multiple-choice questions. They start with the topic *Logistics and Safety.* By *clicking* students move from one subtopic to another subtopic. Each topic is supported by video clips and literature, but is also differently elaborated.

Primary evaluation of students (n = 11)

The pre-departure module has started in academic year 2014-2015. Eleven students followed and evaluated the module. The visiting countries for their internship were: India (n = 3), Indonesia (n = 2), Malaysia (n = 1), South Africa (n = 1), Surinam (n = 1), Tanzania (n = 2), and Uganda (n = 1). Six students spent 21 or more hours on the e-learning part of the module. For eight students the structure or the module was clear and 10 students did not have any technical problems. Both following modules, *Infectious diseases* and *Mother and Child Health*, were rated as the most liked modules. The topics *Logistics and Safety* and *Culture* were assessed as not difficult. The face-to-face meeting was rated as instructive; it had a surplus value to the e-learning component. In conclusion, well-prepared students are a necessity for foreign electives, not only with respect to tropical diseases but also for their personal development. With this module students can reflect on their own possibilities and needs. Also faculty staff can anticipate on the actuality (context), such as information on the ZIKA virus. This blended learning format provides students the possibility to learn in context before the change in their learning environment.

THE BAVARIAN VIRTUAL UNIVERSITY – AN INNOVATIVE APPROACH FOR THE INFORMATION AGE

Corina Erk, Regine Prem, Bavarian Virtual University, Germany

Overview and international perception

The Bavarian Virtual University (BVU) was founded in 2000. It supports its 31 member universities in providing high quality e-learning courses for a growing number of students of higher education. Like its member universities, the BVU is almost fully financed by the Bavarian Ministry of Education. Its aim is to share academic knowledge and thus to increase cooperation between its member institutions in the field of net-based education. The courses offered derive from almost all disciplines; law, medical sciences, business studies and key qualification courses are the most popular of these. All BVU courses run completely online, thus facilitating their exchange among the member universities. However, the aim is not to replace but to complement the offerings of the traditional universities. Students obtain credit points in the courses, but they achieve their degrees at their home universities as the BVU does not offer complete degree programmes.

The BVU was identified as one of seven innovative approaches in higher education worldwide in the *Study on Innovation in Higher Education* section of the European Commission's *Lifelong Learning: Higher Education and International Affairs* (2014). In line with the objectives of the Europe 2020 Strategy, the report aims at contributing to a better understanding of recent developments affecting higher education and at giving proof of how innovation can support higher education in times of change.

Innovative approach of the BVU

In light of the information flood the networked learner is potentially faced with, the underlying concept of the majority of BVU courses focuses on collaborative tasks and extensive tutoring. To this end, the BVU promotes the idea of guided e-learning courses on a cooperative level among Bavarian universities since it is continuous collaboration, the exchange of ideas among students and teachers as well as among students themselves that constitutes education.

Just like MOOCs, BVU courses offer a very high degree of flexibility in terms of time and place of learning to their participants. However, BVU courses comprise different pedagogical approaches and, by doing so, the BVU's fundamental approach goes beyond that of MOOCs: some courses are based on virtual seminars with intensive student cooperation, others are organised as online lectures with tutorials, while some function as virtual laboratories. Moreover, in contrast to the unguided learning concept of MOOCs, it is the key characteristic of BVU courses that students receive tutoring from academic experts of the subject. Furthermore, Bavarian students do not have to pay any additional fees.

At times of potential information overload it is particularly important not to leave learners on their own with the material presented but to offer them, for example, guiding questions to texts, collaborative tasks, tests with individual feedback and a forum to exchange information and thoughts and to encourage discussion among the course participants in a learning environment that is both challenging as well as supportive. Whereas students participating in MOOCs often complain about the impersonal learning situation arising from extremely high numbers of fellow learners, students of BVU courses appreciate the BVU tutoring concept. Furthermore, with the help of BVU courses, students develop their e-literacy, thus enhancing their employability, which is of great importance especially in the information age and in the context of lifelong learning.

Beneficial effects of BVU courses for the teaching staff and the institutions that form the BVU are as follows: by integrating BVU courses into their study programmes, universities can enhance their teaching capacities. The BVU offers financial support for course development and maintenance if at least two member universities state that they have a demand for the course and also decide to replace face-to-face teaching by the course. Hence, courses are only developed if the demand is proven. The cooperation of different universities allows teachers to team up with colleagues from other organizations, building networks and learning from one another. In addition, an elaborate quality management process is applied to course development and course operation: it involves peer and student evaluation, training programmes for new course developers and online tutors as well as financial support for course updates.

DIVERSITY IN LEARNING ENVIRONMENTS AND THE USE OF TECHNOLOGY FOR EDUCATION AT UNAM

Jorge León Martínez, Edith Tapia Rangel, National Autonomous University of Mexico (UNAM), Mexico

Introduction

The late twentieth century and the 2000's brought with them important changes to society due to three important aspects: technological and social; demographic; and industrial and economic. As a result, higher-education institutions are required to prepare citizen with a global consciousness, who are also able to learn by themselves and solve problems collaboratively. The combination of those factors has also driven educators to rethink the way they approach the educational process, therefore, from this perspective, it is possible to envision the construction of a space for rethinking, reimagining and reinventing flexible learning environments that are capable of preparing each person for effective lifelong learning.

Learning environments and institutional policies

A learning environment is the space and the inner or outer place -either formal or informal-, the implicit qualities and the affective and intangible aspects that factor into a scholar experience for each participant in a learning community. Learning environments consist of two nested domains. The inner domain is that of knowledge, which consists of the sum of all the knowledge available for teaching-learning tasks about a particular knowledge area. The second domain consists of the activities and conditions that are established for the student in order for him to conduct his learning activity (either individual or collective) with the support of the available knowledge. Within in the learning environment, processes such as the following take place: orientation; practice; feedback; and an environment's evaluation as a whole. The factors of change have had an impact in society which is reflected in a number of plans, programs and projects that constitute the institutional policies of UNAM for the development of learning environments. Some of the elements included in this frame are the following: The UNAM's Development Plan 2011-2015; The Proposal for Institutional Development Plan 2015-2019; and The Intervention projects through which different learning environments are developed at UNAM.

The UNAM learning environments

UNAM has built not only one learning environments but many diverse environments where the processes of orientation, practice and feedback (either guided by a tutor or self-directed with support of the environment itself) take place along different evaluation practices proper to each environment. *Formal programs*: Likewise, there are three considerable types of learning environments at the undergraduate level: the first type of environment is constituted by twenty online undergraduate programs; the second type is a blended learning environment; and the third one is classroom oriented for the most part. *Lifelong learning*: Different academic entities at UNAM develop their particular offers of continuous education or lifelong learning, what is grounded on the three kinds of learning environments above mentioned. Nowadays, continuous education or lifelong learning gathers over 1,600 online activities (courses, postgraduate courses, seminars and workshops), while the blended-learning activities add 937. *MOOC:* In the case of Massive Open Online Courses (MOOC), courses have been developed under two guidelines: xMOOC (Coursera, edX, MiriadaX); and miniMOOC (Cursos de Cultura General).

Conclusion

UNAM has developed different environments according to the needs of their users, the needs of their educational programs, and to the resources available in the schools and faculties responsible for their development and implementation; such environments are organized in the three categories that have been presented above. While this model allows for flexibility, it is also true that the learning environments always feature the characteristics that guaranteeing their educational quality and functionality. These environments are the result of the UNAM's institutional policies, whose ultimate goals are: to provide higher education, to orient scientific research towards the resolution of national problems, to train professionals and technicians who make contributions to society, to express the national culture of Mexico, and to bring learning to those who are not able to attend to the university campus.

MOVING BEYOND ACCESS: DISTANCE EDUCATION AND CAPACITY BUILDING

Adnan Qayyum, Pennsylvania State University, USA, Albert Sangra, Open University of Catalonia, Spain

Background to the Study

Distance education as a field has strongly been associated with providing students access to education. Indeed, different terms have been used for decades to connote and promote the access advantages of Distance Education (DE), including *flexible* and *distributed*. Currently, the word *open* seems to be ascendant, with the growth and success of open universities, the immense popularity of massive open online courses, and the general enthusiasm for open educational resources. In all these senses, openness is strongly associated with providing students access. Yet, as we move beyond the idea of openness and access, people in the field of DE are increasingly questioning the accomplishments and goals of DE. Weller (2014) argues openness does not feel like victory and is not adequate enough as a goal. Tait (2008) questions what distance education and open universities are for, beyond just providing access.

Access has historically been the *raison d'être* of distance education in response to demands for more equity to education. Implicit in these ideas of equity are conceptions of justice: how can DE help foster equity and justice in society. There are specific approaches to thinking of justice that have tangible implications for distance education.

Purpose of the Study

The goal of this study was to focus on how DE institutions are moving beyond providing access and toward building students' capabilities and society's capacity. Given this interest, the research question for this study is: How does distance education move *beyond access*, and provide capacity building to students?

Research Design

This is an exploratory study for defining *beyond access*, *students' capabilities* and *capacity building* within distance education. A starting point for the survey was Tait's framework (2013) about a capabilities approach to defining the mission of open universities. In it he identifies three areas of focus for a capabilities approach to DE: (a) access and recruitment policies, (b) programmes of study offered, and (c) learning, teaching and student support.

Sampling, Data Collection and Results

These areas formed the categories of survey that will be piloted in two universities with strong DE experience, one in the United States and one in Europe. The survey is currently live and there is not yet a final number of participants. Exploratory factor analysis and correlations will be used to identify key categories that are salient for DE institutions to consider if there is in moving beyond access.

Significance of Study

Many institutions are asking how DE completion rates can be increased and how DE programs can be more successful. As distance education continues to grow and there is increased interest by governments and other agencies to identify the social impact of DE. This study begins to develop categories and an analytical tool for addressing these issues. As such, it will be one of several studies to investigate if and how DE can move beyond an access focus.

10 YEARS OF EXPERIENCE IN VIRTUAL MOBILITY: DEVELOPING COMPETENCIES FOR MASTERING THE VIRTUAL LEARNING ENVIRONMENT AND PARTICIPATING IN VIRTUAL MOBILITY COURSES – THE CASE OF DOBA FACULTY

Nataša Ritonija, Anita Maček, DOBA Faculty for Applied Business and Social Studies, Slovenia

Introduction

DOBA Faculty for Applied Business and Social Studies, Maribor (hereinafter DOBA Faculty) started developing virtual mobility ten years ago. All courses are carried out in the Blackboard virtual learning environment. Course activities are supported with collaborative technologies (other than forums, chats, wiki, OneDrive and Blackboard Collaborate were also used) to encourage participation, collaboration and to maintain motivation. Satisfaction with virtual mobility programmes and developed competencies is measured every year with a survey conducted among students and the obtained results allow us to additionally increase the quality of implementation and thus increase the school's competitiveness.

Virtual mobility at DOBA Faculty

Virtual mobility at DOBA Faculty is implemented in three forms: within the framework of the virtual summer school, within the framework of international week and within the framework of joint implementation of courses with international higher education institutions. So far, over 1,600 students from 31 different countries have participated. According to the surveys during the last 10 years, the main competencies that students expect from international virtual mobility are the improvement of intercultural competencies and an improved knowledge of English. This is followed by the opportunities arising from participation in an international team and improved knowledge of online learning. We were further interested why students decided to take a course in the virtual environment. Students decided to become part of virtual mobility due to a new challenge that virtual mobility brings, for reasons of communicating with students from other countries and because they found the topic of the course interesting. The students pointed out that they joined the virtual mobility course in order to develop the following competencies: personal development, development of linguistic skills, development in the field of culture, academic development and others.

Students have to have specific knowledge and skills in order to be able to take a course in the virtual environment. This predominantly relates to: (a) online learning, where the ability of time and information management and self-discipline are important; (b) communication skills, which include the ability to agree, disagree and summarise as well as intercultural acceptance and awareness of cultural differences and ethics; (c) the knowledge of English; (d) the knowledge of information technologies, especially browsing the Internet and testing different technologies (forums, blogs, chat, etc.).

Managing international groups also requires detailed planning, especially as a number of students are less active, while the groups of students are also very diverse in terms of their cultural background. In virtual mobility, the task of online tutors, whose role is to monitor students' progress and help them with substantive and technical issues, is thus predominantly focused on motivating students.

Our ten years of experience with implementing virtual mobility has shown that during the implementation of a course, individual activities are often adapted to the motivational needs of students. As some students prefer to gain knowledge by observing instead of cooperating, team activities often had to be transformed into individual activities. Experience also shows that dropping out of courses taken in the virtual environment is rather frequent. Considering the average of all years that virtual mobility has been implemented at the school, 20% of students prematurely withdraw from taking the course. Students with little or no experience in online learning also needed more support. Students needed the tutorial as well as the technical support 4 times more than experienced online learners.

A MODEL OF THE DIGITAL MATURITY OF SCHOOLS IN CROATIA

Lucija Dejanović, Croatian Academic and Research Network (CARNet), Croatia

A model of the digital maturity

A model of the digital maturity of schools in Croatia consists of Framework for digital maturity of schools, evaluation of digital maturity of schools and Programme of external evaluation of digital maturity of schools. It is developed through e-Schools national pilot project fully named *e-Schools – Development of the System of Digital Maturity of Schools* in order to raise the digital maturity of schools in Croatia through the development of human resources, e-content, e-services and IT infrastructure. The project is coordinated by the Croatian Academic and Research Network – CARNet due to its mandate to support education system in integration of technology and with the aim of establishing a national system for the development of digital maturity of Croatian schools.

The Framework ensures schools to position themselves on the one of the five digital maturity ranking levels from basic to e-mature. It also describes requirements that should be met by the schools in order to prove their digital maturity covered by several domains:

- Planning, leadership and management;
- ICT in learning and teaching;
- Development of digital competences;
- ICT culture;
- ICT resources and infrastructure.

Methodology that is used in development of the Framework and instrument is comprehensive and based on the qualitative analysis and comparative analysis of existing Frameworks made in several European countries with necessary adjustments to Croatian context. Purpose of the Framework is to serve as a basis for self-evaluation and external evaluation of digital maturity of schools and to help them in the process of planning and implementation of ICT. The Framework is also thought as a model for mapping the scope and activities for raising digital maturity levels during the e-Schools project.

In order to measure levels of digital maturity of the schools in the project it is planned to carry out initial and final measuring through self-assessment tool for schools and external evaluation. Self-assessment tool for schools is made in a form of a questionnaire and it allows schools insight in their own digital maturity level and compares results of initial and final self-assessment. The process of external evaluation is conducted by external evaluators through the on-site interviews with school management, teachers and students. It is the intention that external evaluation of e-Schools serves as a basis for development of a national programme for external evaluation of digital maturity of the schools. At the end of the evaluation process schools will receive a badge in order to increase their motivation and credibility in use of ICT and raising the digital maturity.

Supporting schools in increasing levels of digital maturity is ensured through the project activities which will help principals and school teams in strategic integration of ICT in educational and business processes and in developing strategic policy documents for implementation of ICT on a school level. On the basis of experiences gained during the e-Schools project, the draft strategy of digital maturity of schools will be made on a national level.

QUALITY PACT FOR (E-)TEACHING – AN EXAMPLE FROM THE UNIVERSITY OF BONN

Cornelia Helmstedt, Bettina Graevingholt, University of Bonn, Germany

Introduction

The more universities direct their attention to the quality of teaching, the more important the teaching competence and competence development of lecturers becomes.

This poster will present the newly-created eteaching qualification for lecturers of the University of Bonn, funded by the *Quality Pact for Teaching* (http://www.qualitaetspakt-lehre.de/en/1294.php). This joint programme of the German Federal Government and the Länder is supporting numerous German Higher Educational Institutions (HEIs) to improve study conditions and the quality of teaching in higher education, among them the University of Bonn. One goals of the Pact is to provide support in the qualification or further training of staff and to ensure and further develop the quality of education.

Due to this Pact, the University of Bonn has – amongst other activities – established the Centre for University Teaching (BZH) and extended its eCampus e-learning services in the first funding period from 2012 to 2016. eCampus e-learning services is a joint initiative of Bonn University Library (ULB) and the University Computer Centre (HRZ) led by a steering committee with representatives of ULB, BZH and HRZ. For the design and delivery of an eteaching qualification for lecturers eCampus collaborates with the BZH.

Eteaching Certificate University of Bonn

The BZH together with the eCampus team have developed a formal eteaching qualification, culminating in an eteaching Certificate. Analogous to an already existing qualification in place in the field of university didactics, the eteaching certificate has been organised in three modules - basic, extension and advanced with a total workload of 100 working units à 45 minutes.

All modules can also be booked individually and are to a certain extent as well creditable for the certification scheme in university didactics.

The first workshop *eteaching introduction* started in November 2015 with 15 participants, 7 other workshops will follow until the end of the summer semester 2016.

Conclusion

The newly-created eteaching qualification of the University of Bonn addresses the training needs of lecturers of the University of Bonn in order to integrate e-learning in their teaching practice. First results and lessons learnt will be presented.

CITIUS, ALTIUS, FORTIUS, RETICULIUS: OPENING UP VOLUNTEER TRAINING FOR THE OLYMPIC GAMES TO THE NETWORKED AGE

John P. Egan, University of Auckland, New Zealand

This poster describes the experiences of an eLearning professional at the Vancouver 2010 Olympic Games. It looks at the Games-time training team's work in introducing eLearning to the training of over 19,000 volunteers. It examines key innovations from the Vancouver 2010 Games-time training, which subsequently transformed the Olympic volunteer experience, particularly with respect to training delivered online. It describes how the affordances of available technologies significantly drove (and constrained) online training opportunities for the Vancouver 2010's volunteer workforce.

The motto of the Olympic movement is *Citius, Altius, Fortius*: Olympic athletes endeavour to be faster, higher and stronger. In developing the volunteer training for Vancouver 2010 our team added eLearning – *reticulius*, or networked (learning) – to the volunteer Olympic experience. The following components of the training are analysed:

Games-time curriculum: Drawing up previous organising committees' work, the Vancouver 2010 Games-time training curriculum had five components:

1. *General Orientation*, an overview of the Olympic movement, the Winter Games, and the Vancouver Games;
2. *Service Excellence*, focussed on the service standards for the workforce;
3. *Job-Specific Training*, including skills and knowledges required for specific roles and FAs;
4. *Venue-Specific Training*, where operational aspects of each competition and non-competition venue, included emergency procedures, were addressed; and,
5. *Event Leadership*, for volunteers who would be supervising other volunteers.

Sport event curriculum: Prior to delivering the Olympics, Vanoc (like all Olympic organising committees) was required to successfully deliver a *sport* event, which is an international-level (world cup, world championships or similar) competition for each sport discipline. The sport event curriculum model was compressed into two (rather than five) components:

- Event orientation, including general orientation, venue orientation and service excellence;
- Job-specific training, including elements of venue orientation and event leadership.

Ultimately eLearning was leveraged in preparing the Games-time volunteer workforce for the 2010 Olympics, after overcoming significant barriers to doing so. A limited number of these volunteers were offered a just in time, digitised version of General Orientation and Service Excellence training.

Many of the practices from Vancouver 2010 served as effective pilots for a much wider use of *reticulius*: networked, online learning as part of Olympic volunteer training. As the first Olympics Games that opened up volunteer training to eLearning, Vancouver 2010 shows that online, networked (reticulius) learning can be leveraged and scaled up, despite numerous institutional and resource constraints.

PROFESSIONAL SKILLS IN MANAGEMENT AND LEADERSHIP, ENTREPRENEURSHIP AND COMMUNICATION – THE E-PROFMAN PROJECT

Nataša Ritonija, Nuša Lazar, Pedja Ašanin Gole, Anita Maček, Tina Vukasović, DOBA Faculty of Applied Business and Social Studies Maribor, Slovenia

Introduction

The Joint Online Programme for Professional Development in Innovative Management, Leadership and Strategic Communication – Macedonia, Slovenia and Turkey project (e-PROFMAN) will establish a virtual campus of three higher education institutions from Macedonia, Slovenia and Turkey that will develop and implement a joint online programme for professional development in innovative management, leadership and strategic communication. The fully online programme will promote progressive pedagogical approaches, virtual mobility, intercultural cooperation and internationally recognised competencies.

One of the main objectives of the project is equipping programme participants with appropriate skills and abilities in achieving competitive advantage and effective leadership behaviour in a transnational corporate environment. The participants will acquire a high level of competencies recognised in the partner countries within the Bologna credit transfer system. The programme will further enhance their job prospects in the (trans)national labour market. The paper presents the main findings of the research (phase 1 of the project) which was carried out among working individuals (employers and employees).

e-PROFMAN research

The survey was carried out from 15 January to 15 February 2016 in six countries: Slovenia, Croatia, Bosnia and Herzegovina, Serbia, Macedonia, and Turkey. Answers from 1,305 respondents were received (survey completed by 692 respondents and 623 partially completed). In our study, we are interested in the importance of the following skills to fill the vacancies in companies/organisations:

- *Management and leadership skills*: organisational skills, problem-solving skills, ability to make strategic decisions, strategic planning and creative thinking.
- *Entrepreneurial skills*: creating and analysing business opportunities, entrepreneurial innovation, ability to network, ability to identify strengths and weaknesses, and the ability to focus on customers.
- *Communication skills*: strategic communication planning, digital/social media use, intercultural communication, marketing communication, issues management, and risk and crisis communication.

The paper presents only the findings of the Slovenian survey (26% of valid units). The survey results will help determine the specific needs of organisations in the private, NGO and public sector for knowledge and skills of their employees for effective market presence in the markets from Central Europe to Turkey. They will also help us develop and create the curriculum for the online lifelong learning professional development programme in the field of management, leadership and strategic communication.

Respondents considered that the most frequent obstacles in (and need for) effectiveness of human resources in organisations are problem solving skills, communication skills, creative thinking skills, and leadership skills. Respondents believe that the most relevant skills of innovative management to the job vacancy are business management economics/global economy, creative or critical thinking and digital/social media use. The most relevant skills of leadership are problem solving, communications skills and strategic and systematic thinking, and collaboration and networking. The most relevant professional knowledge/skills of strategic communication according to respondents from Slovenia are communications skills, intercultural communication, strategic and systematic thinking.

The development of skills through education should result from labour market needs. This is also the focus of our research and the project e-PROFMAN. The main findings of the research will be integrated in the fully online program for young working practitioners which will be developed among project partners and carried out in the year 2017.

LEADERSHIP FOR CHANGE IN HE INSTITUTIONS: THE D-TRANSFORM APPROACH

Marta Aymerich, Universitat Oberta de Catalunya, Spain

The current European higher education system was designed to prepare an efficient and technically skilled workforce, a workforce that thrived in a 20th century industrial age of repetitive processes. To master the emergent and disruptive changes of the 21st century we need talents that thrive in processes of innovation, creativity and social impact, and to nurture this talent we need a radically different approach to education. In our knowledge society where information is open and accessible, the way universities can stay relevant is to embed skills such as critical thinking, teamwork, empathy, leadership and change making, skills that our digital students use in their everyday life but that are hidden in their curriculum. In a world changing faster and faster, students need interdisciplinary and entrepreneurial learning and solution-oriented skills to succeed.

Time is pressing. In Europe we may not have yet fully understood the world of our digital students and consequently, we must improve considerably the learning strategies and methodologies adapted to their needs and expectations. Europe is suffering a higher education crisis and is lost in that transition. What are the means deployed by the university governances to conduct this transformation process? What are the strategies needed to increase innovativeness and reactivity in a quickly evolving world?

EU higher education systems are operating in an increasingly fast-changing and competitive environment, dealing with challenging factors such as massification, cost-efficiency, international attractiveness, student mobility, career guidance, and employability, among others. The workshop offers a framework for analysing whether and how ICTs can be a useful tool in responding to these challenges, and what collateral changes their adoption will bring about.

The starting point of the workshop will be two presentations by experts who will share with the audience the first intellectual outputs derived from the D-TRANSFORM European project:

- National policies and Open Educational Resources for digital transition in Higher Education which provides insights into present national policies for digitizing universities.
- Business models for opening up education – Sustainability of MOOCs, OER and related online education approaches in higher education in Europe – which aids decision-making for deploying open education in HE.

Each presentation will be followed by a group activity to discuss the scope of digital transition in HE, and the sustainability of the various Open Education business models, respectively. The workshop aims to develop practical recommendations for educational leaders to drive Higher Education institutions to the level of transformation required for embracing effective digital learning scenarios.

The workshop concludes with a presentation of the upcoming D-TRANSFORM Leadership School – a training program to assist leaders of European universities to develop and use the tools for effective leadership and decision-making for an ICT-facilitated evolution of their institutions.

EFFECTIVE INTERACTIVE WEBINARS: METHODS TO FACILITATE LEARNING IN OPEN COLLABORATIVE LEARNING ENVIRONMENTS. A TOOLBOOK FOR PRACTITIONERS/FACILITATORS

Torhild Slåtto, Flexible Education, Norway, Alastair Creelman, Linnaeus University, Markus Schneider, Karlstad University, Sweden, David Röthler, Projektkompetenz, Austria, Hróbjartur Árnason, University of Iceland, Iceland

Webinars for open and collaborative learning

Webinars are becoming an increasingly popular arena for the dissemination of information, primarily in the form of online presentations to large distributed audiences. However current practice shows a tendency towards largely one-way communication, especially when the number of participants rises above thirty. This happens at a time when one-way presentations or lectures are increasingly being questioned as an environment for effective learning.

Many have experienced large webinars, which are just as tiresome as monotonous lectures, or even worse. As web-conferencing, services get more traction both within the educational and corporate sphere, the need to develop online pedagogies, methods and formats that fit with learning goals and build on what is known about adult learning has become urgent. Universities, adult education centres as well as companies and institutions have been experimenting with the use of web-conferencing services to support learning. However many experiments to increase flexibility and to open the learning arena still seem to be based on replicating on-line what has been done on-site with mostly disappointing results.

During our workshop we will present, demonstrate and discuss pedagogies which can help make webinars vibrant learning environments.

Ways in which the audience is encouraged to participate

Participants will be both online and on-site. They will be encouraged to participate in at least two group work sessions, as well as contributing to plenum discussions and adding material, comments, and group results to an online canvas.

The presentations will be interactive with opportunities for the on-site and the online participants to ask questions as well as engage in discussions with the speakers and with other participants.

Participants will engage with the content in two group discussions. The results will be posted on a common online canvas: an online, public collaborative workspace.

Materials presented, and created during the workshop with recordings will be available and public after the event. Further discussions will be facilitated on the project's open Facebook group (https://www.facebook.com/groups/230337750465944/).

Themes this workshop connects to:

- Visions, concepts about how the new learning environments could be.
- Evolution of the concepts of openness and scalability in education.
- Opening up education: projects, examples of good practices.
- Different ways to understand technological influences, new ways to interpret the collaborative and social-networked society we live in.
- Learning environments – in their widest interpretation: digital, physical, networked, pedagogical, social, cultural, economic…
- Learning environments and learning organisations.

JRC-IPTS RESEARCH ON OPENING UP EDUCATION THROUGH THE USE OF DIGITAL TECHNOLOGIES: DEVELOPMENT OF A SUPPORT FRAMEWORK FOR HIGHER EDUCATION INSTITUTIONS

Yves Punie, European Commission Joint Research Centre, Andreia Inamorato dos Santos, European Commission (JRC-IPTS), Spain

The workshop will present research done by JRC-IPTS, on behalf of DG EAC, on the development of a support framework for HEIs to take strategic decisions and concrete initiatives on opening up education. The OpenEdu research was designed to support the 2013 EC Communication on *Opening up Education: Innovative Teaching and Learning for all through New Technologies and Open Educational Resources.*

The OpenEdu project contains a number of studies to provide data and information on the state-of-the art of open education in Europe. *OpenCases* is an analysis of opening up education practices of nine institutions in Europe which offer open education either via MOOCs, OER or a combination of these and other open practices. *OpenCred* is a study on credentialisation and recognition of non-formal learning via MOOCs, based on desk research and in-depth interviews, out of which case studies were produced. *MOOCKnowledge* is an ongoing study of MOOC learners from European MOOC providers consisting of a series of surveys in different time periods (pre-course, post-course and follow up questionnaire at least one year after the finalisation of a MOOC) to better understand the profiles of MOOC learners, their motivations and attitudes and the impact of MOOCs on professional and/or academic career and personal life. *OpenSurvey* was a representative survey of higher education institutions in five selected EU member states (France, Germany Spain, Poland and UK) carried out by IPTS in collaboration with the Academic Cooperation Association (ACA) on practices, beliefs, and strategies related to MOOCs, OER and other dimensions of openness (data from spring 2015).

These studies are the backbone for the development of the OpenEdu framework for HEIs presenting 10 interdependent dimensions for opening up education. It offers a holistic view of open education to embrace different areas in which a university can be more open. It has been developed with the extensive involvement of institutional stakeholders, being scrutinised by 40 experts in open education from Europe and abroad as well as universities managers from 18 European Member States. There are 6 core dimensions (access, content, pedagogy, recognition, collaboration and research) and 4 transversal dimensions (strategy, technology, quality and leadership).

NEXT GENERATION LEARNING ENVIRONMENTS: HOW TO MAP LEARNING METHODOLOGIES TO LEARNING TECHNOLOGIES

Francesc Santanach, Universitat Oberta de Catalunya, Spain, Jeff Merriman, Massachusetts Institute of Technology, Tom Coppeto, Boston College, United States of America

Description of workshop

Over the past decade and a half, the Learning Management System (LMS) has emerged as the enterprise answer to the delivery of education, while managing the impact on Information and Communications Technology (ICT) organizations by offering a single system for supporting the rudimentary functions of online education.

Looking forward, with the almost ubiquitous reach of the Internet and increasing digital literacy, educational institutions find they now need to offer more than one system. There is a growing call for diverse educational functions, like assessment, accreditation, personalization, and analytics. Newer architectures have to be designed around and offer a wider range of functions to support newer learning methodologies and business models.

Foreseeing the future is risky. Learning methodologies have and will continue to evolve. While we can only describe the state of the art as it is known today, we can no longer afford to design systems based on a specific way of doing things. A system architecture ought to allow for the necessary changes and rearrangements to prevent its obsolescence upon entering new methodologies developed from ongoing observation and study from different disciplines.

The aim of this practical workshop is to illustrate and demonstrate a vision of next generation digital learning environments (NGDLEs) that will be stable yet flexible to changing functional thinking, and evolving learning methodologies and business models. This realistic and innovative vision consists of a marketplace of educational applications based on a flexible infrastructure of independent services, and supportive of numerous, evolving learning methodologies.

Ways in which the audience is encouraged to participate

The workshop is open to researchers and practitioners both from a technology and a pedagogy background and from any sector of education. Educators, the educational sector, industry representatives as well as students are welcome. Therefore, all Eden attendees are very welcome. A balance between researchers/experts and experienced users is key for a rich interchange so interdisciplinarity is welcome.

Attendees will be introduced to processes for de-constructing learning methodologies to define a variety of educational experiences and required infrastructure for defining a NGDLE, and will participate in an exercise illustrating how this vision can support pedagogy and technology working more effectively together.

All workshop activities are open to online attendance, the presentations will be distributed through streaming and for the work in groups activities a Google hangout for each group will be set up. Workshop activities will be captured via Google Docs, which will be available to and editable by streaming participants in addition to those in the room. The interactivity between the participants – both, in room and online – is required specially for the working in groups activities and the final discussion.

Format of the session

This 90 minutes workshop is divided in three parts. The first one is a presentation showing the vision and approach from workshop moderators about the next generation learning environments. The second one is a practical and interactive session where attendees – in place or online – will work in groups to define and map learning methodologies to this technology approach. The final part is open discussion about the activity and their outcomes.

THE GLOBAL CLASSROOM LEARNING CONCEPT

Kristian Madsen, Flemming Nielsen, Laila Emiliussen, VUC Storstrom, Denmark

In 2008, VUC Storström (please see the presentation in the end of this text) sought to break down distances and barriers that prevented students to get the education they wanted by developing the concept of parallel teaching, which ultimately became a core element of the Global Classroom – synchronous distance learning with high-end video conference technology. VUC Storström was awarded a Silver medal at USDLA annual conference in 2013 for this concept which is now shared with educational partners in Europe, Asia and North America.

Global classroom opens possibilities for participants to attend classes from home, and gives them the opportunity to participate actively in the class. (VUC Storstrøm provides home-based students with laptop computers.) They can see and hear the class and vice versa. The concept of extended parallel instruction also provides new opportunities to invite guest teachers who live far away to contribute with teaching in the class.

Teaching in Global Classroom requires special competences, and teachers are trained in a two-level program:

1. The basics: Mastering the technology; digitalizing the learning design and creating relations;
2. The IT-pedagogical Think Tank for Teacher teams; training innovative skills while developing interactive learning designs – for instance integrating virtual games in Global Classroom.

The training program is developed with the experiences from parallel teaching and Global Classroom. Since 3 years VUC Storström cooperates with a PhD student, Mrs. Weitze, from Aalborg University, Denmark, on innovations in teaching in Global Classroom. Mrs. Weitze developed especially level two in the training program, and data from this is an important part of her PhD Thesis to be defended in April 2016.

At the concurrent workshop, the participants will learn about the Global Classroom training program by interacting with the instructors. The challenge to the participants is to integrate video conference in teaching with use of a digital learning design.

Located in the Zealand region in southern Denmark, VUC Storström is comprised of five campuses, employs 200 teachers and serves 6,000 students. VUC Storström holds classes from 8 am to 10 pm to accommodate our students' busy lives, which often include holding down jobs and caring for families. Some also care for sick parents or children, and many suffer from disabilities that prevent them from attending class in person.

The educational programs covers pre-classes for people with reading or calculation disabilities and classes equivalent to the levels K9 – K12. Graduates from 12 classes will typically apply for further education at university.

IS LURKING WORKING?

Joergen Grubbe, The Danish Association for Flexible Learning – FLUID, Denmark, Alastair Creelman, Linnaeus University, Sweden, Hrobjartur Arnason, University of Iceland, Iceland

In this workshop, we will discuss reasons for passive/silent participation in courses and seminars (both online and onsite) and generate methods for encouraging more active participation. We will present the background and initial findings of our current project *Is Lurking working?* (Nordplus, 2015), and the findings of this workshop will provide valuable input to the project's work. We believe that there are similarities between those who are silent learners on campus and online and that although the online environment may make it easier to remain silent the phenomenon is more about learner's feeling of security and sense of belonging than a specific online issue.

This area is receiving increased research interest, notably a study from the Open University UK where they observed an increasing amount of silent learners on their courses and concluded that: teaching and learning strategies need to be reconsidered, to encourage or increase *active engagement*. However, the data, alongside literature, also suggests that some students may find value in engaging *passively*.

Recent studies suggest that many adult learners may find value in engaging *passively*. From the perspective of a Higher Education (HE) institute, this may have implications for the tuition delivery strategy used to deliver the module material, as well as how staff development occurs for the tutors that deliver the material. For example, rather than focus a significant effort on encouraging adult learners to participate in active forum use, the emphasis may need to be shifted to ensuring that appropriate/sufficient material is available to *passive engagers*.

EUROPEAN POLICY AND PRACTICE IN DIGITAL SKILLS AND COMPETENCES – A HANDS-ON WORKSHOP WITH REPRESENTATIVES OF THE ET2020 WORKING GROUP

Deirdre Hodson, DG EAC, European Commission, Belgium, Deborah Arnold, University of Burgundy, France, Sandra Kučina Softić, University of Zagreb, Croatia, Ildiko Mazar, EDEN, United Kingdom

Introduction

As part of the Education and Training 2020 (ET 2020) Open Method of Coordination, the European Commission and Member States cooperate in the form of Working Groups. These groups are designed to help Member States address the key challenges of their education and training systems, as well as common priorities agreed at European Level. The Working Group on Digital Skills and Competences is one of the six new-generation working groups launched in February 2016. Each working group has a specific mandate, meets several times a year and runs Peer Learning Activities for Member States to learn from each other's initiatives.

The digital revolution is boosting demand for digital skills and competences; education and training must address this need, which requires investment in infrastructure, organisational change, digital devices and digital competences of educators and learners, and the creation of digital (and open) educational resources and high quality educational software. Education and training should reap the benefits of new ICT developments and adopt innovative and active pedagogies, based on participatory and project-based methods. Several Member States report initiatives to increase teachers' and learners' digital skills and one third have introduced national strategies for digitalisation of education. Still, huge challenges remain and effective policy and policy implementation plans are lacking to allow the shift at the systemic and educational level necessary to forge a future digital competent society

Focus of the workshop

This workshop at the EDEN 2016 Annual Conference in Budapest will provide participants with insights into EU policy relating to digital skills and competences. It will also enable participants to share their own experience and knowledge and to identify priorities for future work in the field.

Structure of the workshop

1. Introductory presentation on EU policy relating to digital skills and competences, Deirdre Hodson, DG EAC, European Commission
2. Learning café: participants will work in small groups on selected themes from the WG DSC mandate, on two successive tasks, facilitated by moderators from the Working Group and EDEN:
   - Sharing information on related initiatives in different countries / regions / institutions or at EU level.
   - Formulating recommendations for what needs to evolve policy-wise at local / regional / national / EU level.
3. One rapporteur from each subgroup will summarise to the whole group.

The results of this workshop will be presented at the next Digital Skills and Competences Working Group meeting to be held in Brussels in October 2016 and discussed by the representatives of the Member States.

In order to ensure the best possible quality of interaction during this workshop, the number of participants will be limited to a maximum of 25, on a first-come, first-served basis. Participants will be able to sign up on site.

Don't miss this unique opportunity to engage in and contribute to high-level discussions in the field of digital skills and competences!

IMPLEMENTING INQUIRY BASED SCIENCE EDUCATION IN EUROPEAN SCHOOLS

Thomas Fischer, Sofoklis Sotiriou, Ellinogermaniki Agogi, Greece, Christian Stracke, Open University in the Netherlands, The Netherlands, Sally Reynolds, Mathy Vanbuel, ATiT, Belgium

Introduction

Inspiring Science Education (ISE) is all about providing the tools to make Science Education more challenging, more playful and above all more imaginative and inspiring for today's students, the citizens of tomorrow's world. Inspirational science teachers are at the heart of successful science teaching – ask any scientific Nobel prize-winner who had the greatest influence on their decision to become a scientist and invariably the answer will be – my Science Teacher! So what is it that makes a science teacher truly inspirational? That's one of the conundrums we aim to unravel in the Inspiring Science Education (ISE) project.

ISE is aiming for large-scale take-up of these opportunities amongst European science teachers. The mission of ISE is therefore to provide digital resources and opportunities for teachers to help them make Science Education more attractive and relevant to students' lives. Through the ISE Community Portal, the ISE Website and its Social Media presence, teachers can help students make their own scientific discoveries, witness and understand natural and scientific phenomena and access the latest, interactive tools and digital resources from within their classrooms.

During the ISE pilots, teachers are accessing interactive simulations, educational games and eScience applications and integrating them with extra-curricular activities, such as field trips to science centres and discovery parks, and virtual visits to research centres. Teachers also have the possibility to access remote and online labs, and relevant Demonstrators, Educational Scenarios and Lesson Plans for their use in the school classroom. Students are inspired to use eLearning tools and other digital resources to learn Science, Technology, Engineering and Maths (STEM) related subjects in a practical and exciting way.

Workshop Description

The highly interactive ISE Workshop on 'Success Factors and Barriers to the Implementation of Inquire Based Science Education in European Schools' is aiming at (a) identifying supportive elements as well as challenges for Inquiry Based Science Education (IBSE); (b) further building and expanding the IBSE Communities of Practice (CoP); (c) contributing to the mid and long term sustainable planning of Inquiry Based Science Education; and iv) supporting the development of the European Science Education Academy (ESEA), which promotes IBSE learning in Teachers Training (TT) programs and Continuous Professional Development (CPD) initiatives. The ISE Workshop at the EDEN Annual Conference 2016 will include the following activities:

- Introductory Flash Presentations on Inspiring Science Eduaction (ISE); access, use and attitudes to technology in European schools; Current Situation of Inquire Based (Science) Education in Europe.
- Interactive Workshop with free brainstorming and ideas generation; ad-hoc interactive Learning Cafés; and a concluding plenary discussion (15 minutes).

The ISE Workshop will be opened for virtual participation. The Workshop will be available online through webinar facilities. Furthermore a chance to participate in the idea's generation and the subsequent discussions will be offered. Before the Workshop, potential participants can already start preparations by sharing their insights virtually. The online (collaborative) writing document (Google Docs) for the generation of ideas is available at: http://tinyurl.com/ISE-EDEN-2016.

Target Audience

The ISE Workshop is targeted to:

- School communities of teachers, students, administration, teacher trainers;
- eLearning / digital tools developers from universities, research centres, companies;
- Educational policy makers in science education and research.

LEARNING ANALYTICS: EXPLORING THE PUTTING IN PLACE OF A SYSTEM THAT SUPPORTS LEARNING WHILE STILL RESPECTING PRIVACY

Tore Hoel, Oslo and Akershus University College of Applied Sciences, Norway, Dai Griffiths, Bolton University, United Kingdom, Sally Reynolds, ATiT, Belgium

Great expectations have been raised by learning analytics, among researchers, teachers and managers. Enthusiasts hope that learning analytics will be help in optimising educational planning, personalising learning experiences, and enhancing teaching. However, it is not possible to make any progress towards these potential benefits without access to the data generated on computer systems by the various activities of the learners and those who support them in their studies.

The LACE project (http://laceproject.eu) was funded to coordinate work in the learning analytics in Europe. In the course of its activities over the past two years, the project has talked to many people from a wide range of sectors engaged with learning analytics. Part of this work has involved investigating Visions of the Future of learning analytics, in order to identify the drivers which policy should take into consideration. In consultation with experts in learning analytics and others engaged in the field, it became clear that the great majority were convinced that it was important to give greater control to data subjects. There was also a consensus that opens architectures and infrastructure should be used in analysing data, which would increase transparency of the means whereby judgements were made. The full Visions of the future results are available at http://www.laceproject.eu/wp-content/uploads/2016/02/LACE_D3_2.pdf.

LACE engagement with the learning analytics community has also shown that there is widespread uncertainty about the policies which should be applied to manage the collection of data about learners, and the ways in which that data should be used. Nor is there clarity about the moral, ethical and political criteria which could inform such strategy. A LACE review paper *Is Privacy a Show-stopper for Learning Analytics? A Review of Current Issues and their Solutions* examines this issue, and describes some of ways that problems are currently being addressed. (http://www.laceproject.eu/learning-analytics-review/is-privacy-a-show-stopper/). Related LACE work has examined the emerging landscape of interoperability specifications and open infrastructures for learning analytics, and this is available at http://www.laceproject.eu/d7-4-learning-analytics-interoperability-requirements-specifications-and-adoption/.

Work on LACE has confirmed the proposition underlying the project that design of learning analytics systems must be based on requirements from the learners and teachers that will use the tools. Therefore, there is a need to engage these stakeholders in a discourse on benefits and constraints, ensuring that the conversation is documented and made available as input to design. An EDEN 2016 workshop will serve this purpose well, as traditionally this community is representing a wide range of interests and views, covering most countries in Europe, also countries where the discussion on learning analytics has not yet started.

This workshop will build on the results of the LACE project described above, and other lessons learned over the last 30 months of project activity. An update will be given on the development of LA applications in schools and higher education, and concerns about data sharing and privacy, control of data and trust will be explored. In discussion with participants, we aim to understand the issues with greater clarity, and to find ways of overcoming the issues and research challenges related to ethical and privacy aspects of learning analytics practice. The workshop is highly interactive and will through a simple, but structured and well-tested process engage the participants in finding solutions that could be accepted in European schools and universities.

ABC RAPID BLENDED COURSE DESIGN FOR EDUCATORS

Clive Young, Nataša Perović, University College London, United Kingdom

Overview

How do we best help our time-pressured academics design rich blended and online courses? To address this, University College London (UCL) has developed ABC, an effective and engaging hands-on workshop that has now been trialled with great success over a range of programmes. In just 90 minutes using a game format teams work together to create a *visual storyboard* using cards to outline the type and sequence of learning activities (online and offline) required to meet the course's learning outcomes. ABC is particularly useful for new courses or those changing to an online or more blended format.

UCL's ABC Method

ABC facilitates an activity-based approach to learning design. Adapting the University of Ulster's *Viewpoints approach*, a UCL card-set was developed in 2014 based on Diana Laurillard's notion of six *learning types*, derived from her well-known Conversational Framework. The six learning types are acquisition; inquiry; practice; production; discussion and collaboration, and these form the ABC six-card set. The Viewpoints workshop sequence was shortened and the documentation adapted. At least two members of the team involved in programme or module development attend a workshop. They bring the module specifications (or programme overview) with learning outcomes to the workshop. Several, if not all, modules in a programme are usually addressed in a single session.

Workshop format:

- Brief presentation introducing the toolkit elements and the pedagogical rationale.
- The first task for the teams is to agree on a tweet size description (strapline, unique selling point, value proposition etc.) of the module/programme and write it on the workshop graph sheet. Team leaders also report this back to the facilitators.
- The participants then draw the rough "shape" of their programme as they envisage it initially as represented by learning types on a spider graph (e.g. how much practice, or collaboration) and the envisaged blend of face-to-face and online.
- Next the team plan the distribution of each learning type by selecting and arranging the postcard-sized learning types cards along the timeline of the module, represented by a large A1 sized paper '"canvas".
- With this outline agreed participants turn over the cards. On the back of each card is a list of online and conventional activities associated with each learning types and the team can pick (by ticking) from this list or write in their own. The type and range of learner activities soon becomes clear and the cards often suggest new approaches. The aim of this process is not to advocate any "ideal" mix but to stimulate a structured conversation among the team.
- Once learning activities are selected and agreed, participants identify opportunities for formative and summative assessment, represented by affixing silver (formative) and gold (summative) stars to the activities.
- By this point module/programme development team have a *visual storyboard* of the sequence and type of learning and assessment activities on the module/programme.

Benefits of ABC

By necessity this rapid-development approach focuses on a simple set of pedagogic principles. Rather than being restrictive this has been found to generate discussion about the fundamental purposes of the programme and foregrounds the student experience. The workshop itself is structured to encourage collective discussion with a focus on collaboration and consensus, starting with the initial "tweet" exercise. An important aspect of ABC is the staged progression from broad abstraction to concrete activities. Storyboarding provides a visual narrative that teams find easy to work with and the paper-based format encourages creativity and adaptation. The cards themselves act as an aide memoire of potential activities, helping to bring pedagogic diversity to the design. Assessment and feedback also become a natural element of this form of activity-based design rather than driving the module structure.

OPEN COURSES AS VIRTUAL MOBILITY AND THE ROLE OF COLLABORATIVE LITERACY IN STAFF DEVELOPMENT

Alastair Creelman, Anders Gerestrand, Linnaeus University, Lars Uhlin, Maria Kvarnström, Karolinska Institute, Maria Hedberg, Lotta Åbjörnsson, Kenneth Johansson, Lund University, Stefan Stenbom, Royal Institute of Technology, Sweden, Anne Whaits, IIE Varsity College, South Africa

Aims of the workshop

- To collaboratively draw up critical success factors for virtual mobility in staff development
- To raise awareness of the need for a focus on collaborative literacy as a critical element of digital literacy

Background and justification

Open Networked Learning (ONL) https://opennetworkedlearning.wordpress.com is an open online course that is offered both as an internal professional development course at the partner universities (Karolinska Institute, Lund University, Linnaeus University, KTH in Sweden and IIE Varsity College in South Africa) as well as being open to learners from all over the world. The course has been derived from an earlier model that has in turn led to several other online courses. The primary target group is university teachers, educational technologists and course designers but it also attracts educators from other educational sectors both public and private. Using an open collaborative learning environment learners investigate aspects of connected, collaborative learning with modules based around topics such as digital literacies, collaborative and flexible learning, teaching in open spaces and course design.

ONL uses a problem-based learning approach with most interaction taking place in small groups each with a facilitator from one of the host universities as well as a co-facilitator who is a volunteer former participant. These study groups consist of 7-9 learners from different institutions mixing institutional learners (from the host universities) with open learners. They collaborate synchronously and asynchronously to discuss, write and present solutions to weekly problem scenarios using a variety of digital tools and media. This group work is enhanced by individual reflection on personal blogs. The course design has a similar foundation to the earlier iterations but is constantly being revised and adapted as more partner institutions join (2-3 more universities are expected to join during 2016) and as more experience and learner feedback is gained.

Internationalization in higher education is increasingly a mix of physical and virtual mobility to enable all students and staff to learn to work in a global context. Concepts such as *virtual mobility*, and *internationalization at home*, are already well-known and implemented in many universities and a course like ONL fully meets the criteria. Collaborative cross-institutional courses and communities like ONL have a key role to play in the full internationalization of university staff development, both for teachers and administrators and offer an opportunity to work in an international context without necessarily engaging in physical mobility. This type of virtual mobility can also facilitate future physical mobility by acclimatizing staff to working with colleagues from other countries.

From our surveys we have found that ONL participants have seen the internationalization element of the course as a clear added value. We have also positive experience of the collaboration between course facilitators and co-facilitators, also from a wide variety of countries (e.g. Sweden, South Africa, Philippines, Poland, Denmark, Sudan, Portugal). However the key to participation in virtual mobility activities is both digital literacy (the ability to use online tools and spaces to communicate, access information and create) and collaborative literacy (the ability to truly collaborate online). We have seen on all courses that participants find it difficult to move from the traditional perspective of learning as consumption of content to the perspective of learning as collaboration and co-creation. Only when this collaborative literacy is developed can participants truly benefit from this form of virtual mobility.

Participation and outcome

The workshop will offer a combination of input from project members and group discussions. The results of these discussions will be compiled using a common digital workspace and made publically available. The session will be accessible via Adobe Connect and project colleagues in the course team will contribute online. We will also invite all participants to follow the autumn iteration of ONL either as a registered participant or as an observer.

FROM HESTON BACK TO JAMIE: DESIGNING AN APPETISING RECIPE WITH AN EVER-CHANGING ARRAY OF INGREDIENTS (DESIGNING LEARNING FOR A WORLD IN FLUX)

Lisette Toetenel, Wendy Fowle, Tom Olney, Open University, United Kingdom

Context

This workshop follows on from *From Beans on Toast to Molecular Gastronomy (and a Bit of MasterChef): Linking Learning Design with Learning Analytics*, delivered at EDEN in 2014. In 2014 we explored Heston's hyper-experimental approaches for providing evidence-based Learning Design. Our intention for 2015 is to return to our roots by creating an inspirational design based on what's already in the fridge.

Significant changes made to funding in Higher Education in the UK have led to notable changes in the student population. When designing learning materials in a distance-learning context, especially when working with large populations of students, these changes are less evident than for educators that work solely in a face-to-face or blended setting. Learning Design puts the students at the heart of the design process through an evidence-based approach focussed on student activity, which helps address this issue. Conole (2012, p212) describes *learning design* as 'a methodology for enabling teachers/designers to make more informed decisions in how they go about designing learning activities and interventions, which is pedagogically informed and makes effective use of appropriate resources and technologies'. These issues are expected to become more prominent as increasing numbers of institutions move towards a blended and/or distance-learning model.

In order to make informed decisions for large student populations, the relationship between learning analytics and learning design is important. Changes in society include demographic variables, but also differences in learners' behaviour, which can be captured through applying Learning Analytics approaches. By combing these data sources, it might become possible to provide more insights into combinations of learner and institutional related issues, which need to be captured in a way that can inform the design process. This is important, as Learning Design has an impact on satisfaction and retention of students (Toetenel & Rienties, 2016).

Workshop outline

The workshop will provide a brief outline of the changes in the Higher Education landscape in the UK, followed by the changes in the OU's student population and the use of technology. This approach addresses the issues raised by the concept of unconscious bias (Equality Challenge Unit, 2015) whereby module designers may inadvertently make design decisions which reinforce their own assumptions without recognising the bias that this may ensue. By explicitly prompting learning design teams to think about the needs of a range of students in terms of religion, culture, sexuality or gender, it is anticipated that those hidden biases are brought to the surface, enabling more inclusive module content to be developed from which students of all backgrounds can benefit. The implications of these demographic changes for Learning Design will then be explored. After this brief introduction, participants will be invited to consider the contents of their own institutional fridge and customise the recipes based on each of the ingredients they find. Colleagues will be given the opportunity to use two Learning Design resources in order to visualize the needs of the learners by creating a detailed student profile.

SO CLOSE, BUT STILL OUT OF REACH – ALTERNATIVE EDUCATIONAL PROGRAM FOR YOUNG EARLY SCHOOL LEAVERS

Taru Kekkonen, Otava Folk High School, Johanna Juvonen, Valteri Centre for Learning and Consulting, Finland

So Close, but Still out of Reach – An Alternative Educational Program for Young Early School Leavers

Research shows how young people who leave mainstream school early without achieving certification, limit their opportunities and risk social exclusion. Early school leaving is a complex issue and often an outcome of multiple factors which always cannot be dealt with basic educational systems. Reasons for staying at home instead of going to school can be numerous: psychiatric problems (anxiety, depression, panic disorder), bullying, falling ill due to indoor air, lack of motivation etc. Often local schools are doing their best in tailoring various paths for these pupils to carry out the studies from home. Most often the pupils study the learning content independently at home and make their learning visible in exams at school. Anyway, the reality is that too many of these kids don't complete their comprehensive school studies, they leave school without the diploma and thus also miss their chances for further education.

When studying from home, the support of the parents is critical: the more capable the parents are to support the pupils' learning, the better the chances are for him/her to complete the studies. Bigger cities have more possibilities to provide and support tailored learning paths than small municipalities. This means that pupils are not in equal situation when it comes to their social background as well as their national location.

Two Finnish schools, Otava Folk High School and Valteri Centre for Learning and Consulting, both located in eastern Finland but working nationwide, decided to do something about this. The schools joined their strengths – experience in online education and expertise in special needs education – and launched a project called Monni. Monni Online aims at developing and providing a national model of supported distance studies for those pupils who have difficulties in completing their studies at comprehensive school. The project looks for, develops and pilots models that could help the final grade pupils who already get intensified or special support but still need further individualised, tailored solutions in order to complete their studies and get the school leaving diploma.

Monni Online studies include online courses provided by Otava Folk High School as well as the support of a special needs teacher from Valteri Centre for Learning and Consulting. Our experience from the first pilots has shown that it is essential to compile personal learning plans for each pupil. Another important thing has been to agree on sharing the responsibilities between the two organizations and the local schools. The latter is especially important as the pupils remain enrolled in their local schools. At the moment there are 13 pupils with the aim of achieving the school leaving certificate. During the first pilot year, seven pupils out of eight achieved the certificate.

In the demonstration session, we will show in practise how the cooperation between three organizations works and how the learning plans are followed. We will also introduce our online learning environment as well as the learning materials to the participants of the demonstration. Additionally, we will show how (time bound) cooperational courses and (non-stop) independent studying are interlinked and how the interaction between the pupils and teachers works.

EVOLVING MATERIALS FOR THE FLIPPED E-CLASSROOM

Antonio Perez-Navarro, Marta Aymerich Martinez, Victor Garcia, Quelic Berga, Israel Conejero-Arto, Jordi Conesa, Enric Mor Pera, Universitat Oberta de Catalunya (UOC), Spain

Transmitting, sharing and storing knowledge is a key process for culture ever since the origins of humanity. Teaching and learning are part of this human process and they involve several media, from oral communication to interactive applications. For the longest time most media employed in residential and distance education – from print, to radio, television… – have been unidirectional, not allowing feedback or interaction between students and learning facilitators, and amongst students; the process of learning was still very much a self-teaching experience. Opportunities for overcoming the barrier of unidirectionality appeared with the irruption of the Net at the end of the 20th and the beginning of 21st centuries, also bringing about new ubiquitous possibilities.

The twinning of a progressive popularization of high bandwidth Internet connections and a "new" medium – video – engendered Vimeo (2004) and later YouTube (2005) among other platforms, thus transforming video into a household item, available anytime anywhere. With time, amateur recordings filmed by teachers began rivalling expensive videos produced by universities, and the advent of Smartphones proletarianised video creation.

Inexpensive classroom video lecture recordings pinned on the Internet and originally meant to reinforce student's learning comprehension ushered a pedagogical evolution known as the *flipped classroom*. Although this learning model is generally associated with f2f universities' imaginative use of video, it has been in use in some online universities, as well; one in particular, the Universitat Oberta de Catalunya (UOC), was, in a most visionary design, born a *flipped classroom* institution 20 years ago, where students have always learned through text-based *lectures* on the privacy of their screen, and then entered their *classroom* for forum discussions, group projects, and other collaborative competence development interaction.

In order to enhance the virtual *flipped classroom* model, use of media has been subject to ongoing innovation and the various media – seen as complementary rather than mutually exclusive – have been made to interact. Video is a core element of this evolution, especially since it is becoming an important source of Internet-based knowledge for today's students.

However, the UOC has gone, once more, a step further. In the present work we will show how the UOC has introduced video at the beginning and at the end of the process of flipping classroom. It has been made possible by a UOC-designed application called Present@, which allows video to incorporate comments, quizzes, still images and audio, and, furthermore, to host student feedback. Thus, students can use the video as the first contact with the subject, as well as to interact with teacher via video throughout the learning process.

Nevertheless, *flipped classroom* is not an issue of technology, but rather a philosophical one. Therefore, although Present@ is the technology that allows to use video in all the steps of the process of flipping a classroom, there are several questions that need to be addressed: (a) which role is video to play in the learning process? Will it facilitate the first contact between users and the subject? Will it be the primary learning material of the subject, or only a support to other material? (b) in which steps of the learning process will the video be used?; and (c) how should the video be in order to satisfy the requirements of questions (a) and (b)?

The answer to these questions will be illustrated with a pilot in a physics subject. This subject was chosen because of its high level of difficulty for many students, making it a challenging environment to test new techniques. The experiment has been performed analyzing three variables: (a) kind of student: it has been performed with face-to-face students as well as with online UOC students; (b) kind of videos: after a classification of videos by objective and subjective items, the most suitable kinds for the specific subject were chosen and developed; (c) interactivity: introduced via Present@ by means of comments, quizzes and the possibility of question within the video itself.

The main contributions of the present work are: a classification of the pedagogic videos oriented to teacher creation; a recommendation of which videos are most useful to students; which role interaction plays in videos, when can video be a supporting tool in the course, and, finally, Present@ – the tool that allows to introduce video in all the steps of a flipped classroom.

IVIDEO.EDUCATION – A TOOL FOR INTEGRATING HYPERVIDEO IN EDUCATION

Florinda Sauli, Alberto Cattaneo, Swiss Federal Institute for Vocational Education and Training, Switzerland

iVideo.education is a system which gives teachers and students the possibility to create, access and share hypervideos. A hypervideo is a video enriched with additional materials (e.g. images, links, files, audio tracks, etc.) directly hyperlinked within the video through special markers or hotspots, and integrating the possibility to annotate the video, individually or collaboratively, directly within the interface. Finally, iVideo.education constitutes a versatile learning environment, allowing for creative usage in education. It comprises three interfaces: (a) the player, which allows the user to watch hypervideos and annotate them, (b) the editor, i.e. the authoring tool to realize hypervideos, and (c) the website, which allows the users to publish their own hypervideos, sharing them with other users in order to constitute a common repository. iVideo.education can be used both online and offline, both on desktop computers and on mobile devices.

Given its versatility of use, iVideo.education aims at creating a varied learning environment. It can be used in very different ways, the most common of which are: (a) by the teacher in front of the class as a support to her/his lecture, (b) by students individually, e.g. in a computer lab or in an e-learning course, (c) by students in groups in a Learning by Design approach; in this last case, students build together the interactivity in the video.

iVideo.education gives the possibility to fill the gap between different learning locations (e.g. between formal and informal / non-formal learning contexts). In the context of Swiss dual Vocational Education and Training (VET), which is based on an alternation of school-based and work-based tracks, iVideo.education is an example of good practice: learning resources based on video can be a very useful tool for showing apprentices concrete, real and authentic professional situations or procedures, as well as for asking them to capture or reproduce such situations from their professional daily life. Based upon these user-generated (interactive) videos, a teacher at the vocational school can plan learning activities in order to foster the link between theory and practice, abstract and practical knowledge, and thinking and acting. Moreover, videos favour learning across sites through processes like, for example, reflecting, sharing and comparing involving students more actively and opening new frontiers of learning environments. Through the iVideo.education website (www.ivideo.education) materials and examples of good practices can be shared between teachers and trainers.

BOOK OF PROJECTS

Collection of “Synergy” Synopses

Thematic focus and relevance of the Synergy initiatives

	Acronym	COOP	DPED	GUID	ICT	ILSD	INNO	MIND	MLS	NETW	QFIC	QLTY	RISK	ROI	SCL	STRU	SVET	TASS	VWC	WBCD
B5	D-TRANSFORM						X							X						
	ARMAZEG		X													X				
	eQTel											X								
	OpenMed							X												
	SP4CE																X			
	LACE				X															X
	BigEdData															X				
	Y1 Feedback																X			
	Student Success Toolbox			X													X			
	Digital Laboratory of Open Learning						X									X				
	MOOQ				X		X					X				X		X		
	OERUp!		X				X									X				
	OpenPROF		X			X		X		X							X			
F4	OntoTechnology					X				X					X			X	X	X
	EDUWORKS					X				X				X	X					X
	eLene4work		X	X	X		X				X		X			X	X			X
	OBN					X					X									X
	LEHO												X							
	EBE-EUSMOSI										X	X	X							
	PBL 3.0	X			X					X	X			X				X		X
	EDADCC		X				X			X										
	ENGAGE			X																
	DICHE										X		X						X	
	Learning21						X	X		X										
	FORESIGHT				X							X								
	tMAIL								X				X							
	m-commerce								X											

Conference themes and their related tags

COOP	Enterprise-education (Academia, VET) co-operation
DPED	Digital pedagogy in adult and lifelong learning
GUID	Student guidance services and their effectiveness at universities
ICT	ICTs in support of transitions from school through vocational and higher education into the world of work
ILSD	Informal learning and self-development at the workplace
INNO	Innovation in e-learning business models, management processes
MIND	Educational mindset for the workplace
MLS	Mobile learning solutions at the workplace
NETW	Working and learning in networks, communities of practice, social media – social interactions in workplace based e-learning
QFIC	Qualification, competence validation and recognition issues
QLTY	Quality aspects: assessment and evaluation, retention techniques, performance support
RISK	ICT-enhanced teaching/training of excluded or at-risk groups
ROI	Economic aspects of education and training: ROI, benchmarking, performance indicators, success factors
SCL	Scaling up work based learning by ICTs
STRU	Distance and e-learning and the restructuring of educational levels - vocational, post-secondary, and higher education
SVET	E-learning solutions for vocational education and training
TASS	Evaluation and pre- and post-training assessments: specificities in the work based learning environment: what and how to measure
VWC	Best practices adaptable by other white-collar VET stakeholders
WBCD	Measuring competence development in work based learning

INNO ROI

D-TRANSFORM

DigiTal Resources As a New Strategical Factor for a Renovation of Modernization in higher education

Website: http://www.dtransform.eu

Runtime: 01 Sep 2014 – 31 Aug 2017

Supported / co-funded by: Erasmus+

Partners: Fondation Maison Des Sciences De L'Homme, FR (coordinator); Université de Lorraine, FR; Sero Consulting Ltd, UK; Fundacio per a la Universitat Oberta de Catalunya, ES; Politecnico di Milano – METID, IT; European Distance and E-Learning Network, UK; Budapest University of Technology and Economics, HU.

Project representative to be contacted for further info: Angela Procoli (procoli@msh-paris.fr)

The D-TRANSFORM project is a first attempt to set up a *University Leader Program* at the European level, addressed to university presidents and vice-presidents on the role of e-Education in shaping University strategies. It gathers together specialists of e-Education from various institutions (University, higher education ministries, consultancy in learning innovation, e-Education networks) and primarily considers that digital technologies, like Massive Open Online Courses, (MOOCs) and Open Educational Resources are an essential lever for transforming the higher education systems and adapting them to the new needs of youth and requirements of work-market (lifelong training).

D-TRANSFORM intends to produce recommendations on various aspects of a university strategy on the use of digital tools. Based on these recommendations, D-TRANSFORM will set up two "leadership schools", dedicated, for the 1st time in Europe, to the university governances.

Main target groups of the project: HE Institutions and schools, presidents, vice-presidents and staff involved in management at the highest level

Significant public results:

Guidelines of a training program for university leaders on the base of state-of-the art and context analysis of European and national public policies, a business model for online training, rationalising the costs of HE through the use of digital teaching by evidence-based analysis and case studies:

- Public Digital Policies in Higher Education – A comparative survey between Spain, France, Italy and the United Kingdom.
- Business models for opening up education – Sustainability of MOOCs, OER and related online education approaches in higher education in Europe.
- Open Educational Resource, a lever for digital transition of higher education?

Organisation of *two leadership schools* for university leaders (presidents and vice-presidents) of partner universities, establishing an *online training kit* based on assessment of training outcomes

Integration of the leadership school program and the online training kit into the lifelong training programs of the partner universities and national and European associations of university presidents.

3 multiplier events, organised yearly.

DPED STRU

ARMAZEG

Developing Tools for Lifelong Learning in the Transcaucasus Region: e-Learning

Website: http://www.armazeg.com/en

Runtime: December 2013 – November 2016

Supported / co-funded by: Tempus

Partners: Katholieke Universiteit Leuven, BE (coordinator); State Engineering University of Armenia, AM; Ministry of Education and Science of the Republic of Armenia, AM; Institute of Informatics & Automation Problems of NAS RA, AM; Orbeli Institute of Physiology of NAS RA, AM; Armenian State Pedagogical University after Kh. Abovian, AM; St. Andrew the First-Called Georgian University, GE; Georgian Technical University, GE; Università degli Studi di Firenze, IT; University of Granada, ES; European Distance and E-Learning Network, UK; Ivane Javakhishvili Tbilisi State University, GE.

Project representative to be contacted for further info: Ilse Op de Beeck (ilse.opdebeeck@kuleuven.be)

Financed by the European Commission within the TEMPUS program the ARMAZEG project aims to stimulate educational reform in Armenian and Georgian partner universities by establishing e-Learning centres and training for their staff members – with special attention to lifelong learning methodologies.

The project involves twelve partners from Europe and Transcaucasia with a clear vision to establish new links in the educational sphere between the two regions. With the assistance of four European partners ARMAZEG's Armenian and Georgian institutions will import and adapt e-Learning practices in their educational agenda to realise a flexible organisation of higher and adult education locally. A thorough needs analysis accompanied by study visits to the state of the art European universities will help the Transcaucasian partners improve learning by supporting student-centred methodologies, support research-based higher education and enable the internationalisation of their higher education services.

Amongst the most important outcomes of the project will be the establishment of e-learning centres in 7 partner universities of Armenia and Georgia and the implementation of pilot projects in different disciplines. To ensure the sustainability of the concept in Transcaucasian partner institutions, the project also includes, besides the above mentioned policy makers' study visits, trainings of trainers and regional and national workshops.

Main target groups of the project: Higher education stakeholders (University management, lecturers, administration staff, students)

Significant public results:

- Documents:
  - State-of-the-Art report on Armenian and Georgian e-learning (available)
  - Policy recommendations regarding e-learning and ICT for LLL in Armenia and Georgia
  - Long-term capacity building strategy regarding e-learning competences for staff
  - Quality assurance framework for e-courses
- Established e-learning centres with trained staff and specific business strategy
- Training material for teachers regarding e-learning and ICT for lifelong learning
- Pilot projects (implemented e-courses)

QLTY

eQTel

Enhancing Quality of Technology-Enhanced Learning at Jordanian Universities

Website: http://eqtel.psut.edu.jo/Home.aspx

Runtime: 12.2013 – 11.2016

Supported / co-funded by: Tempus, EU / Structural Measures in Governance Reform 2013-4568

Partners: Coordinating institution: Princess Sumaya University for Technology, JO; Full list of partnership: http://eqtel.psut.edu.jo/Lists/UniversitiesOverview/Universities.aspx

Project representative to be contacted for further info: Abdullah Al Zoubi (zoubi@psut.edu.jo), Christine Appel (mappel@uoc.edu)

eQTeL is a Structural Measures project which completely addresses *Governance Reform* under the theme: Introduction of Quality Assurance. This is a national priority for Jordan. It will modernise and reform teaching methodologies. The project has been designed to improve the quality and relevance of technology-enhanced in Jordan through developing and implementing new accreditation standards, guidelines and procedures for distance learning study programs according to EU practices. This proposal has been instigated and is highly supported by Ministry of Higher Education and Scientific Research as well as the Higher Education Accreditation Commission. eQTeL focuses on developing a quality assurance framework to foster technology-enhanced learning in university education in Jordan, and establishing a sustainable capacity building programme to support faculty implement technology in education. The wider objective of the project is to promote reform and modernization of higher education in Jordan through the introduction of a national quality assurance system for technology enhanced learning.

eQTeL aims to improve the quality and relevance of technology-enhanced learning (TeL) at Jordanian higher education institutions and to enable the country's easier inclusion into European Higher Education Area. The main project objective is to improve, develop and implement accreditation standards, guidelines and procedures for quality assurance of TeL courses and study programs at a national level. The new standards will assimilate the quality of Tel courses offered by higher education institutions in Jordan, and would consequently be incorporated into existing legal acts and regulatory documents at both institutional and national levels. Implementation of the new standards will be ensured through establishing a capacity building programme that provides extensive training for all levels of staff involved in accreditation or delivery of TeL programs, from teaching staff, trainers, evaluators, official accreditation reviewers and higher education public authorities. This will result in (a) improving staff competences in defining and applying a standardized quality assurance system; (b) defining national standards for TeL taking into account quality references and guidelines commonly shared with the Ministry of Higher Education and Scientific Research as well as the Higher Education Accreditation Commission.

The specific objectives of the project are: (a) improve, develop and implement accreditation standards, guidelines and procedures for quality assurance of distance learning study programs according to EU practices; (b) establish a framework for improving the quality of technology-enhance learning (TeL) and eLearning methodology on higher education institutions in Jordan; (c) provide training for relevant public authorities personnel responsible for accreditation and evaluation of distance learning programs and build the capacity of trainers involved in distance education in Jordan; and d) disseminate good practices on assuring the quality of technology-enhanced learning courses, degrees and programmes.

Main target groups of the project: Jordanian Higher Education Institutions

Significant public results: The main significant public results which are being developed during the project are: (a) development and implementation of accreditation standards, guidelines and procedures for quality assurance of distance learning study programs according to EU practices; (b) a framework for improving the quality of technology-enhance learning (TeL) and eLearning methodology on higher education institutions in Jordan; (c) training programme for relevant public authorities, personnel responsible for accreditation and evaluation of distance learning programs and increased capacity of trainers involved in distance education in Jordan; and (d) dissemination of good practices on assuring the quality of technology-enhanced learning courses, degrees and programmes, including the reports on 3 pilot courses developed within the project (English skills, Renewable Energy Systems, and a Communications Engineering Lab).

OpenMed

Opening up Education in South-Mediterranean countries

Website: http://www.openmedproject.eu

Runtime: 10.2015 – 10.2018

Supported / co-funded by: Erasmus+ KA2 – Capacity Building in the field of Higher Education

Partners: UNIMED – Mediterranean Universities Union, IT (coordinator); POLITO – Politecnico di Torino, IT; UNIR – Universidad Internacional de La Rioja, ES; US – University of Seville, ES; DMLL, Coventry University, UK; CU, Cairo University, EG; AU – Alexandria University, EG; UCA – Cadi Ayyad University, MA; UIZ – Université Ibn Zohr, MA; BZU – Birzeit University, PS; ANNU – An-Najah National University, PS; AarU – Association of Arab Universities, JO; GJU – German Jordanian University, JO; PSUT – Princess Sumaya University for Technology, JO; EDEN – European Distance and E-Learning Network, UK (associated partner).

Project representative to be contacted for further info: Cristina Stefanelli (stefanelli@uni-med.net)

The overarching goal of OpenMed is to raise awareness and facilitate the adoption of Open Educational Resources (OER) and Open Educational Practices (OEP) in the South Mediterranean region, with a particular focus on Egypt, Jordan, Morocco and Palestine.

OpenMed fosters the role of universities as knowledge providers not only to their on-campus students but also beyond the walls of institutions, especially towards disadvantaged groups (e.g. low income peoples, disabled students, people living in rural areas, learners at risk of low achievement, refugees).

The initiative also opens the possibility to provide free educational resources for self-learners, in terms of informal and lifelong learning.

Main target groups of the project: Higher Education managers and educators

SVET

SP4CE

Strategic Partnership for Creativity and Entrepreneurship

Website: http://www.sp4ce.piap.pl/index.php

Runtime: September 2014 – August 2017

Supported / co-funded by: ERASMUS+

Partners: PIAP, PL; TUKE, SK; PRO-MED, PL; ASTRA, SK; TREBAG, HU; IDEC, GR.

Project representative to be contacted for further info: Jacek Zieliński (jzielinski@piap.pl)

Project aims at design and elaboration of innovative common tools for collaboration between students, enterprises and schools. Those tools are available as ICT solution with WWW interface.

The portal concept is based on the following coaching and mentoring principles:

- Companies willing to find young workers (preferably students entering the labour market) submit/send a case (e.g. problem to be solved).
- The case is presented to students who try to find a solution.
- Based on proposed solutions the company selects the student(s) and give them coach(es) who support and co-work with students.
- Mentors (teachers) from universities or high schools supervise the process and guide students inside so called Learning Rooms.

The main impact of SP4CE is connected with influence on potential portal users such as students, enterprises staff and teachers:

- Students have an opportunity to learn about enterprises' activities and they can interact with coaches. They are able to enter the labour market having real professional experience.
- Enterprises receive required knowledge and possibility to recruit students who have concrete skills and competences.
- Teachers receive information about students' progress and real enterprises needs. Both items are important for developing training programs and further training activities.

The project has a big impact on partners' approach to training content creation, training activities and utilization of ECVET opportunities.

It must be emphasized that knowledge sharing as a main part of partnership activities supports changing of partners' educational strategy.

Main target groups of the project:

- Students from vocational schools and universities, entering in the near future the labour market.
- Enterprises staff from companies looking for the new workers. The staff will be supported by training materials about coaching and will be in direct contact with students interested in establishing a co-operation with the company.
- Teachers (mentors) from different institutions dealing with education. They will be provided training materials about mentoring and they will help students to establish the successful co-operation with coaches from companies.

SVET

Significant public results:

- SP4CE learning portal;
- SP4CE pedagogical concept;
- Guidelines for consultants (enterprises);
- Guidelines for mentors (teachers);
- Guidelines for general public *How to use SP4CE portal.*

Erasmus+ Project *Strategic Partnership for Creativity and Entrepreneurship (SP4CE)* has been funded with support from the European Commission under the ERASMUS+ Programme. This publication reflects the views only of the authors, and the National Agency and the European Commission cannot be held responsible for any use which may be made of the information contained therein.

ICT WBCD

LACE

Learning Analytics Community Exchange

Website: http://www.laceproject.eu/

Runtime: Jan 2014 – Jun. 2016

Supported / co-funded by: FP7

Partners: Open Universiteit Nederland, NL; Cetis – The Centre for Educational Technology and Interoperability Standards at the University of Bolton, UK; Institute for Educational Technology at the Open University, UK; Infinity Technology Solutions, IT; Skolverket, the Swedish National Agency for Education, SE; Kennisnet, NL; Høgskolen i Oslo og Akershus, NO; ATiT, Audiovisual Technologies, Informatics and Telecommunications, BE; EDEN – European Distance and E-learning Network, UK.

Project representative to be contacted for further info: Sally Reynolds (sally.reynolds@atit.be).

LACE partners are passionate about the opportunities afforded by current and future views of learning analytics (LA) and educational data mining (EDM) but we are concerned about missed opportunities, undesirable consequences of mis-application, investment funding failing to realise value, market failure, etc. LACE is our response, a project to reduce risk and to increase benefit through an approach that accounts for the necessary unity of research, policy and practice.

- Organise a range of activities designed to actively and passively integrate communities that are conducting LA/EDM research, early practitioner adopters, and those who are building first-generation commercial or open-source software. This integration is to be used to stimulate creativity and accelerate the identification of viable and effective solutions to real problems, and hence to drive both current research and technology transfer.
- Create and curate a knowledge base of evidence. This will capture evidence for the effectiveness and the relative desirability of the outcomes resulting from use of various tools and techniques.
- Actively participate in the exploration of plausible futures for learning analytics and EDM by combining the creation of imaginative scenarios with participatory workshops and structured methods including a Policy Delphi to assess differences of opinion about the feasibility and desirability of possible future states, thus informing future research and policy agendas.
- The LACE project brings together existing key European players in the field of learning analytics & EDM who are committed to build communities of practice and share emerging best practice in order to make progress towards four objectives.

Objectives: (a) Objective 1 – Promote knowledge creation and exchange; (b) Objective 2 – Increase the evidence base; (c) Objective 3 – Contribute to the definition of future directions; (d) Objective 4 – Build consensus on interoperability and data sharing.

The LACE project received *Excellent* rating on its second year review.

Main target groups of the project: Researchers, practitioners and stakeholders interested in learning analytics and how learning analytics can be used to enhance ICT-supported learning in particular. LACE targets schools, higher education and workplace learning separately while helping to support cross-sector learning and exchange where relevant in the area of learning analytics.

ICT WBCD

Significant public results:

- The LACE Evidence Hub: it brings together evidence about learning analytics from all around the world and relates it to four propositions concerning learning, teaching, uptake and ethics (http://www.laceproject.eu/evidence-hub/).
- Learning Analytics Review: a series of articles and briefings for those working in the schools, workplace and higher education with an interest in the impact of learning analytics in the short to medium term (http://www.laceproject.eu/learning-analytics-review/).
- Interoperability studies (http://www.laceproject.eu/data-interoperability/) and studies in Ethics & Privacy (http://www.laceproject.eu/ethics-privacy/).
- Evaluation Framework for Learning Analytics (EFLA) (http://www.laceproject.eu/evaluation-framework-for-la/).
- FAQ on learning analytics (http://www.laceproject.eu/faqs/learning-analytics/).
- Workshops and learning opportunities both on and off-line.
- Community and network support.

STRU

BigEdData

The MOOCs Story Deconstructed

DCU | NIDL National Institute for Digital Learning

北京师范大学 BEIJING NORMAL UNIVERSITY

Website: http://www.dcu.ie/nidl/research/current-projects.shtml

Runtime: 3.2016 – 3.2017

Supported / co-funded by: Office of Vice-President for Research Business Innovation Platform, Dublin City University; Centre for Big Data in Education, Beijing Normal University;

Partners: Dublin City University, Ireland; Beijing Normal University, China

Project representative to be contacted for further info: Professor Mark Brown (mark.brown@dcu.ie); Dr Eamon Costello (eamon.costello@dcu.ie)

Short description

This project builds on a current line of research critically analysing the portrayal of MOOCs in traditional media (Brown, Costello, Donlon, Nic Giollamhichil, & Kirwan, 2015a). Arguably no other educational innovation in the last century has generated the same level of media attention and there remains considerable debate on the future of MOOCs (Sharrock, 2015). While the portrayal in traditional media of this debate and the wider story about the growth of MOOCs more generally has been the focus of serious research (see for example, Kovanovi, Joksimovic, Gaševic, Siemens, & Hatala, 2015; Selwyn, Bulfin, & Pangrazio, 2015), a gap exists in our knowledge of how the story is being told through social media. To date there is limited research on the coverage of MOOCs in social media with the exception of an analysis of the public response through Sina Weibo in China (Zhang, Perris, Zheng, & Chen, 2015). Specifically this project seeks to deconstruct the MOOC story being told through social media—namely Twitter and in a sub project in partnership with Beijing Normal University the Sina Weibo platform.

In broad terms the research questions seek to explore: Who is telling the MOOC story? How are they telling the MOOC story? What is the story being told about MOOCs? What story is missing? Whose story is not being told? More specifically the study is framed to answer the following research questions:

- What is the story being told about MOOCs through Twitter?
- What can we learn from an analysis of the major patterns, themes and trends evident in Twitter about MOOCs?
- How does the story about MOOCs being told through Twitter compare and contrast with Sina Weibo?

In an initial pilot phase, Twitter data for the MOOC dataset was extracted from GNIP API for the period of September – December 2015 and augmented with additional data including Klout Score (a Social Network Influencer Score), geographic location and URL expansion. The keyword '#MOOC' was used to extract the required data. The GNIP API provides a GZIP file containing data for every 10-minute interval for the specified period. There were 12,373 GZIP post-extraction files. Complex analytics on the data was performed mainly in R (an open-source statistical tool) which accessed data from MongoDB through database instances. This methodology is in line with current state-of-the-art frameworks for descriptive analytics, content analytics and network analytics on Twitter data outlined by Chae (2015) and extended by Lynn et al. (2015).

The MOOC dataset for this pilot analysis phase had 32,309 tweets of which 17,910 were original tweets and 14,399 were retweets. Replies constituted 8 percent (1,434) of the total number of the original tweets. The dataset had 4,980 unique hashtags. Content analytics is primarily concerned with uncovering the patterns hidden inside the content. Word analysis, hashtag analysis, sentiment analysis and URL analysis are the analyses which were performed in this category.

From preliminary analysis of the findings there is evidence to suggest that the term MOOC may be problematic, especially to derive a deeper understanding of how the MOOC story is being told. The promotional nature of many tweets suggests this term may be used more for marketing and informational purposes rather than as a social network. Moreover, it may be that the term MOOC has particular currency only within particular communities such as the academic one. In other words, the MOOC story being told through Twitter is restricted to a relatively small population of users. At this stage it is unknown how widely prevalent the term "MOOC" is in other popular social media platforms and hence many MOOC related tweets by learners may go undetected. More particularly this issue may limit the value of using the term MOOC to make inferences about learners. Using other search constructs such as comprising course, platform, provider or some combinations of these might bring more learners into the dataset, which is one of the key lessons from this pilot phase. In this regard the study has already contributed to our understanding of the methodological challenges and opportunities of analyzing social media as a source of data.

Main target groups of the project: MOOC Specialists, Social Media Researchers, Policy-Makers

Significant public results:

- Brown, M., Costello, E., Donlon, E., Nic Giolla Mhichil, M., & Kirwan, C. (2015a). *Hold the front page: The story of MOOCs in the Irish media.* Invited paper at WOW Conference: Europe Embraces MOOCs, Rome Italy, 30th November.
- Brown, M., Costello, E., Donlon, E., Nic Giolla Mhichil, M., & Kirwan, C. (2015b). *MOOCs in the media: The story behind the story.* Paper presented at The Online, Open and Flexible Higher Education Conference, Hagen, FernUniversitat, 29th October.

References

- Brown, M., Costello, E., Donlon, E., Nic Giolla Mhichil, M., & Kirwan, C. (2015a). *Hold the front page: The story of MOOCs in the Irish media.* Invited paper at WOW Conference: Europe Embraces MOOCs, Rome Italy, 30th November.
- Chae, B. K. (2015). Insights from hashtag# supplychain and Twitter Analytics: Considering Twitter and Twitter data for supply chain practice and research. *International Journal of Production Economics, 165*, 247-259.
- Kovanovi, V., Joksimovic, S., Gaševic, D., Siemens, G., & Hatala, M. (2015). What public media reveals about MOOCs: A systematic analysis of news reports. *British Journal of Educational Technology, 46*(3), 510-527.
- Lynn, T., Kilroy, S., van der Werff, L., Healy, P., Hunt, G., Venkatagiri, S., & Morrison, J. (2015). Towards a general research framework for social media research using big data. *Proceedings of the Professional Communication Conference (IPCC), 2015 IEEE International*, 1-8. IEEE.
- Selwyn, N., Bulfin, S., & Pangrazio, L. (2015). Massive open online change? Exploring the discursive construction of the 'MOOC' in newspapers. *Higher Education Quarterly, 69*(2), 175-192.
- Sharrock, G. (2015). Making sense of the MOOCs debate. *Journal of Higher Education Policy and Management, 37*(5), 597-609.
- Zhang, J., Perris, K., Zheng, Q., & Chen, L. (2015). Public response to "the MOOC movement" in China: Examining the time series of microblogging. *The International Review of Research in Open and Distributed Learning, 16*(5). 144-160.

SVET

Y1Feedback

Enhancing Assessment Feedback in First Year Using Digital Technologies

Website: http://y1feedback.ie

Runtime: 01.2015 – 12.2016

Supported / co-funded by: National Forum for the Enhancement of Teaching and Learning

Partners: Maynooth University, Athlone Institute of Technology, Dublin City University, Dundalk Institute of Technology, Ireland.

Project representative to be contacted for further info: Lisa O'Regan (lisa.oregan@nuim.ie)

The transition into Higher Education (HE) is challenging for many learners (Thomas, 2012). Although feedback can play a critical role in fostering student motivation, confidence and success in the first year, as well as in supporting retention (Tinto, 2005; Nicol, 2009), current feedback practices are not consistently supporting these aims, particularly in large cohorts. Irish students express dissatisfaction with perceived deficiencies in the timeliness, scope, and usefulness of feedback (ISSE, 2014; Y1Feedback, 2016a) concerns that are mirrored by students in the UK, Australia and Asia (Carless, 2006; James et al,. 2010; HEFCE, 2014; 2015; Jessop et al., 2014; Mulliner & Tucker, 2015; Radloff & Coates, 2010), while teaching staff point to the lack of student engagement with feedback (Price et al., 2010; Y1Feedback, 2016a).

Y1Feedback is a multi-institutional change project that seeks to investigate the potential for digital technologies to support feedback practices in the first year of study. Informed by an analysis of current feedback practices across the four partner institutions (Y1Feedback, 2016a), as well as a comprehensive review of recent literature, the Y1Feedback project team have identified eight features of effective feedback in the first year:

- promote feedback both within and beyond assessed work;
- support the embedding of student assessment and feedback literacies;
- foster student competence, motivation, and belonging;
- provide opportunities for dialogic feedback;
- feed forward to future work;
- support the development of digital literacies;
- employ consistent and co-ordinated approaches to feedback across programmes of study; and
- foster sustainable feedback practices that encourage self-regulated learning.

We have also identified a range of specific pedagogical approaches that have potential to support effective feedback practices in the first year. These include: peer feedback; in-class and real-time feedback; feedforward strategies (such as flipped feedback, multi-stage assignments, and linked assignments); separating grades and feedback; provision of generic feedback; the use of exemplars, rubrics and marking guides; provision of anticipatory feedback; and programmatic approaches to feedback provision. We are currently collaborating with teaching staff across the four participating institutions to pilot technology-supported solutions to enabling such approaches. Supporting technologies under exploration include: peer feedback tools; audio-visual technologies; e-portfolios; automated feedback technologies; in-class technologies such as clickers and text walls; and learning analytics. Twenty six pilots are currently in progress, involving sixteen academic departments and thirty two academic partners. The design of each pilot study has been informed by particular contextual issues and needs, and each incorporates a range of pedagogical approaches and technologies. An iterative Design Based Research approach is being employed in order to refine the approaches employed (Amiel & Reeves, 2008), and where possible, students are involved as active partners.

Main target groups of the project: Institutional Leaders, Centres for Teaching and Learning, Educational Developers, Learning Designers

SVET

Significant public results:

- Y1Feedback (2016a). Feedback in First Year: A Landscape Snapshot. Available from http://y1feedback.ie
  This report provides a snapshot of current feedback practice in first year undergraduate programmes across the four Y1Feedback partner institutions.
- Y1Feedback (2016b). Technology-Enabled Feedback in the First Year: A Synthesis of the Literature. Available from http://y1feedback.ie
  This report synthesises contemporary thinking in relation to enhancing feedback practices in HE, with a particular emphasis on the affordances that technology may offer in supporting effective approaches in the context of the first year of study.
- Learnings from the pilot studies will be disseminated by way of video case studies, to be disseminated via http://y1feedback.
- An international Symposium on Feedback in Higher Education is planned for early 2017.

Previous conference presentations:

- O'Regan, L., Walsh, E., Brown, M., Maguire, M., Gallagher, G., Harding, N., & McDermott, G. (2015). *Supporting transition: Enhancing (assessment) feedback in first year using digital technologies - A current practice review.* Paper presented at The Online, Open and Flexible Higher Education Conference, Hagen, FernUniversitat, 29th October.
- O'Regan, L., Brown, M., Maguire, M., Harding, N., Walsh, E., Gallagher, G., & McDermott, G. (2015). *Assessment feedback in first year using digital technologies - Preliminary findings from an Irish multi-institutional project.* Poster session (Best Poster Award) at International Assessment in Higher Education Conference, Birmingham, 25th June.
- O'Regan, L., Brown, M., Maguire, M., Harding, N., Walsh, E., Gallagher, G., & McDermott, G. (2015). *Assessment feedback in first year using digital technologies – A baseline review.* Presentation at EdTech 2015, Irish Learning Technology Association Conference, Limerick. 27th May.

GUID SVET

Student Success Toolbox

Supporting Transitions from Thinking about Study to the First Weeks

Website: http://studentsuccess.ie

Runtime: 01.2015 – 06.2016

Supported / co-funded by: National Forum for the Enhancement of Teaching and Learning in Higher Education

Partners: Dublin City University, Maynooth University, Dundalk Institute of Technology, Sligo Institute of Technology, Ireland

Project representative to be contacted for further info: Dr James Brunton (james.brunton@dcu.ie)

Short description

The Student Success Toolbox project seeks to address the problem of effective transitions and the foundations for student success during the initial stages of the study lifecycle with a specific focus on flexible learners. In the context of this project a broad definition is adopted of flexible learners, which includes adult learners engaged in part-time and online/distance learning. Enhancing retention and completion rates of this group of flexible learners is a significant problem globally (Simpson, 2009). The particular focus of this project is on supporting flexible learners through key transitions in the early stages of the study lifecycle: from thinking about study, making choices, the registration process and through to the first few weeks. A basic premise of the project is that the foundations for student success are laid early in the study lifecycle, and that insufficient attention has been given in the literature and within institutions to the importance of the period before flexible learners formally commence their study. A related underlying assumption is that this crucial transition period may be enhanced by the availability of appropriately designed digital readiness and preparation tools, which help to scaffold both prospective students and those about to embark on part time or online/distance study for the first time.

There are five phases to this project:

- Phase 1 – Project establishment, including formalizing the project team, partner agreements and scope of the work packages;
- Phase 2 – Analysis of relevant literature and audit of digital readiness tools currently available internationally to support successful transitions for flexible learners;
- Phase 3 – Design and development of a strategically targeted suite of eight research-informed digital readiness tools for flexible learners;
- Phase 4 – A series of pilot evaluations of the digital tools across the partner institutions to gather feedback on their fit for purpose;
- Phase 5 – A guide for institutions on how to support flexible learners and effectively deploy the suite of digital readiness tools along with a series of dissemination workshops.

An agile, iterative, Design-based Research (DBR) methodology (Reeves, 2006) was adopted to plan, develop and pilot a total of eight digital readiness tools (Figure 1). The project began in February 2015 with the design of the digital readiness tools phase commencing in August through the development of initial storyboards. These storyboards went through several iterations over the next few months as the wider project team peer reviewed proposed solutions and our design specialists provided expert advice on particular features within each tool. Based on both the Phase 2 synthesis of existing literature, and on the analysis of existing tools in use internationally, five overarching principles were adopted for the design of a suite of eight digital readiness and preparation tools for flexible learners: (a) self-regulation, (b) personalization, (c) customization, (d) information at the point of need, and (e) language and framing of the tools in the world of the prospective learner.

Figure 1. The Eight Digital Tools for Student Readiness and Success

Tool 1, *Am I Ready for Study?*, invites prospective flexible learners to self-assess if they are ready to commit to part-time online/distance study. The tool involves a brief quiz comprising six sections: (a) Previous Study, (b) Work and Family, (c) Study Intentions, (d) Study Skills, (e) Computer Skills and (f) Work Habits. The second tool, *Do I have Enough Time?*, provides a self-reflective 'life calculator' where prospective flexible learners are encouraged to think about the amount of time they can realistically spend on different activities during a typical week. More to the point this tool is intended to help people make better choices in terms of how much spare time they might have to allocate to study. The third tool, *Who can I Ask?*, offers prospective flexible learners the opportunity to think about their support network and how they might garner support to help them successfully complete their studies. In Tool 4, *Am I Computer Ready to Learn?*, prospective flexible learners are given guidance on the necessary computer skills needed in higher education. They are also informed of the technology they will need, and the computer services offered by colleges and universities. The fifth tool, *My First Assignment*, navigates through a narrative relating to what it is like to plan out and develop a first assignment in higher education. Advice on how to start an assignment, develop a plan, break down a research question is also provided, with key elements within a plan being presented.

Tool 6, *Get Ready to Learn*, is a five week openly available online course that provides prospective flexible learners with key tips and lessons about how to prepare for studying at higher education level. This tool, which is built on a new MOOC platform, incorporates a number of the other tools within its structure. The seventh tool, *Study Tips for Me*, is designed to provide support for flexible learners from crowd sourced tips and suggestions from other flexible learners. This tool is based on the Tumblr platform. Finally, Tool 8, *Online Orientation*, takes a different form in providing a guide for those who wish to create an online orientation for new online/distance learners. This guide describes the elements that should be present in an effective online orientation for their program or institution.

The eight tools that have been developed in this project have been short-listed for the IMS 2016 Learning Impact Awards and will be openly available through the most accommodating Creative Commons Licence (CCL) for other institutions to take, augment, customize and use to enhance the success of flexible learners. Guidelines will also be provided alongside of the tools to help facilitate the effective implementation process. Finally, the research team is committed to undertaking further research on their implementation as our experience in this project has reinforced the basic premise that the foundations for student success are laid early in the study lifecycle.

Main target groups of the project: Online/Distance Providers, Programme Leaders, Learning Support Officers, Student Success Advisors.

GUID SVET

Significant public results:

- Brunton, J. (2015). *Use these digital readiness/preparation tools to support your new flexible learners!* Poster presented at the 45th Annual Conference of the Psychological Society of Ireland, Galway, Ireland, 25th November.
- Brunton, J., Brown, M., Costello, E., Delaney, L., & Fox, S. (2015). *Student success toolbox: Digital tools for use in supporting flexible learners.* Poster presented at OER15, 14th April, Cardiff. Retrieved from https://oer15.oerconf.org/sessions/student-success-toolbox-digital-readiness-tools-for-use-in-supporting-flexible-learners-900/
- Brunton, J., Brown. M., Costello, E., Delaney, L., Fox, S., Galvin, C., & Lonergan, N. (2015). *Digital readiness tools for use in supporting flexible learners: A research and development transitions project.* Presentation at EdTech 2015, Irish Learning Technology Association Conference, Limerick. 28th May. Retrieved from http://www.slideshare.net/JamesBrunton/digital-readiness-tools-for-use-in-supporting-flexible-learners-a-research-and-development-transitions-project
- Brunton, J., Brown, M., Costello, E., Delaney, L., Fox, S., Galvin, C., & Lonergan, N. (2015). *Free, focused and flexible: A suite of online transition tools for supporting student success.* Paper presented at The Online, Open and Flexible Higher Education Conference, Hagen, FernUniversitat, 29th October.

References

- Reeves, T. (2006). Design research from a technology perspective. In J. V. D. Akker, K. Gravemeijer, S. McKenney & N. Nieveen (Eds.), *Educational design research* (pp. 52–66). New York: Routledge.
- Simpson, O. (2009). Motivating learners in open and distance learning: Do we need a new theory of learner support? *Open Learning: The Journal of Open and Distance Learning, 23(2),* 159-170.

INNO STRU

Digital Laboratory of Open Learning

An Exploration of Future Trends in Digital Learning Environments

Website: http://kd.coolking.cn

Runtime: From July, 2013

Supported/ co-funded by: Shanghai Science and Technology Commission, Shanghai Municipal Commission of Education

Partners: Lianhua Wang, Jun Xiao, Li Cai, Yibin Zhang, Ye Yu, Zhen Xu, Lamei Wang, Guang Liu, Chunni Qian, Shanghai Engineering Research Center of Open Distance Education, Shanghai Open University, China.

Project representative to be contacted for further information: Jun Xiao (xiaoj@sou.edu.cn)

The Digital Laboratory of Open Learning, is an open educational research service platform supported by advanced information technologies, and is in combination with learning, experience, test, analysis, research and innovation.

The digital learning resources is constructed and shared in the digital laboratory of open learning through the cloud computing application environment, and the applications and tests of all kinds of learning patterns of open and distance learning can be carried out. That is, it provides an intelligent digital teaching and learning environment, offering a variety of learning scenarios and simulations, with all kinds of learning terminals for mobile learning, using multi-screen interactive technology to carry out cross-screen collaborative learning, using 3D, hologram, AR technology to support experiential learning. Recorded or live broadcast and telecommunication are applied.

The digital laboratory possesses the function of open learning test and analysis, which can conduct usability tests on the teaching and learning products such as online courses, micro lectures, E-books and so on. The learning analysis of digital learning is involved as well, using advanced laboratory equipment to conduct interdisciplinary experiments and assessment from the perspectives of network environment, learner behavioural signs, EEG, equipment power consumption, and online learning behaviour. Open teaching digital laboratory is expected to integrate the new digital learning environment, interactive teaching and learning resources, open learning test and analysis, and so as to improve the research and support of open teaching and learning.

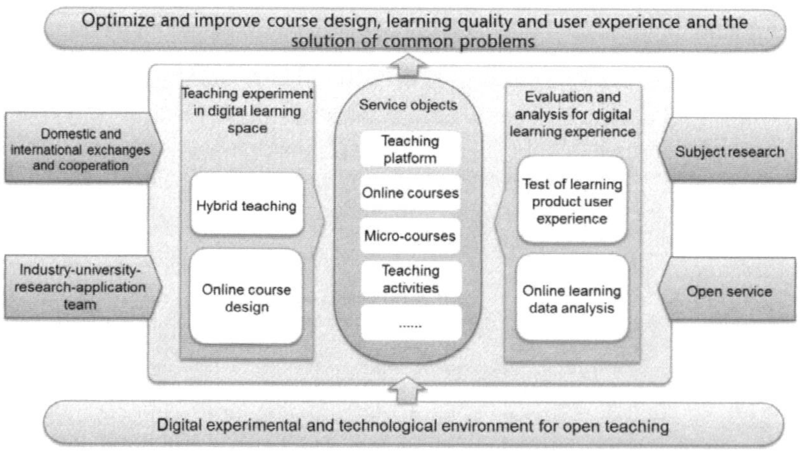

Main target groups of the project: lifelong learners

Significant public results:

- *U-Learning model and Its Applications for Lifelong Education* supported by Innovative Key project of Shanghai Municipal Commission of Education.
- *The Construction and Operation Mode of Digital Education Public Service Platform for Shanghai Learning Society* and *Big Data Analysis of Online Education* supported by Shanghai Educational Science Research Key Projects.

ICT INNO QLTY STRU TASS

MOOQ

Massive Online Open Education Quality

Website: http://www.MOOC-Quality.eu

Runtime: September 2015 – August 2018

Supported / co-funded by: European Union / Erasmus+

Partners: Open University of the Netherlands (OUNL), NL (coordinator); Hellenic Open University (HOU), GR; National Quality Infrastructure System (NQIS), GR; Universidade Aberta (UAB), PT; Ecole Normale Supérieure de Lyon (ENS), FR.

Project representative to be contacted for further info: Associate Professor Dr. Christian M. Stracke (christian.stracke@ou.nl)

Short description of the initiative:

MOOQ is the European Alliance for Quality of Massive Open Online Courses, called MOOCs. The vision of MOOQ is to foster quality in MOOCs leading to a new era of learning experiences.

MOOQ's mission is to develop a quality reference framework for the adoption, the design, the delivery and the evaluation of MOOCs in order to empower MOOC providers for the benefit of the learners.

The main goal of MOOQ is therefore the development and the integration of quality approaches, new pedagogies and organisational mechanisms into MOOCs with a strong focus on the learning processes, methodologies and assessments.

To enhance the unique digital market in Europe, MOOQ will lead to new Q-generation of MOOCs that will be designed, organized and tested as qMOOCs. This will be done in close collaboration with all interested partners and stakeholders in Europe and beyond.

MOOQ promises: We will make MOOCs better!

Thus, MOOQ invites all interested MOOC designers and providers as well as all learners, organizations and public authorities interested in MOOC to join our unique initiative to improve the quality of MOOCs!

More information about MOOQ online: http://www.mooc-quality.eu

Main target groups of the project:

- All learners and citizens interested in online courses and MOOCs;
- MOOC designers and providers;
- Higher Education institutions interested in online courses and MOOCs;
- Certification and accreditation agencies;
- National, regional and local public authorities and decision makers in educational systems.

Significant public results:

- Quality Reference Framework for the quality of Massive Open Online Courses (MOOCs);
- A MOOC about the quality of MOOCs as open discussion among MOOC experts, designers, providers and learners;
- A simple web-based tool to compare MOOCs and their quality.

DPED | INNO | STRU

OERup!

Open Educational Resources uptake in adult education

Website: http://www.oerup.eu/home/

Runtime: 09/2014 – 08/2016

Supported / co-funded by: Erasmus+ Programme of the European Union / strategic partnerships KA2

Partners: MFG Baden-Württemberg mbH (MFG), DE; Universitad Oberta de Cataluny (UOC), ES; Learning & Work Institute (L&W), UK; SOPHIA Research & Innovation (SOPHIA), IT; Institutul Roman de Educatie a Adultilor (IREA), RO.

Project representative to be contacted for further info: Fabio Nascimbeni (fabio.nascimbeni@gmail.com)

OERup! takes up the need to promote and foster the successful implementation of OER (Open Educational Resources) and OEPs (Open Educational Practices) in adult education in Europe in order to widen participation in Open Education. In order to reach this goal, the project has developed, and tested a training package (including online learning material, webinars, and self-assessment as well as OER project management tools) for anyone involved in adult learning. The OERup community provides a space, where anyone involved can network and exchange ideas: http://bit.ly/1XfKRHi

All material of the training package has been released under an open license, and can be found on http://www.oerup.eu/the-training/

The overall aim of the project is to provide all actors with knowledge about Open Educational Resources, but also to enable them to easily incorporate OER in their daily work life, which means successfully and sustainably adapting Open Educational Practices. The pilot of the training includes the first step of an OER initiative development. These initiatives are being supported by the project partners, and finally integrated as practice examples into the training package, for others to learn from.

At the EDEN conference, the OERup! project will emphasize on the presentation of our developed OER-project development and management tools, and the discussions about good practice examples.

Main target groups of the project: Teachers or trainers, as well as managers of adult education institutions.

Significant public results:

- Need analysis on OER in adult education, for download on: http://www.oerup.eu/reading-material/
- Online learning material for the basic knowledge of OER, openly accessible via http://oerup2.teachable.com/courses
- Self-assessment and project management tools, openly accessible via http://www.oerup.eu/the-training/oer-jams/

DPED ILSD MIND NETW SVET

OpenPROF

Open Professional Collaboration for Innovation

Website: http://www.openprof.eu

Runtime: Sepember 2014 – August 2016

Supported / co-funded by: Erasmus + Key Activity 2, Cooperation for innovation and the exchange of good practices, Strategic Partnerships for VET

Partners: Lithuanian Association of Distance and E. Learning, Siauliai Vocational Education and Training Centre, The European Distance and E-Learning Network, Fondo Formación Euskadi, Auxilium pro Regionibus Europae in Rebus Culturalibus, Universidade Aberta (UAb)

Project representative to be contacted for further info: Airina Volungeviciene, LieDM (info@liedm.net)

Designing innovative and sustainable curriculum is a new challenge for the majority of teachers, trainers and adult educators. Professionals supporting innovative services at institutions contribute substantially to developing professional identify, self-esteem, and self-potential. Online learning and open educational resources meet these needs and suggests solutions for innovative, quality work – based learning curriculum designing.

The project addresses key innovations in training of teachers and trainers, as well as adult educators: open educational resource and open curriculum development and licensing, open collaboration, as well as designing curriculum for diverse target groups including the mode of work-based learning. The project aims to foster open and international professional collaboration for innovation by training them to openly collaborate in the development of online innovative curriculum designing using open educational resources. The requirements raised in this project for the innovation of curriculum will allow to create learning services suitable for diverse learners and target groups, including work-based learning.

Main target groups of the project:

1. Institutional level: teachers and trainers, as well as adult educators at partner institutions
2. Local and national level: VET / CVET organizations, adult training organizations, companies, higher education institutions
3. International level: European adult learning community consisting of organisations/institutions listed above, Professional networks

Significant public results:

- Training material on OER and sustainability models: http://openprof.eu/training-material/OER_and_sustainability_models
- Training materials on ICT tools: http://openprof.eu/training-material/Training_material_on_ICT_tools
- Training material on innovative curriculum designing for work: http://openprof.eu/training-material/Innovative_curriculum_designing_for_work-based_learning
- 48 OER in the national and English languages (24 created and 24 adapted): http://openprof.eu/oer
- Curriculum for work - based learning: http://moodle.liedm.net/course/index.php?categoryid=3
- Webinars, multiplier events and presentations at national and European conferences: http://openprof.eu/node

ILSD NETW SCL TASS VWC WBCD

OntoTech

OntoTechnology

Website: http://ontotech.eu

Runtime: 11.2013 – 02.2016

Supported / co-funded by: EU-Funded Lifelong Learning Programme (LLP)

Partners: Coordinator: CVO Antwerp, BE; Full partners: University of Amsterdam, NL; Netpositive, HU.

Project representative to be contacted for further info: Dr. Gábor Kismihók (g.kismihok@uva.nl)

The OntoTechnology approach believes in utilizing job knowledge as a predictor of future job performance. Job knowledge, as opposed to disposition, has the major advantage of being malleable, thus allowing a person a centered approach to personnel selection. The main aims and objectives of this project are to provide detailed personalized assessment and training of essential technical competencies and related job knowledge elements that are required for a certain position. Characteristics of the consortium: Center of Job Knowledge Research (University of Amsterdam), CVO Antwerpen, Netpositive Ltd.. A general description of outcomes includes: – a customizable, adaptive job knowledge test – a general mental ability test – an applicant ranking based on integrated job knowledge and GMA test performance – an automatic and tailored e-Learning content delivery on the basis of test results – a cutting-edge semantic technology for job knowledge structuring, testing and evaluation.

Main target groups of the project: Academia, Industry, Policy

ILSD NETW ROI SCL WBCD

EDUWORKS

Crossing borders in the comprehensive investigation of labour market matching processes: An EU-wide, trans-disciplinary, multilevel and science-practice-bridging training

Website: http://www.eduworks-network.eu

Runtime: 10.2013 – 09.2017

Supported / co-funded by: EU-Funded FP7 Marie Curie Initial Training Network

Partners: Coordinator: University of Amsterdam, Netherlands; Central European University, Hungary; Corvinno Technology Transfer Center, Hungary; University of Salamanca, Spain; University of Siegen, Germany; Trinity College of Dublin, Ireland; associated partners: http://eduworks-network.eu/pages/associated-partners

Project representative to be contacted for further info: **Dr. Gábor Kismihók** (g.kismihok@uva.nl)

The objective of EDUWORKS is to train talented early-stage researchers in the socioeconomic and psychological dynamics of the labour supply and demand matching processes at aggregated and disaggregated levels. EDUWORKS brings together researchers from several academic disciplines, namely: Labour Economics, Sociology of Occupations, HRM, Lifelong Learning, and Knowledge Management.

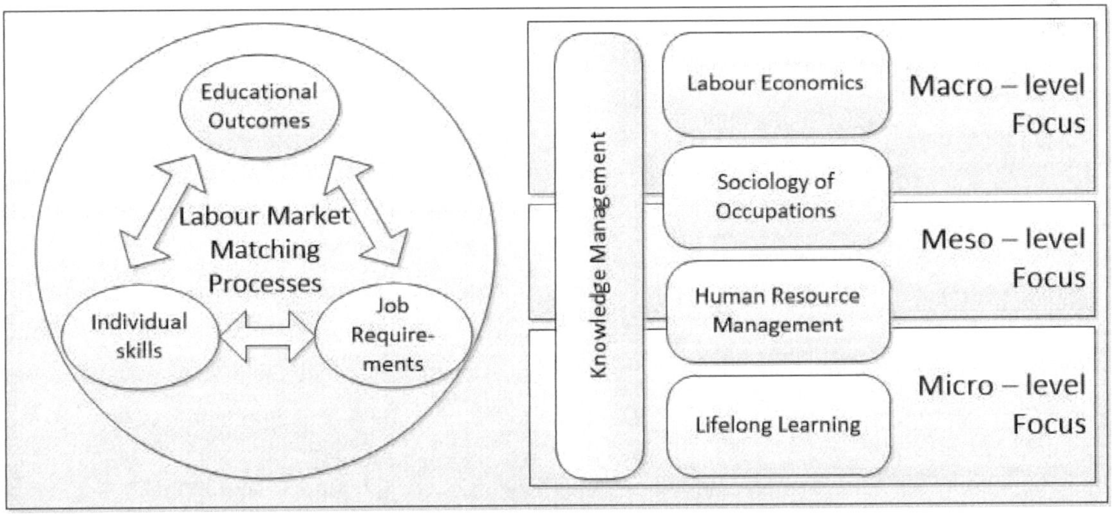

EDUWORKS focuses on matching processes at three levels and on one overarching topic:

- Individual level fit between job demands – persons' abilities
- Meso-level employers' demands for occupational skills versus occupational dynamics
- European and national level labour supply and demand matches and mismatches
- Knowledge Management for supply and demand matches

The specific research training aims of the research in the ITN are to develop expertise in:

1. Investigating demands - abilities fit, that is the extent to which individual skills and abilities match the demands (tasks) and requirements of organizations, and the ways in which organisations allocate tasks to jobs.
2. Investigating the mechanism concerning the division of work reflected in task sets of occupations and the shaping of occupational boundaries, the skill sets related to these occupations and the ways in which organisations define their skills need.

3. Investigating the wide range of mechanisms causing skills mismatches in national and European labour markets, including the impact of the 2008 crisis on skills-occupation mismatch in Europe, and workers' responsiveness to labour market shortages concerning gender, age, and ethnicity.
4. The establishment of a common language on the basis of which future investigations on the topics may draw to further facilitate training and knowledge exchange.
5. The strengthening of interdisciplinary research cooperation so as to advance our understanding of the matching mechanisms and the interactions between different levels of aggregation, including research cooperation with private and academic organisations.

Main target groups of the project: Academia, Industry, Policy

eLene4work

Learning to learn for new digital soft skills for employability

Website: http://www.eLene4work.eu

Runtime: 12.2014 – 10.2017

Supported / co-funded by: Erasmus+ Cooperation for innovation and the exchange of good practices, Strategic Partnerships addressing more than one field

Partners: eLene4Work Coordinator: Fondazione Politecnico Di Milano, IT; see more at: http://elene4work.eu/project-description-2/list-of-partners/

Project representative to be contacted for further info: Project coordinator: Matteo Uggeri (info-eL4w@eden-online.org)

The aim of the eLene4work project is to help students and new entrepreneurs develop soft skills (often also referred to as 21st century skill, such as problem solving in a creative way, learning to learn, cooperation, effective and clear communication, adapting to different cultural contexts, managing conflicts, showing endurance in complicated or stressful situations, etc.) skills required by companies of all sizes nowadays. The eLene4work outputs and services, therefore, are also aimed to help companies exploit the digital talents of young employees. The project proposes a strategic partnership whose goal is to test and monitor the possibility offered by various means of open and distance learning opportunities such as MOOCs and OER to address the demand for digital soft skills (like e-collaboration, digital communication, social network participation, social media management and web 2.0 activities in general) formally not taught at universities but desirable by most employers on the labour market.

The aim of the eLene4work project is to allow students to:

- autonomously identify their own:
  - gaps in soft skills and competences, in order to develop or improve them;
  - potential in digital soft skills, to increase their professional attractiveness on the labour market;
- autonomously learn how to:
  - fill their skill gap using MOOCs (and other OERs);
  - include in their CV their soft skills and digital soft skills in order to enhance the opportunity to enter the labour market.

Students will learn to learn how to use and exploit their own digital competences and soft skills on the labour market.

Main target groups of the project: The various project outputs are being developed to bridge a clearly identifiable gap between what employers seek and job seekers can offer in terms of today's essential digital skills. From the educational point of view both VET institutions and universities (deans, presidents, rectors, teachers as well as students) can benefit from the eLene4work services, while on the other hand managers, HRs, entrepreneurs, chambers of commerce and company associations are also primary target stakeholders. The project's secondary target audiences include instructional designers, e-learning experts, researchers and policy makers.

Significant public results: The main results of *eLene4work* will be the following:

Comparative analysis on state of the art on soft skills and soft skills 2.0:

This report provides a cross-institutional analysis focusing on the identification of the most important soft skills needed for successful transition from university education to the labour market. It is based on the partners experience in the field and puts together and compares all the studies, initiatives, practices emerging in each single country on the following topics:

1. soft skills gap in students approaching the labour market;
2. digital soft skills (soft skills 2.0) in students, new workers and youngsters in general. However, the information on digital soft skills is not explicitly mentioned in the analysis of every country, but in some cases it can be referred to more indirectly, as for example, when the document gives information on online training.

Focus groups with the stakeholders

This report describe and compare the qualitative data about *soft skills* gathered through focus groups carried out in 9 partner country: Belgium, Finland, France, Germany, Greece, Italy, Poland, Spain, UK.

The aim of Focus Groups meetings was to find out what we mean by "soft skills" and if they are recognized in partner countries and to check which soft skills are really important and needed in labour market, in which areas students and young workers have biggest gaps and what should be done to change this situation.

Focus Group meetings were organised with 2 stakeholders groups:

1. Students (especially closed to graduation) and young workers (FG1)
2. Employers, HR managers, teachers (FG2)

In each partner countries the same set of questions was used during meetings to make it possible to compare results and situation in all countries.

In the report we present results of meetings with both groups and general conclusions.

- *Self-evaluation tool*: an online questionnaire for students' self-assessment of soft skills and digital soft skills resulting in a *Personal development plan*.
- *Orientation tool for students and young workers*: a coordination tool specifically being developed for the students, who will approach their personal development in soft skills and soft skills 2.0, drawn on the results produced within the project primarily the Comparative analysis on state of the art of soft skills and soft skills 2.0, the 2 rounds of Focus groups.
- *Personal Journal*: a template to give a method to students about how to learn autonomously and further develop themselves and to evaluate the whole learning path held through the MOOCs.
- *Lesson learned kit*: a set of recommendations targeted at different groups, with a collection of all the experience developed within the project, with a particular attention to the filled evaluation of the students' learning experience and the tutoring and monitoring of the students' path.

ILSD QFIC WBCD

OBN

Open Badge Network

Website: http://www.openbadgenetwork.com

Runtime: September 2014 – August 2017

Supported / co-funded by: Erasmus+

Partners: Beuth-Hochschule fuer Technik Berlin, DE; Cambridge Professional Development, UK; EDEN – European Distance and E-Learning Network, UK; Dienst Uitvoering Onderwijs, NL; Institute for Sustainable Technologies – National Research Institute, PL; Digitalme, UK; ARTES – Applied Research into Training and Education Systems, IT.

Project representative to be contacted for further info: Ilona Buchem (buchem@beuth-hochschule.de)

The Open Badge Network (OBN) is an Erasmus + project which brings together organisations from across Europe to support the development of an Open Badge ecosystem, promoting the use of Open Badges to recognize non-formal and informal learning.

Mozilla Open Badges is an open standard that allows all skills and achievements to be recognised and shared across the web. Schools, Universities, Employers and informal learning providers globally are using open badges to capture lifelong learning which is currently unrecognised.

This project aims to provide a trusted source of independent information, tools and informed practice to support people who are interested in creating, issuing and earning badges across Europe.

You can see who is already issuing badges on the Inventory of Open Badge Projects map (http://www.badgetheworld.org) and share your planned or active badge projects too.

We are looking for organisations and individuals from across Europe to join us and help build the Open Badge Network. It doesn't matter whether you are a badge novice or expert, you can become a member of the Open Badge Network by registering here: OBN community registration (http://www.openbadgenetwork.com/members/).

Main target groups of the project:

- Educational and human resource professionals;
- Employers and self-employed professionals and organisations;
- Organisations and learning communities where educational practitioners and leaders operate (educational institutions, businesses, public and private, small and large);
- Local, regional and national authorities, policy makers;
- Citizens at different stages of their education and life in a perspective of lifelong and life-wide learning;
- Professionals working with disadvantaged groups (learners with special needs, school push/drop out, women back to work, unemployed, migrants, etc.);
- Sister initiatives / projects (e.g. ODS, LeHo, VM-PASS, OpenPROF, etc.);
- Institutions, organisations who have influence and/or commitment in the recognition of informal learning and in-demand workplace skills.

Significant public results:

- Creation of an Open Badges European professional network;
- Open Badges MOOC (Massive Open Online Course);
- Open Badges initiatives to support learning regions and cities;
- Open Badges infrastructure;
- Integration of Open Badges at policy level, in particular with the Europass initiative.

RISK

LeHo

Learning at Home and the Hospital

Website: http://www.lehoproject.eu

Runtime: January 2014 – December 2016

Supported / co-funded by: LLP-KEY3 Networks / 543184-LLP-I-2013-I-IT-KA3-KA3NW

Partners: FPM: Fondazione Politecnico di Milano, IT (applicant); University of Perugia – Department of Education and Human Sciences, IT; Bednet vzw, BE; Staatliche Schule für Kranke München, DE; MMB – Institute for Media and Competence Research, DE; EDEN – European Distance and E-Learning Network, UK; FUNDITEC, ES; Leicester Children's Hospital School, UK; Children's Cancer Hospital, EG.

Project representative to be contacted for further info: Matteo Uggeri (matteo.uggeri@polimi.it)

LeHo - financed by the Lifelong Learning Programme of the European Commission - is developing an online hub that will provide tools and resources for those engaged or involved in home and hospital-based education for children with medical conditions. The initiative is coordinated by the Fondazione Politecnico di Milano and involves 9 organisations that include universities, hospital schools, IT solution providers and European networks.

In the first phase of this 3-year project, a definition of the key educational factors and highlighting good practice in the field are the initial outcomes that will be used to access further aims, such as providing a Practical Guide and a Toolkit for everybody involved in Home and Hospital Education (HHE) including medical staff, nurses, volunteers, teachers, parents, etc. By the end of the project, the resulting resource will target the policy makers and will conclude the experiences of the participants and contributors of LeHo, highlighting strengths, challenges and weaknesses that may require further development across the partner countries.

The LeHo online hub is already available and open for everybody involved and interested in the topic and includes resources that are being developed or collected by the LeHo team. A Board of Experts was founded in order to support LeHo's work. Members of the BoE include professionals with a high level of experience in the field of HHE who also take on a liason role between the teachers, medical staff and the decision makers at policy level. Focus group discussions are and will be also presented on the online hub.

Main target groups of the project:

- teachers already involved or potentially involved in HHE;
- other personnel/workers of schools not directly involved in the education process:
- technicians (IT administrators, usually) in charge of ICT structures (from computers to webcam to printer, scanners or cables...);
- medical staff (nurses, doctors...);
- volunteers and volunteers associations;
- students, not only with medical needs but in general: this is because in many cases the students themselves are the main 'engine' and helpers for their classmates with medical need and even for their own teachers, especially in the use of technology;
- schools directors and decision makers (in hospitals and schools): 90% of the times any project of home tuition or in general variations in the normal teaching path has to be evaluated and accepted by the school and hospital decision makers.

Secondary target:

- policy makers;
- representative of institutions related to education (at local, regional and national level);
- parents and parents associations;

RISK

- supporting institutes providing ICT solutions (i.e. Bednet (Be), KlasseContact (Nl), PSO (ITA)...;
- high and higher education students representatives;
- students with a disability: even if the focus is not specifically on them, we need to take into account the needs of people suffering from some specific form of disabilities (e.g. special high contrast, bigger letters, audio transcriptions of videos, etc.).

Significant public results:

- The LeHo online hub, including international and national communities: http://wwLeho w.lehoproject.eu/
- LeHo on Facebook: https://www.facebook.com/groups/677222725654610/
- LeHo on Linkedin: http://www.linkedin.com/groups/LeHo-Learning-Home-in-Hospital-4966339
- Examples from the LeHo Repository's content:
  - LeHo Board of Experts and their report on the state-of-the art of HHE in their country: http://www.lehoproject.eu/en/board-of-experts
  - First Focus Group Discussion Report: http://www.lehoproject.eu/en/documents/viewdownload/17-international-community/170-focus-groups-with-hhe-teachers-and-medical-staff-full-report-of-the-first-round-v-6-2
  - Glossary of terms in use in the Home and Hospital Education: http://www.lehoproject.eu/en/glossary
  - LeHo International Community: http://www.lehoproject.eu/en/home-international
  - Training action at HOPE in Vienna: http://www.lehoproject.eu/en/vienna-training

QFIC QLTY RISK

EBE-EUSMOSI

Evidence Based Education European Strategic Model for School Inclusion

Website: http://www.inclusive-education.net

Runtime: September 2014 – August 2017

Supported / co-funded by: European Union / Erasmus+

Partners: University of Perugia, IT (coordinator); Open University of the Netherlands (OUNL), NL; University of Udine, IT; University of Barcelona, ES; University of Zagreb, HR; University of Ljubljana, SI.

Project representative to be contacted for further info: Associate Professor Dr. Christian M. Stracke (christian.stracke@ou.nl)

Short description of the initiative:

New Initiative to Use Proven Evidence-based Education in School Inclusion

EBE-EUSMOSI Aims to Support and Promote Inclusion Strategies in Europe through Interactive Portal, Dynamic Quality Framework, Open Educational Resources

Which is the best way to assess the elements which compose inclusive and high-quality learning environments using evidence-based education (EBE)? The forward-thinking new Erasmus+ project *Evidence Based Education – European Strategic Model for School Inclusion (EBE-EUSMOSI)* has set out to develop the great potential of EBE in inclusive educational approaches in schools across Europe.

Taking their cue from the recommendations made in many international studies supporting evidence-based policy-making, EBE-EUSMOSI will address problems in assessing the effectiveness and efficiency of school inclusion practices. Furthermore, the project will work to overcome the difficulties in promoting methodologies suitable for special education and inclusion.

As any good decision-making should be based on empirical research, EBE-EUSMOSI plans to integrate procedures based on such to develop a European reference model to evaluate the quality of school inclusion, especially regarding EBE. The project will also create and validate a tool to assess school inclusion strategies in different organisational and cultural contexts.

In order to ensure the long-term impact of its efforts, EBE-EUSMOSI will foster a research network to integrate, define, and disseminate specific training models internationally, including open educational resources and practices.

More information about EBE-EUSMOSI online: http://www.inclusive-education.net

Main target groups of the project:

- All teachers, parents, learners and citizens interested in inclusive education;
- Inclusive education teachers, designers and providers;
- Schools and headmasters interested in inclusive education;
- Evidence-based education;
- National, regional and local public authorities and decision makers in educational systems.

Significant public results:

- European Teacher Trainings on Prosociality and Social and Emotional Learning;
- European Reference Model able to assess the quality of school inclusion in an EBE perspective.

COOP ICT NETW QFIC ROI TASS WBCD

PBL 3.0

Problem-based Learning 3.0

Website: http://pbl3-project.eu

Runtime: January 2015 – December 2018

Supported / co-funded by: European Union / Erasmus+

Partners: University of Macedonia, GR (coordinator); Open University of the Netherlands (OUNL), NL; Aalborg University, DK; University of Alcalá, ES; BOC Asset Management GmbH, AT.

Project representative to be contacted for further info: Associate Professor Dr. Christian M. Stracke (christian.stracke@ou.nl)

Short description of the initiative:

The overall aim of the project is to enhance Problem Based Learning (PBL) with Learning Analytics (LA) and Learning Semantics (LS) in order to produce a new educational paradigm and pilot it to produce relevant policy recommendations.

To this end, the cooperation will aim at reaching the following objectives and corresponding specific goals:

Construct a new educational approach that combines a well-established learning strategy like PBL with novel technologies in learning like LA in PBL respecting legal and ethical considerations (PBL_LA). This approach will take into consideration the whole LA lifecycle:

- Data gathering, by identifying educational data that is generated in each and all steps of PBL.
- Information processing, by analysing processes and techniques that transform educational data to meaningful, multi-modal information.
- Knowledge application, by identifying all intervention mechanisms that could be put into practice based on all LA feedback during course design and course execution.
- Design a semantic model for PBL_LA, which will enable the annotation of learning resources in order to easily integrate them to the PBL approach and enable their discoverability when setting personalized learning pathways.
- Adapt a set of open source software tools for supporting PBL_LA and the semantic model based on existing LMS (e.g. Moodle), analytics tools (e.g., RapidMiner, Gephi, etc.) and an intuitive semantic annotation tool.
- Create a number of relevant, semantically annotated educational materials and perform trials at various sites in order to draw evidence-based conclusions.
- Produce relevant policy recommendations for PBL_LA that could raise the quality in education and training.
- Create an organic ecosystem of organizations, researchers, students, etc., with an interest in PBL_LA. To this end, we will develop a Community of Practice, where institutions and individuals from across Europe will be able to exchange knowledge and expertise on LA, learning semantics, innovative learning tools and approaches etc. This aims to address the call's objective to "support transnational cooperation and mutual learning on forward-looking issues between key stakeholders to provide solutions to current challenges in education and training".

More information about PBL 3.0 online: http://pbl3-project.eu

COOP ICT NETW QFIC ROI TASS WBCD

Main target groups of the project:

- All teachers, parents, learners and citizens interested in problem-based learning.
- Problem-based learning designers and providers.
- Schools and headmasters interested in problem-based education.
- National, regional and local public authorities and decision makers in educational systems.

Significant public results:

- Educational approach combining PBL with LA respecting legal and ethical considerations (called *PBL_LA*).
- Semantic model, adapted open source tools and educational materials for PBL_LA.
- Policy recommendations for PBL_LA.

DPED INNO NETW

EDADCC

Digital environments for argumentation, debate and collective knowledge

Website: http://www.uned.es

Runtime: 10.2015 – 09.2017

Supported by: Gobierno de España, Ministerio de Economía y Competitividad. Programa Estatal de I+D+I orientada a los Retos de la Sociedad. Acciones de dinamización "Europa Investigación" 2015. Ref.: EUIN2015-62461

Partners: Universidad Nacional de Educación a Distancia (UNED), ES; Universidad Autónoma de Madrid, ES; Universidad Politécnica de Madrid, ES; Ikerbasque, ES.

Project representative to be contacted for further info: José Francisco Álvarez (jalvarez@fsof.uned.es)

This project is intended as a preparatory work for submitting a proposal to the European H2020 Program. We are in the process of identifying a call for proposals to which apply, as well as on the conformation of a European consortium of partners and on the preparation of the proposal itself.

The current partnership is conformed by members from four Spanish institutions, coordinated by Universidad Nacional de Educación a Distancia (UNED). Participants work in the fields of Philosophy, Education, Computer Science and Philology.

As an initial approach to the final proposal, we intend to design, develop and implement a set of digital functionalities in real and concrete situations that helps us to enhance a collective production of knowledge in the Internet with high reliability. Those digital functionalities are designed to facilitate processes of collective work by managing the communication and structuring the available information. At the same time, they allow participants to classify, tag, comment, annotate or highlight materials. Moreover, users can start a debate among themselves while accessing and leveraging the activity of others. We have already developed a basic functionality to organize digital debates as digital spaces for argumentation. The next step will be to add emotional expressive elements as well as dialectic and rhetorical components, as they are very relevant in argumentative processes.

The expected output will be the merger of the previously mentioned functionalities into computer applications, development service frameworks, open APIS and communication protocols that can be applied in processes related to collective knowledge management in digital spaces (in academic, business, organizational environments). Particular cases of development would be: (a) the organization of conferences and meetings (for academic or business purposes) in a rich digital environment that expands the capabilities of the analogue world; (b) the development of digital narrative structures and itineraries that surpass the usual type of e-books; (c) the enrichment of learning environments. The functionalities will be integrated in a toolkit with a double structure: (a) the front-office layer with tools aimed at end users and directly applicable; (b) back-office profits, aimed at generating knowledge about social processes from the massive data collected.

The conceptual framework of the project assumes that adding different approaches and knowledge, opening participation to large numbers of people, allowing the integration of epistemic variety and facilitating the aggregation of positions of diverse groups encourages the production of collective knowledge [Page, Scott E. (2008). *The Difference: How the Power of Diversity Creates Better Groups, firms, schools and societies*. Princeton University Press]. A design capable of providing adequate functionality to digital spaces will overcome simple quantitative groupings, common in social networks, and move towards the organization of intelligent collectives with multiple scenarios of possible applications.

Digitization has already made progress in many areas related to knowledge management and education, dissemination and popularization of science, organization of research and organizational management of public goods. However, such actions usually occur as a single copy or translation of the analogue world. This project aims to experiment with specific social interaction conferences, meetings, courses, enriched books to finally offer an open store of unrestricted digital resources designed to overcome the stage of simple aggregation of individual activities in digital spaces.

Main target groups of the project: academic, business and organizational environments

DPED INNO NETW

Significant public results: Project members have already developed the following related products:

- Oxford Debate WordPress plugin: https://wordpress.org/plugins/oxford-debate/

It is a plugin that allows to incorporate Oxford-Style debates on your website. An Oxford-Style debate is a communication process in which participants argue for and against a given topic.

Publications:

- Álvarez, J. F. (2015). La argumentación en los espacios digitales. *Actas I Congreso internacional de la Red española de Filosofía, Vol. XI*, 27-39.
- Domínguez, D., & Álvarez, J. F. (2012). Social networks and University Spaces. Knowledge and open Innovation in the Ibero-American Knowledge Space. *Revista de Universidad y Sociedad del Conocimiento (RUSC), 9*(1), 245-257. Retrieved from http://rusc.uoc.edu/index.php/rusc/article/view/v9n1-dominguez-alvarez/v9n1-dominguez-alvarez-eng
- Gil-Jaurena, I., & Domínguez, D. (2012). Open Social Learning y educación superior. Oportunidades y retos. *Revista Iberoamericana de Educación, 60*, 191-203. Retrieved from http://rieoei.org/rie60a12.pdf

GUID

ENGAGE

Engaging Science, Innovative teaching for responsible citizenship

Website: http://www.engagingscience.eu

Runtime: 01.2015 – 04.2017

Supported / co-funded by: FP 7 / Infrastructure, Grant agreement 612269

Partners: Centre for Science Education – Sheffield Hallam University, http://www.shu.ac.uk/research/cse/ (Coordinator); http://www.engagingscience.eu/en/consortium/

Project representative to be contacted for further info: Sonia Hetzner (Sonia.hetzner@fau.de)

Science Education plays an important role for responsible citizenship in the contemporary age. Technology and Science progress are the basis for a better future. However innovations must address societal needs in accordance with societal values in order to maximize the benefits and reduce any harmful impact.

Therefore, citizens must be equipped at an early age to understand socio-scientific issues, applying science knowledge, ethical values and inquiry skills to form evidence-based opinions.

The 21st century is marked by the fast scientific advancement. Latest discoveries related to various emergent fields such as nanotechnology, artificial intelligence, biotechnology are frequently announced to citizens through science-in–the-news. These daily innovations indicate various issues closely connected to people' lives, for instance, food security, enhanced health, energy and environment. On the other hand, the impact of scientific innovations is unpredictable and implies scientific knowledge and skills for reflecting on social and ethical implications. This requires societies being able to deal with promises and uncertainties, particularly to develop better understanding of its potential benefits and risks.

The European Commission has highlighted the importance of Responsible Research and Innovation (RRI) in Science Education through its Science in Society programmes (FP7 and Horizon 2020). Various European projects have been helping teachers foster students' inquiry based learning (IBL) skills for them being able to discuss socio-scientific issues. Some of recent initiatives have been also highlighting the importance of innovative teaching for students being able to make decisions based on informed opinions and Science applied to their life, such as the ENGAGE project.

The ENGAGE project aims at spreading the teaching and learning of RRI at scale, by connecting cutting-edge Science and Technology with educative materials. Our goal is to reach 12.000 teachers and 300.000 students in 14 countries. For that, ENGAGE platform (EngagingScience.eu) combines Open Educational Resources (OER) for students, Open Online Courses (MOOC) and Community of Practice (CoP) for teachers. It targets three components: students' interest, science knowledge and inquiry skills.

The ENGAGE team aims to help teachers develop new strategies collaboratively to equip students for active engagement in science. A big challenge is to change how science is taught in European Science curricula. This means moving from teaching focused only on science as a body of content to equipping students with knowledge, skills and values to use science in society [9]. In order to tackle this issue, we invite you to discuss challenges and opportunities for innovating teaching's practice and join our community.

Main target groups of the project: Secondary School Teachers, Mainly STEAM subjects

Significant public results:

1. A repository of currently 28 Classroom activities in 12 languages integrating Responsible Research and Innovation, innovative pedagogies and science from the news (e.g. Zika, Three Parents, Two degrees, Fracking, etc.);
2. Online teachers' Community in 12 Countries;
3. A MOOC to teach teachers on how to use the materials in the classroom, how to adopt innovative pedagogies in the classroom, how to promote responsible Research and Innovation in the classroom.

QFIC RISK VWC

DICHE

Digital Innovation in Cultural and Heritage Education in the light of 21st century learning

Website: http://diche-project.eu

Runtime: 09/2015 – 02/2017

Supported / co-funded by:

Partners: Stichting Protestants Christelijk Hoger Beroepsonderwijs Utrecht, Marnix Academie (MARNIX), NL; Stichting Landschap Erfgoed Utrecht (LEU), NL; ATIT BVBA, BE; Loughborough University, UK; Società Cooperativa Culture (COOPCULTURE), IT; Universita degli Studi Roma TRE, IT.

Project representative to be contacted for further info: Antonella Poce (antonella.poce@uniroma3.it)

DICHE project's aim is to integrate digital resources and opportunities in primary education in general and in cultural and heritage education in particular.

The project addresses the following *priorities*:

1. Enhancing digital integration in learning, teaching, training and youth work at various levels.
2. Developing basic and transversal skills using innovative methods.
3. Strengthening the profile of the teaching professions.

The project is innovative as it brings together 3 *fields*: (a) cultural and heritage education, to experiment with (b) digital integration and innovation, in (c) primary education.

The *methodology* applied in this project is based on the logic of converting a theoretical basis for digital innovation in cultural and heritage education into a practical menu of teaching scenarios and digital resources, testing the menu and using the test outcomes to enrich the theoretical basis. This methodology is applied through 6 steps:

1. The development of a common research agenda, includes pending academic questions and matters that require additional research, in the field of digital innovation and integration in cultural and heritage education (Part of intellectual output O1).
2. The partner organisations formulate a set of desirable, long-term directions of development in the use of digital tools and resources in cultural and heritage education, which are in line with the theoretical research agenda and with the best practices partner organisations share in the partnership (Part of O2).
3. Partner organisations make an action plan for the development of a pilot menu of teaching scenarios that include the use of digital tools and resources in primary education. The action plan for the menu is in line with the desirable, long-term development direction and can be seen as a first practical step towards the realization of these development directions (Part of O2).
4. Partner organisations carry out the action plan for the development of the menu, by adapting the existing teaching scenarios and digital resources in such a way that they are suitable to use in cultural and heritage education regardless of the theme, and by producing tutorials that instruct teachers when and how to use which teaching scenario and digital resource, as well as a framework for evaluation (Part of O2).
5. Partner organisations test the menu in primary school teaching settings, both in The Netherlands and in Italy, and both in classrooms and in museums/at cultural heritage sites. A framework for evaluation is drawn up before the testing itself. Evaluation takes place on a continuous basis throughout the pilot phase, in cooperation between all four organisations carrying out the pilot phase (MARNIX, LEU, COOP, UNIROMATRE) and with the professional guidance of ATIT (Part of O3).
6. Based on the pilot phase, an end evaluation of the menu takes place, based on which recommendations for the use of digital tools and resources in cultural and heritage education is drawn up. On the one hand, this set

of recommendations serves as a practical guideline for (prospective) teachers, primary schools, teacher's colleges and educating parties in the culture and heritage sector seeking to integrate digital tools and resources in their activities. On the other hand, the recommendations relate back to the initially created research agenda, thereby closing the project "circle" of moving from a theoretical agenda to a practical menu and back to the theoretical agenda (Part of O3).

Main target groups of the project: Approximately 1050 persons will be target of the activities organized by DICHE project or will benefit indirectly from it: 50 participants are prospective teachers who are instructed about the menu of teaching scenarios that include the use of digital resources; 800 participants are pupils at primary (and in Italy middle) schools who attend the cultural and heritage classes; 40 participants are primary school teachers of the pupils mentioned above; approximately (at least) 160 participants attend one of the 7 multiplier events organized throughout the course of the project.

Significant public results: Most of the expected project results are listed in intellectual outputs and multiplier events: 2 local multiplier events on pilot locations: 1 in Utrecht, by LEU for educators in the field of culture and cultural heritage and 1 in Rome, by COOPCULTURE for all teachers and cultural educators belonging to their network; 5 multiplier events are meant to involve international stakeholders, and take place at international conferences organized all around Europe.

However, in addition, an important expected project result is the creation of a long-lasting international partnership of organisations active in digital innovation and integration in cultural and heritage education. By formulating desired long-term directions for development and innovation in the use of digital resources in cultural and heritage education, the partnership has a long-term basis for continuous cooperation.

INNO MIND NETW

Learning21

Shaping the Future

Website: http://shapingthefuture.dcu.ie/project/learning-futures-labs/

Runtime: 10.2015 – 12.2019

Supported / co-funded by: Dublin City University, DCU Education Trust

Partners: Dublin City University, Ireland

Project representative to be contacted for further info: Professor Mark Brown (mark.brown@dcu.ie)

Short description:

The Learning21 project involves the redesign of physical learning spaces at Dublin City University (DCU) with a particular focus on the development of Digitally Enhanced Active Learning Spaces (DEALS). There is a growing body of literature on the design of new active and collaborative learning spaces that help institutions better harness the potential of flexible pedagogies and the affordances of new digital technologies. Barnett (2014), for example, proposes a useful set of conditions of flexibility as yardsticks by which higher education providers can guide their commitment towards flexible learning experiences and flexibility more generally as a valued feature of institutional culture. More specifically in the area of learning design, Keppell, Souter and Riddle (2011) suggest the following Seven Principles of Learning Space Design:

- Aesthetics – recognition of symmetry, harmony, simplicity and fitness for purpose (http://www.skgproject.com/what-are-aesthetics/);
- Comfort – a space which creates a physical and mental sense of ease and well-being (http://www.skgproject.com/design-principles/comfort/);
- Blending – supporting a mixture of technological and face-to-face pedagogical interactions (http://www.skgproject.com/design-principles/what-is-blending/);
- Affordances – the *action possibilities* the learning environment provides the users, including such things wifi, seating, writing surfaces, natural light, and so on (http://www.skgproject.com/design-principles/what-are-affordances);
- Flow – the seamlessness of learning when totally involved in the experience (http://www.skgproject.com/what-is-flow/);
- Equity – consideration of the needs of cultural and physical differences (http://www.skgproject.com/design-principles/what-is-equity/);
- Repurposing – the potential for multiple usage of a space (http://www.skgproject.com/design-principles/what-is-repurposing/).

Above all the fundamental principle is that quality teaching requires high quality learning environments, which by definition in the 21st Century need to support teachers to exploit the affordances of new digital technologies. A decade or so ago the classroom was the primary focus for learning in higher education but since then a great deal has changed and the virtual space has taken its place alongside physical spaces ranging from conventional classrooms to the Library and even the café. With this point in mind the literature emphasizes the value of designing for seamlessness between spaces, and flexibility as different teachers are likely to use the same space in different ways. Importantly, we know from the literature that students are drawn to both physical and virtual spaces that are inviting, aesthetically pleasing and conducive to interaction where they can become fully engaged in the excitement of generating new knowledge through a blend of technologies (JISC, 2007). Although refurbishing existing physical spaces usually requires some compromise due to existing physical and technical constraints, the Learnig21 project is firmly anchored in the aforementioned literature.

INNO MIND NETW

A notable feature of the project is the way it brings together different units and stakeholders within the University to share ideas and resources. More specifically the Learning21 project involves collaboration between Estates, Information Systems Services (ISS) and the National Institute for Digital Learning (NIDL). In phase 1 of the project, an online survey gathered data in August 2015 on how staff perceived the current state of physical learning spaces at DCU. Figure 1 shows that a minority of staff rated the current state of DCU's lecture theatres and classrooms as 'good' or 'very good'.

Table 1: How staff rated the current state of DCU's learning spaces

	Very Good	Good	Adequate	Poor	Very Poor	Total	Weighted Average
Lecture Theatres (i.e., tiered spaces)	**4.39%** 5	**23.68%** 27	**48.25%** 55	**17.54%** 20	**6.14%** 7	114	2.97
Classrooms (i.e., flat spaces)	**1.63%** 2	**25.20%** 31	**43.09%** 53	**24.39%** 30	**5.69%** 7	123	3.07

The staff survey also sought views on the preferred designs, configurations and technologies of DCU's learning spaces in the future. Table 2 shows that flat classroom spaces were rated as the highest priority for future developments.

Table 2: Highest priority in terms of the future development of physical learning spaces

Answer Choices	Responses	
Lecture Theatres (i.e., tiered spaces)	**31.30%**	36
Classrooms (i.e., flat spaces)	**42.61%**	49
Computer Labs	**6.09%**	7
Other (please specify)	**20.00%**	23
Total		**115**

In light of this response, Phase 2 of the project in September 2015 involved the redevelopment of three flat classrooms to support more active and collaborative learning spaces. Figure 1 illustrates the traditional design of one of the chosen spaces for redevelopment.

Figure 1. Traditional configuration of classroom

This phase of the project had a relatively small budget and particularly tight deadlines in order to ensure the three classrooms were available for teaching at the start of the new academic year. Figure 2 illustrates the level of transformation achieved through the redevelopment process including new collaborative furniture, new whiteboards, new projectors, air media wireless connectivity, new carpet, new ceiling and new paint colour scheme.

Figure 2. New DEALS classroom

A formal evaluation of the larger Learning21 project will be undertaken later in the project but initial feedback from staff was very positive, as evidenced by the following comment:

> *"The work you guys did on C167 is amazing. I had two classes in there yesterday, we used all the whiteboards, we moved the tables to be a u-shape for the start then back to the circles. It was quick and easy and the 'Air Media' thing sounds superb, I can't wait to have the freedom to move around and teach."*

The next phases of the project involve further developments, including the intention to pilot new collaborative chairs (Senator Ad- Lib Scholar) in a number of unusually shaped environments and the design of two 'Learning Futures Labs' as innovation classrooms for exploring, harnessing and shaping the future of new generation learning spaces.

Main target groups of the project: Institutional Leaders, Learning Space Managers

Significant public results:

- Brown, M., Donohue, F., Doyle, J., Glynn, M., & Spillane, I. (2015). *New generation learning spaces: Investing in the digital campus.* Presentation at EdTech 2015, Irish Learning Technology Association Conference, Limerick. 28th May.

References

- Barnett, R. (2014). *Conditions of flexibility: Securing a more responsive higher education system.* York: Higher Education Academy. Retrieved from https://www.heacademy.ac.uk/resource/conditions-flexibility-securing-more-responsive-higher-education-system
- JISC (2007). *Learning Spaces InfoKit.* Retrieved from http://www.jiscinfonet.ac.uk/infokits/learning-spaces/
- Karnad, A. (2013). *Student use of recorded lectures: a report reviewing recent research into the use of lecture capture technology in higher education, and its impact on teaching methods and attendance.* London School of Economics and Political Science, London, UK. Retrieved from http://eprints.lse.ac.uk/50929/
- Keppell, M., Souter, K., & Riddle, M. (2011). *Physical and virtual learning spaces in higher education: Concepts for the modern learning environment.* Hershey, Pennsylvania: IGI Global.

ICT QLTY

FORESIGHT

FORESIGHT
ICT in Higher Education

Access, Equity and Quality: Envisioning the Sustainable Future of Postsecondary Education in a Digital Age

Website: http://iite.unesco.org/foresight/

Runtime: October 2014 – December 2016

Supported / co-funded by: UNESCO

Partners: UNESCO, EDUCAUSE, International Council for Open and Distance Education (ICDE), New Media Consortium (NMC), Skoltech, universities from Australia, Brazil, China, South Africa.

Project representative to be contacted for further info: Svetlana Knyazeva (s.knyazeva@unesco.org)

Objectives of the project:

- to strengthen UNESCO's function as an international laboratory of ideas capable of rethinking education and a platform for the global debate and reflection on critical emerging trends and challenges;
- to identify how the technological, social and economic context for postsecondary education is changing and what are the key implications for decision and policy makers in governments, universities, companies and civil society;
- to develop a better understanding of how postsecondary education can contribute to the realization of the Sustainable Development Goals.

Project activities:

- Future thinking, debating and shaping the future development of HE in relation to ICT;
- Mapping and assessment of relevant foresight and major relevant trends;
- Focus groups to discuss major issues and preparing next phases of the foresight;
- Online survey among high-level decision-makers and experts in postsecondary education, including education practitioners;
- Virtual panels of policy makers and experts;
- Analysis/generalization of the results of the panel/survey and feedback from UNESCO Chairs.

Main target groups of the project: policy- and decision-makers

Significant public results:

Project events:

- The meeting of experts "Access, Equity and Quality: Envisioning the Future of Higher Education in a Digital Age" (March 2015, Paris).
- Conference of UNESCO Chairs held in St. Petersburg (June 2015, Russian Federation).
- Global High-Level Policy Forum "Online, Open and Flexible Higher Education for the Future We Want: from Statements to Action: Equity, Access, and Quality Learning Outcomes", which was held by UNESCO and ICDE (June 2015, Paris).
- 26th ICDE Conference (October 2015, Sun City (South Africa) – focus group discussion.

The online survey yielded interesting results for the following major issues:

- The need for curriculum reform due to such changes as the availability and development of open educational resources.
- The readiness to acceptance, use and recognition of learning outcomes for OER and MOOCs.

ICT QLTY

- The fastening technological change of society and economy necessitates integration of self-learning competence with the use of digital technologies.
- The impact of these developments on the change of the roles of teachers and institutions and the urgent need to (re)train teachers.
- The consequences of these developments for the way in which (informal and formal) learning results are translated into credits and can be transferred and used in the globalizing society.
- Price and quality expectations for the production of resources and delivery of education services, including those for people with disabilities.

MLS RISK

t-MAIL

Teacher Mobile Application for Innovative Learning

TMAIL PROJECT.EU

Website: http://tmailproject.eu

Runtime: November 2015 – October 2017

Supported / co-funded by: Erasmus+ Programme, Support for policy reform; Prospective initiatives; Forward looking cooperation projects

Partners: Vrije Universiteit Brussel, BE (Coordinator); Universidad Autonoma de Madrid, ES; University of Hull, UK; Universitaet Wien, AT; Youth Entrepreneurial Service Foundation, MK; HET Gemeenschapsonderwijs, BE; European Distance and E-learning Network, UK; Kidimedia bvba, BE; ETUCE-CSEE, BE.

Project representative to be contacted for further info: Jeltsen Peeters (jeltsen.peeters@gmail.com) – project coordinator

t-MAIL aims to develop and test a mobile application supporting primary school teachers, teacher educators and educational decision makers in implementing classroom practices that stimulate students' self-regulated learning (SRL). The project aims to address the needs of these different target groups by designing activities to support the development and testing of a mobile app. It delivers a personalized training course on SRL for in-service primary school teachers. Data generated through the mobile app will be processed through learning analytics and semantics. This approach, in support of data-driven teacher education, will enable the personalization of teachers' and students' learning, ultimately facilitating evidence-based policy making pathways. The mobile training app and associated feedback loops will be piloted and evaluated in three European countries, the UK, Belgium and Spain. Materials will be available in English, German, French, Spanish, Dutch, and Macedonian.

Main target groups of the project:

- Primary school teachers;
- Teacher educators, trainers;
- Decision makers.

Significant public results: Expected project results:

Deliverable	Expected time of delivery
Theoretical framework report	31 March 2016
Stakeholder study report	31 March 2016
Repository course material	31 March 2016
Country reports educational policy	31 March 2016
Algorithm	April, 2016 (draft) July, 2017 (final)
Mobile application	October, 2016 (draft) July, 2017
Data warehouse and learning analytics procedure	October, 2016 (draft) July, 2017 (final)
User manual learning analytics	October, 2016 (draft) July, 2017 (final)
Teacher training course	October, 2016 July, 2017
Implementation plan	December, 2016 (draft) July, 2017 (final)
Pilot study	31-Jul-2017
Evaluation plan	31-Oct-2016
Evaluation report	31-Jul-2017

MLS

m-commerce

m-commerce

Website: https://www.m-commerce.enterprises

Runtime: 09.2014 – 09.2016

Supported / co-funded by: Erasmus+ Strategic partnership KA2

Partners: FH Joanneum Graz (Austria), University of Alcala (Spain), Politehnica University of Timisoara (Romania), Center for Knowledge (Macedonia)

Project representative to be contacted for further info: prof. Radu Vasiu (radu.vasiu@upt.ro)

The project m-commerce focuses on the training of staff and employees of Small- and Medium-sized Enterprises (SMEs) in order to develop the further development and expansion of m-commerce activities.

The project is divided into different phases that build up on each other. The first phase includes a state-of-the-art analysis of m-commerce activities and its demands, which is based on online surveys, controlled interviews and the evaluation of secondary data. The results, which are unified due to the country-dependent findings, are the basis for the development of the training course m-commerce. Another result of this phase is a best-practice database, in which already existing as well as successful m-commerce solutions are displayed.

In phase 2, the training course as such is developed on the lessons learned in phase 1. The training course is developed by the project partners: FH Joanneum Graz (Austria), University of Alcala (Spain), Politehnica University of Timisoara (Romania), Center for Knowledge (Macedonia).

Phase 3 is characterized by the implementation of the training curse. The training course is conducted in all partner countries. In this context, the choice of participating companies is taking into consideration in order to achieve a balanced mix of trades and industry.

In the project m-commerce, the following activities are conducted:

- Survey of the current status quo of m-commerce in different European regions
- Collecting best practice examples from different regions
- Development of teaching and learning materials for the training course m-commerce
- Implementation of the training course in all seven partner countries, having a minimum of 10 participating employees of SMEs each training cycle
- Participating SMEs of each training cycle are equipped with m-commerce strategies and first possible solutions for m-commerce implementation

Main target groups of the project: SMEs employees

Significant public results:

The **m-commerce training course**, a holistic approach, includes economic, legal and technical topics that are necessary for the switch to m-commerce.

Block 1 aims at familiarizing the participants with the topic m-commerce. In this context, e-business models and business processes are addressed. The second part of this block deals with country specific legal and safety-related issues of online businesses. A basic understanding of the processes and procedures in e-commerce and m-commerce is the basis for customer satisfaction as well as an increased turnover.

Block 2 deals with the aspects of online marketing in the first place. Further, possibilities of social media marketing are discussed. Not only the usage of different marketing channels, but also the critical reflections concerning the results of these activities, as well as the personalization of offers enlarge the range of customers of the participating enterprises.

Block 3 deals with the technical aspects of m-commerce. In this context, usability, responsive design and mobile first approaches are considered for already existing e-commerce applications. The goal of this block is it to optimize current e-commerce tenders for mobile devices. In this context, we can speak of a holistic system tuning, ranging from the representation, to performance and storing of data.

MLS

In Romania the training course was run online using the (MOOCs model) on the UniCampus Romanian platform http://www.unicampus.ro in the spring of 2016. The online participants were involved in several online activities with regard to increase their ability to develop m-commerce applications and 12 of them also participates at the face-to-face training and final evaluation and were awarded a certificate.